Recultivating the Vineyard

Figure 1. Lucas Cranach the Younger. *The Vineyard of the Lord* (1556). Epitaph for Paul Eber. Stadtkirche, Wittenberg.

Recultivating the Vineyard

The Reformation Agendas of Christianization

Scott H. Hendrix

Westminster John Knox Press
LOUISVILLE • LONDON

© 2004 Scott H. Hendrix

Scripture quotations from the New Revised Standard Version of the Bible are copyright © 1989 by the Division of Christian Education of the National Council of the Churches of Christ in the U.S.A. and are used by permission.

Book design by Sharon Adams
Cover design by Eric Handel, LMNOP
Cover illustration: Lucas Cranach the Younger, The Vineyard of the Lord (1556). Epitaph for Paul Eber. Stadtkirche, Wittenberg. Used with permission of the Evangelische Stadtkirchenge-meinde Lutherstadt Wittenberg.

First edition
Published by Westminster John Knox Press
Louisville, Kentucky

This book is printed on acid-free paper that meets the American National Standards Institute Z39.48 standard. ∞

PRINTED IN THE UNITED STATES OF AMERICA

04 05 06 07 08 09 10 11 12 13 — 10 9 8 7 6 5 4 3 2 1

Library of Congress Cataloging-in-Publication Data

Hendrix, Scott H.
    Recultivating the vineyard : the Reformation agendas of Christianization / Scott H. Hendrix.
        p. cm.
    Includes bibliographical references.
    ISBN 0-664-22713-9 (alk. paper)
    1. Reformation. I. Title.

BR305.3.H46 2004
274'.06—dc22   2004041292

In Memory of

Heiko Augustinus Oberman (1930–2001)

For
John and Rocky

Making conversation, sharing a joke, doing kindnesses for one another, reading good books, jesting about trifles and sharing the deepest things, disagreeing without animosity, . . . teaching one another and learning from one another, longing with impatience for those who are absent.
—Augustine, *Confessions*, iv.8.13

Contents

Illustrations

Preface

The ideas for this book germinated ten years ago when I read some familiar works of Martin Luther with fresh eyes. For the first time I noticed something simple: how often he used the term "Christian." That should have been no surprise. After all, Luther was a religious reformer and the people whom he addressed were Christian believers. Teaching the Reformation in confessional settings, however, had apparently blinded me to the fact that the Reformation was a reform of Christianity and not only a process of confessionalization in early modern history. Ecumenically minded scholars were already insisting that Luther was a reformer of the church catholic, but even they seemed to think in confessional rather than historical categories. As I taught the Reformation, I realized that other sixteenth-century reformers—Zwinglians, Calvinists, Radicals, Catholics, Spiritualists—also used the same term for themselves and their audiences. I also became aware of the growing literature on the subjects of Christianization and secularization as they pertained to the medieval and modern periods of European history. Gradually the general thesis of this book became clear. Although confessional categories have an important place in our interpretations of the Reformation, the reformers themselves thought they were bringing a Christianity to their society that was deeper and more effective than the medieval process of Christianization. In their minds, that process either had failed (as Radicals thought), or had serious deficiencies (as Protestants thought), or needed new forms and energy (as Catholics thought). The Reformation ended with the establishment of religious confessions, but those confessions grew out of the different agendas by which reformers sought to realize their visions of a renewed Christian Europe.

I presented early forms of my argument to a Renaissance and Reformation seminar at Harvard University in 1998 and in my inaugural
address at Princeton Seminary in 1999. At that point I was still using the
term "re-Christianization," and the address was published in two versions:
in the *Princeton Seminary Bulletin* (n.s., 21 [2000]: 63–80), and in *Church
History* (69 [2000]: 558–77). I presented some of the material in chapter 4
of this book at a joint conference of the German and North American
societies of Reformation research in Wittenberg in 1999. That essay
appeared subsequently, under the title "Radical Agenda, Reformation
Agenda: The Coherence of the Reformation," in a special supplement of
the *Zeitschrift für Historische Forschung* (Beiheft 27, ed. Han-Jürgen Goertz
and James M. Stayer [Berlin: Duncker & Humblot, 2002], 43–60). Some
material on Geneva in chapter 3 first appeared in an essay entitled "The
Reform of Marriage in Calvin's Geneva" in the *Festschrift* for Carter Lindberg (*Caritas et Reformatio*, ed. David M. Whitford [St. Louis: Concordia
Publishing House, 2002], 113–31).

Over the years many people have contributed to the development and
refinement of my arguments as presented in this volume. They include
the student at Gettysburg Seminary, Gretchen Cranz, who submitted a
paper on the frequency of Luther's use of the term "Christian," as well as
the most recent readers of my manuscript—some known and some who
remain unknown. I would like to thank those who graciously read parts of
this work at various stages and supplied helpful suggestions and information: my colleagues in the History Department at Princeton Seminary,
especially James Deming, Paul Rorem, and Richard Young; also Scott
Bruce, Giles Constable, Berndt Hamm, Sigrun Haude, Daniel Jeyaraj,
Anna Johnson, John Maxfield, M. Douglas Meeks, Steven Ozment,
Suzanne Sisoler, James Stayer, John Van Engen, Andrew Walls, and Timothy Wengert. I also wish to thank Jennifer Selwyn for permission to cite
a source from an unpublished manuscript that will appear in *A Paradise
Inhabited by Devils: The Jesuits' Civilizing Mission in Early Modern Naples*
(Burlington, Vt.: Ashgate, 2004).

Several libraries have assisted with the location of material essential to
this project. I express my special appreciation to the staffs of the following institutions: the Wentz Library at Gettysburg Lutheran Seminary, the
Speer and Luce libraries at Princeton Theological Seminary, the Fire-
stone Library at Princeton University, the Institute for Advanced Study
in Princeton, and the Herzog August Bibliothek in Wolfenbüttel. The
first draft of this book was written on a sabbatical and research leave
funded in part by a Henry Luce III Fellowship in Theology from the Asso-

ciation of Theological Schools. I wish to thank the Association and the Luce Foundation for their support, and I am grateful to the colleagues in the class of 2000–2001 who gave helpful responses to the presentations of my project. The administration and Board of Trustees of Princeton Theological Seminary approved and funded the sabbatical and I express my appreciation to all of them, especially to President Thomas Gillespie and Dean James Armstrong for their encouragement.

This volume is dedicated to the memory of my teacher at the University of Tübingen, Heiko A. Oberman, who died during the first year of writing. He was continually supportive of my work, even when it departed from his own way of thinking, and for that I am deeply grateful. I also dedicate this book to my oldest friends, John R. Ellsworth and Wilfrid P. ("Rocky") Hendrix Jr., who have regularly expressed interest in my work and helped me to keep it in perspective. I recall with special pleasure the hours in a New York hotel room in August 2001, when they forced me to formulate carefully and clearly the contours of this book. I also wish to thank my wife, Emilee, and my children, Selinde and Giles, for their ongoing love and support even when this project took time away from them.

Finally, I wish to thank the executive editor of Westminster John Knox Press, Stephanie Egnotovich, for her encouragement and editorial acumen. She happened upon the manuscript when several chapters had been written and graciously read it and expressed interest. She also willingly reviewed it when I did offer it for consideration and has provided very helpful recommendations through the process of revision and publication.

Scott Hendrix
Princeton, New Jersey
November 2003

Introduction

In the study of history, it is hard to see the forest for the trees. The more details we discover about a period, the more difficult it is to fit them into a single coherent picture. Recent study of the European Reformation has been dominated by the trees. Scholars have invested enormous amounts of energy and skill in the study of reform movements in early modern Europe. They have studied reform in villages and towns, parishes and bishoprics, territories and entire countries. In addition to the traditional Protestant, Radical, and Catholic reformations, they have discovered and debated reformations of the cities and the countryside, princes and peasants, laity and clergy, women, men, and the family. So many reform trees have grown up, in fact, and the differences among them have multiplied so rapidly, that historians now tend to speak of reformations instead of Reformation.[1]

This development is understandable and fits the trend of historical studies in general. Although interest in macrohistory is very much alive, in recent years microhistory has also become popular. Local history is essential because it provides the building blocks of larger theories. The analysis of religious change in one place over time makes a fascinating story and highlights the concreteness that surveys and grand theories can supply only in anecdotes.[2] The appeal of analyzing one life or one event is also easy to comprehend. We identify more readily with the daily existence and struggle of people in the past than with general theories about their era, just as we know our own lives and struggles much better than we can understand our age as a whole. Journalists have long realized that one person's experience makes a better story than a hundred generalizations about what happened.

Generalizations, nevertheless, are important, and it is the business of history to supply them. We need to see the forest as well as the trees in order to understand what happened and how it has affected us. This book is about the forest of the Reformation, but it employs a different image, one that was used by people in the sixteenth century: the Reformation as a vineyard. No sooner was the Reformation underway than the people involved tried to make sense of what was happening. They not only wrote about the Reformation, but they also made pictures; the new printing technology produced hundreds of engravings and woodcuts alongside traditional paintings.[3]

One of these paintings emerged around 1556 from the workshop of Lucas Cranach the Younger in Wittenberg; it was fashioned for the epitaph of Paul Eber (d. 1569), a professor at the university and superintendent of the Wittenberg clergy.[4] Using the parables in Isaiah 5:1–7 and Matthew 20:1–16, Cranach explains the meaning of the Reformation by portraying the medieval clergy and Lutheran reformers as laborers in the vineyard of the Lord. The vineyard is split down the middle. On one side, the vineyard has withered from neglect and mismanagement by the pope and his clergy who, at the bottom, try unsuccessfully to collect their wages from Christ. On the other side, the vineyard is flourishing under Lutheran cultivation: eight reformers associated with Wittenberg, ranging from Martin Luther (d. 1546) to the young Matthias Flacius Illyricus (d. 1575), clear the land and prune and irrigate the new, healthy plants.

This picture poses two problems for historians. First, it is obviously one-sided and polemical. It is a narrow Protestant portrayal of the Reformation that exalts the Wittenberg reformers at the expense of the Roman clergy. Medieval Christianity looks worse than it was, while the Reformation appears to be a more cooperative and successful enterprise than it was. There were not only many contented laypeople in medieval Europe, but many dedicated clergy and not a few reformers as well. By the same token, Reformation Europe contained scrawny plants alongside healthy ones, and a host of clergy and reformers who disagreed with one another as stridently as they condemned the Roman Church. A half century ago the German historian Franz Lau used the term *Wildwuchs* (unruly growth) to describe the vitality and diversity of the early Reformation.[5] Lau used the metaphor in a constructive sense, but on the Reformation side of the Cranach painting the healthy diversity and the disruptive growth have all been ignored.

Second, because the picture is so one-sided, it fails to display adequately the continuity between medieval and Reformation religion. Instead of a solid hedge between the two halves of the vineyard, a more accurate portrayal would have carved paths through the hedge along which sixteenth-century reformers would carry healthy stalks from medieval Christianity into the Reformation. These stalks would represent the basic doctrine and rituals of the faith from which reformers derived their knowledge of Christianity in the first place. The indebtedness of the Reformation to early Christianity is portrayed on the extreme right by Philip Melanchthon (d. 1560) drawing water from the well. Melanchthon was the most celebrated humanist of the Lutheran movement, and his very action is meant to illustrate the humanist program of returning to the sources of antiquity and drawing from them new life and knowledge.[6] On the opposite side, the well is being filled with stones—a symbol of the reformers' accusation that the medieval church had shut off access to the religion's earliest and most authoritative texts.

Despite its shortcomings, the Cranach painting shows one thing very well, however. It depicts the mentality of Protestant reformers and vividly illustrates how they understood the Reformation. They thought they were replanting authentic Christianity in the vineyard of the Lord, that is, in the same European Christendom which, they believed, had been devastated by the medieval church. Its clergy, according to the painting, were unfaithful laborers who had practically destroyed the vineyard and eradicated the faith. The reformers, by contrast, were faithful laborers who had recovered genuine Christianity from the original sources and restored the vineyard to productivity. The fruits of their labor were the flourishing vines and the dedicated laity kneeling devoutly in the lower-right-hand corner of the painting. They are the true Christians whom the Reformation sought to create, in contrast to a negligent clergy and lax laity whom it censured as no better than pagans.

The sixteenth-century reformers thus set for themselves the goal of Christianizing Christendom. Although Cranach's portrayal of their task has limitations, it captures their intention. Despite differences among the reformers, which led to harsh polemical exchanges and prolonged religious warfare, that goal gave coherence to the Reformation as a historical movement. In this book I describe that goal and claim that it was in fact common to prominent sixteenth-century reformers. I also argue that studying the goal of Christianization enables us to see the forest of the Reformation despite its many trees and to understand it as a whole. The effort to Christianize Europe was only part of the Reformation, and I make no attempt to present here a complete political and religious history of the sixteenth century. Nevertheless, the mentality of Christianization is essential to a full appreciation of the Reformation and to an evaluation of its impact.

To argue that the Reformation was a coherent movement does not deny its diversity or the conflict that it generated. According to Berndt Hamm, the "real Reformation," in contrast to the idealized Reformation portrayed by Cranach, for example, entailed both unity and diversity.[7] I show that the most important unifying element was the vision of replanting Christianity in a European culture that was judged by Protestant reformers to be riddled with idolatry and by Catholic reformers to be in need of more explicit Christian faith and devotion. The diversity arose from the different agendas that were developed to realize that vision. These agendas were shaped by the divergent convictions that reformers held about theology and practice, and those differences generated the conflict that resulted in the restructuring of Christianity and the redrawing of the religious and political map of Europe.

The sixteenth-century attempt to Christianize Europe had different consequences for laity and clergy, princes and subjects, towns and rural communities, men and women, and we can say accordingly that these groups had, or did not have, their own reformations. I believe it is more accurate and conceptually useful, however, to speak of one Reformation and to locate its diversity in the various theological and practical agendas that sought to realize the goal of Christianization. These agendas led to a variety of political and social outcomes that historians now call confessionalization. These outcomes went beyond the original intention of reformers, however, who envisioned a new kind of Christianized European society and did not foresee the rise of conflicting confessions. The rise of confessions spelled the end of the Reformation vision. Subsequent reforms might be undertaken in the name of true Christianity, but they could only be pursued within the bounds of the new confessionalism.

The debate over the best way to describe the Reformation is, admittedly, a disagreement about the best use of words to describe a complex historical period. It also involves decisions about which aspects of the period to emphasize: the common features of sixteenth-century religious change or the differences and conflicts generated by that change. Instead of a common goal or vision, one could argue that reformers had different visions of a newly Christianized Europe as well as different agendas for achieving that end. To a certain extent that was true. New agendas were devised only as the old forms of being Christian were judged inadequate, new concepts arose, and new models were tried. Still, these agendas were rooted in the need for a new campaign of Christianization that was broadly perceived and pursued by the Reformation. Prior to 1525 in Zurich, for example, the supporters of Huldrych Zwingli who became Anabaptists deviated from his vision of a Christian city and developed under duress new forms of Christian existence. Nevertheless, they shared Zwingli's original conviction that believers had to be free of unbiblical regulations in order for their faith to take deeper root and to flourish. The debate among Protestants over the destruction or retention of statues and pictures derived from a common conviction that unchristian attitudes toward the saints had to be changed, but the different strategies approved by Lutheran (to re-educate the people) and Reformed leaders (to abolish the images) crystallized only after iconoclastic riots forced them to examine the issue more closely. Before that time, Luther and Karlstadt, or Luther and Zwingli, did not necessarily have different convictions on this issue.

By and large I appreciate the model of interpreting Reformation differences that has been proposed by Miriam Chrisman on the basis of German lay pamphlets from the early Reformation. She argued that lay pamphleteers harbored conflicting visions of reform which corresponded to their social ranks: nobles wanted to "reform the empire," peasants to "gain more autonomy in the villages," magistrates to "create greater civic order and harmony," and the artisans to apply Christian love to care for the poor. "All agreed on the need for change," but "how change was defined, what it should include, laid bare the fundamental divisions in the society."[8] While that may have been true for laity, it was not as true for the primary reformers, most of whom were clergy and cherished a similar theological vision before they had to adapt that vision to the different social and political realities they encountered. That vision was more religiously specific than the need for change but not yet as specific as the definite social ends of lay pamphleteers. Even when those goals changed, in the case of Zwingli's radical supporters, for example, a common vision of changing and intensifying Christianity was present and perceptible.

Different words can be chosen to express both the common features and the diversity of the Reformation. One can speak of different agendas and a common vision or of conflicting visions and a common need for change. In this book my agenda is to emphasize the common concern of the reformers rather than the better-known conflicts that developed among them, and I have chosen the term Christianization for that concern because it reflects the vocabulary of the reformers themselves. Reformers did not describe their goal primarily in confessional terms but in Christian ones. I have also chosen "Christianization" because it expresses both continuity and discontinuity between the Middle Ages and the Reformation. The project of the medieval church was certainly the Christianization of Europe, but this term also captures the way in which the agendas of the Reformation adapted and intensified the medieval project. Substantial alterations in medieval theology, ministry, and piety were conceived and enacted, and the outcome was a new structure of Christianity in Western Europe that did not exist prior to the 1520s. Nevertheless, the intention was not fundamentally different from what medieval missionaries and reformers had always desired, namely, a more Christian Europe.

The Reformation was not a new drama, but the second act of the same drama, the act in which the plot thickened and took an unexpected and unprecedented twist. I borrow this image from Constantin Fasolt, who makes a larger argument about European history in which the Reformation enables the nation to assume the spiritual leadership roles exercised earlier by the church.[9] He contends that the Reformation was a "continuation (*Fortpflanzung*) of spiritual dominion in worldly hands" that overshadowed the local, temporal, and conceptual differences between nations and between confessions without extinguishing them.[10] Despite his emphasis on what was common across confessions, Fasolt is making a point that is different from mine. His argument concerns mainly the impact of the Reformation upon European society, while my argument concentrates on the intention of the reformers that embraced both continuity and discontinuity with medieval Christendom and is thus nicely captured by Fasolt's image of a "second act."

This book is more descriptive than explanatory, although I do argue that the goal of Christianization explains features of the Reformation like its harsh polemics, its missionary urgency, and the idealism and the disappointments of the reformers. In general, I agree with Brad Gregory's affirmation that "understanding others on their terms is a completely different intellectual endeavor than explaining them in modern or postmodern categories."[11] In this book my primary aim is to understand the reformers on *their* terms and to construct an argument about the Reformation in those same terms. I have tried to prove that prominent reformers in the major camps thought they were improving and intensifying

Christianity even when they disagreed with one another. Although that may seem obvious to us, it is seldom noted in studies of the Reformation; yet without this awareness it is impossible to understand their eagerness to expand the reforms, their willingness to condemn one another or to die for the cause of eternal salvation, and their swings between optimism and disappointment as they observed the reactions to their work.

My concern for the forest as well as the trees has led me to set broad limits to the Reformation. Limits do exist nonetheless. In contrast to the terms Middle Ages or medieval Christianity, which were not used by people who lived in them, the term Reformation was selected by some sixteenth-century authors to describe not just reform in general, as the term had been used before them, but the specific restructuring of Christianity of which they were a part. I am therefore allowing the Reformation to extend throughout the sixteenth century and well into the seventeenth; but I am not setting its beginning in the fifteenth century despite the keenness of late medieval reform and its own goal of Christianization. Although medieval reformers yearned for the reformation of the church "in head and members" and criticized facets of medieval piety like indulgences, one seldom finds in their writings the widespread denunciation of religious life as unchristian that one sees especially in Protestant and Radical sources. Furthermore, despite some defections from the Roman Church like the Hussite movement, prior to the sixteenth century no comprehensive restructuring of Western Christianity occurred that is comparable to the Reformation. On the other end, as I argue in chapter 6, the rise of confessions only gradually heralds a new age that was substantially different from the Reformation. At first, confessionalization was a process of implementing the Reformation vision by embedding Christianity more deeply in the religious cultures of Europe. It soon became clear, however, that competing claims to embody true Christianity led to a confessional awareness that was erasing a common Christian identity.

Another factor that extends the Reformation well into the seventeenth century is my contention that the goal of Christianization embraced Catholic as well as Protestant reform. To be sure, Ignatius Loyola did not consider himself to be a colleague of John Calvin, but the efforts of new orders and reforming bishops to create a devout society in the Catholic areas of Europe corresponded to the efforts of Calvin and others in Protestant towns and territories.[12] In the long campaign to replant vibrant Roman Christianity in areas like France during the seventeenth century, one finds not only a Counter-Reformation strategy but the dedicated pursuit of the Reformation vision in its Catholic form.[13] In England, too, the Reformation lasted almost to the end of the seventeenth century. At stake during the long conflict between Puritans and Anglicans were not only issues of jurisdiction but also the forms of worship, ministry, and discipline that the different parties could recognize as Christian. When the dates of specific edicts and settlements are compared, it appears that the Reformation officially ended in the various parts of Europe at different times, but the distinct pursuit of the Reformation vision and the ecclesiastical consequences of that pursuit lasted well into the seventeenth century.

Most of this book, however, is about the sixteenth century. In chapter 1, I review the Christianization of medieval culture and discuss its depth in light of charges by Protestant reformers that medieval religion was full of superstition and paganism. I also call to mind monasticism and humanism as agents of Christianization in the Middle Ages and as essential sources of the Reformation vision. In chapters 2 through 5 I try to show how the medieval Christianizing vision was modified and adapted by major reform movements of the sixteenth century. That modification, an intensification or second act of the medieval agenda, envisioned a more devout Europe that all reformers desired, even while they adapted that vision to their own theologies, circumstances, and political possibilities. In this sense, a common Reformation vision was shared by Martin Luther, by the city reformers of Germany and Switzerland, and by radical and Catholic reformers, even though they shaped their own agendas to actualize that vision. These chapters form the heart of my argument. Finally, in chapter 6 I evaluate the impact of the Reformation in light of its Christianizing agendas. Some older issues, like the success and failure of the Reformation, are revisited, but I also risk a broader discussion of the Reformation's effects. At the end, I suggest that Reformation theology was agenda-driven and that its historical context made it more than the sum of the arguments leveled by reformers against one another.

The Reformation of the sixteenth century is filled with more trees than I can identify here and with more unruly growth than one book can control. Disagreement may well be Christianity's "central feature" in the Reformation period,[14] especially when that growth is the main object of attention. There was so much disagreement among reformers, however, because for them there was so much at stake: not only eternal salvation in the next world, but the survival and renewal of Christendom that would make that salvation, in their eyes, available to people in this world for generations to come. While they were disagreeing over the best way to produce healthy vines, reformers had to make sure that the entire vineyard continued to thrive. Likewise, the best way to understand their disagreements is to recall their common root in the Reformation vision.

Figure 2. Lucas Cranach the Younger. *The Vineyard of the Lord* (1556). Detail: Medieval clergy devastating the vineyard. Stadtkirche, Wittenberg.

Chapter 1

The Medieval Vision

A Christian Europe

The Christianization of Europe

The Reformation took place in a European society that was Christianized over the course of more than a thousand years. During the early Middle Ages, the rulers of European peoples inside and outside the Roman Empire were gradually converted to the faith and their people began to live in a network of Christian parishes and dioceses. Told many times, the story of the conversion of Europe[1]—before and after the last Western emperor was deposed in 476—featured both famous bishops, like Gregory the Great (pope, 590–604), and enterprising missionaries like Patrick (fifth century) in Ireland and Boniface (d. 754) in Germany. Conversion often came from the top down. The Frankish king Clovis, who ruled from 481 to 511, was hailed as "another Constantine" when he "advanced to the baptismal font to terminate the disease of ancient leprosy and wash away with fresh water the foul spots that had long been borne."[2] Although three thousand members of his army allegedly followed him into the baptismal waters, Clovis was in all likelihood drawn gradually and gently to the Catholic faith of the Gallo-Romans around him.[3] Over eight hundred years later, the conversion of Europe formally came to an end with the dynastic merger of Poland and Lithuania in 1385. Three days after he was baptized in Krakow, the new grand duke of Lithuania married the Catholic princess of Poland and brought his land into the fold of medieval Latin Christendom.[4]

To say that Christianity was officially accepted, however, is not to say that Christian faith and practice were uniformly entrenched in the society. This observation has been confirmed by dramatic changes in the study

1

of medieval Christianity over the past half century. The featured characters are not prominent bishops, monks, and rulers, for whose lives we have explicit sources, but ordinary people who populated the parishes and practiced the faith without revealing their personal data or convictions. New attention has been focused on the process through which these ordinary folk became Christian, and that analysis has in turn raised the question: How Christian did they actually become? Surveying the literature and reflecting on this problem in 1986, John Van Engen phrased it this way: "The question, in the jargon of our day, is the extent of the 'Christianization' of medieval society, that is, the degree to which specifically Christian teachings and practices shaped the cultural milieu of medieval folk both high and low."[5]

Jargon or not, the Christianization of medieval Europe has become the subject of intensive study by scholars of late antiquity and by medieval historians. It is a rich undertaking that highlights several issues pertaining directly to the Reformation of the sixteenth century. For example, what did the terms Christian and Christendom mean when they were used both in Latin and in the vernacular languages of medieval Europe? According to Van Engen, their use described the following dimensions of a Christian culture:

> the ritual, ecclesiastical, and legal mechanisms put in place to plant, foster, and sustain that religious culture at every social level; the dynamic inherent in acting on religious belief; the differing religious obligations and expectations established for a population of baptized Christians; the means and media used to communicate the teachings of written texts to an illiterate religious culture; and finally the inevitable synthesis of old and new in the resultant religious culture.[6]

According to these criteria, the Middle Ages were indeed Christian in the sense of a dominant cultic practice and legal organization. After a certain point, it was expected that almost everyone except Jews and Muslims would undergo baptism as an infant or adult, attend mass on Sunday and feast days, possess some knowledge of the Lord's Prayer and the Apostles' Creed, use the last rites before dying, confess at least once a year and fast on the prescribed days, pay whatever tithes fell due, and give alms to the poor. One could go beyond these minimal expectations and enter a cloister, but all the baptized members of a community passed their lives in this grid of Christian time and space that was laid out around their parish church.

This portrait of a Christian culture contrasts with the picture drawn by historians who have argued for the persistence of a separate folk religion in medieval Europe. Recent books on the history of paganism argue that organized non-Christian practice failed to be obliterated by missionaries and continued to provide strong resistance to Christianization.[7] Was there a pagan Middle Ages? Not in an organized or widespread sense, according to most historians, at least not after the turn of the millennium and perhaps even earlier. If Christianization is defined as the reception of baptism and the adoption of Christian rituals by specific communities, it is possible to say that England, France, Belgium, and parts of Germany were Christianized by 750. About this time, Bishop Daniel of Winchester suggested to Boniface that those "who cling to outworn beliefs are in a very small minority."[8] This claim was too optimistic, for non-Christian belief and practice still existed alongside Christian ritual. Before describing how Boniface exposed the impotence of local Germanic religion by felling the sacred oak at Geismar, his biographer Willibald lamented the attraction of that same religion to some people who had presumably adopted Christianity but who, "not yet strong in the spirit, refused to accept the pure teachings of the church in their entirety":

> Moreover some continued secretly, others openly, to offer sacrifices to trees and springs, to inspect the entrails of victims; some practiced divination, legerdemain, and incantations; some turned their attention to auguries, auspices, and other sacrificial rites; while others, of a more reasonable character, forsook all the profane practices of the Gentiles [i.e., pagans] and committed none of these crimes.[9]

Such reports of non-Christian practices, stylized as they may be,[10] indicate that popular religion was still alive and posed a challenge to the missionaries. Christianity had been defined in the Mediterranean world, but now it had to be taught to Europeans with a different religious heritage and retaught to the same people and their descendants who readily fell back upon the beliefs and practices of their ancestors, especially if they were not kept on a tight leash by Christian rulers and clergy. In the story of Boniface, Willibald revealed how efforts at conversion sometimes had to be repeated:

> He [Boniface] then set out on a journey to Thuringia, having accomplished by the help of God all the things we have already mentioned. Arrived there, he addressed the elders and the chiefs of the people,

calling on them to put aside their blind ignorance and to return to the Christian religion which they had formerly embraced.[11]

The process of removing that "blind ignorance" was complex and it did not look the same in every century or in every region. In eighth-century Thuringia, Willibald alleged that "the devotion of the people to Christianity and religion" died out after the dukes who protected them had lost power and "false brethren" were imported to pervert their minds. The reconversion of the people went hand in hand with the banishment of these "devil's disciples and insidious seducers of the people."[12] Whether the religious competition was always so direct or not, Willibald's account suggests that Christianization was sporadic, not continuous, and other sources indicate that it was difficult to bring the campaign to an end. About a century after Boniface, in the same corner of Germany, Abbot Rabanus Maurus (d. 856) was still admonishing his listeners around Fulda to live chaste lives, to attend church regularly, and to eschew all forms of magic and superstition, including amulets and sorcery.[13] Although it is hard to judge the prominence of non-Christian elements singled out by medieval observers, the whole was in most cases a mixture of official Christianity and popular religion or magic.[14] As the Middle Ages wore on, this mixture looked less and less like a competing, organized paganism.

Magic and pagan practice aside, medieval Christians were also able to distinguish levels of religious activity that modern observers might call commitment. They knew the difference between laypeople who practiced their faith on a regular basis and those who were merely baptized and seemed indifferent to regular practice. The distinction between good or true Christians and the rest of the baptized preceded the Middle Ages and became common in texts such as canon law and commentaries on the Bible. A favorite way of making the distinction was to contrast Christians who were members of the church only numerically (*numero*) with those who could more deservedly (*merito*) be called Christian. This distinction goes back at least to Augustine and was still being used by Martin Luther in the sixteenth century.[15]

Theologians also began to conceptualize various kinds of faith to describe levels of awareness and commitment. Distinctions were made, for example, between formed and unformed faith and between explicit and implicit faith. In the first case, faith formed by love was the goal sought for all people who received through baptism the habit of faith that was expected to grow with the aid of additional grace. Like reformers in every age, medieval preachers urged adults to be diligent in seeking this grace.

Those who sought to do so through the sacraments could be sure that, as long as they put no obstacle in its way, their faith would be formed by love into a virtue worthy of salvation. These "good Christians" were set apart from "false Christians" who had lost sanctifying grace through mortal sin and retained only an unformed faith.[16] In the second case, the distinction between explicit and implicit faith demanded that clergy give conscious assent to specific doctrines while allowing laity to believe in general what the church believed. Implicit faith was regarded as useful for most laypeople, and Thomas Aquinas noted that faith which relied on reason to prompt the will to believe forfeited some of its meritorious character.[17] Later medieval theologians, however, tried to hold laity to a higher standard. Beyond their acceptance of everything revealed in Scripture as true, the Tübingen professor Gabriel Biel (d. 1495) insisted that adults also had to believe specifically in Christ the mediator.[18]

Over the centuries, therefore, the standard of what constituted adequate Christian faith and practice varied according to region and according to the depth and speed with which a local culture was Christianized. Unequal levels of awareness and loyalty existed among the faithful, not only between distinct groupings like clergy and laity or monks and secular clergy, but also among laity and clergy in the same parish. Nevertheless, Christianity gradually became the religion of most people in Europe and their lives were regularly influenced by Christian convictions and ceremonies.

Historians remain alert to this change of medieval culture across time, but few are willing to support the old notion of a golden high Middle Ages (12th–13th centuries) that was preceded by a primitive early Middle Ages and followed by a decaying later period (14th–15th centuries). Though not a heaven on earth, the Carolingian Renaissance (8th–9th centuries) was a remarkable cultural synthesis permeated by Christian ideals, innovation, and scholarship.[19] The twelfth century was both a cultural renaissance and a religious reformation.[20] The late Middle Ages were also a period of intense religious activity and devotion.[21] Historians now cast late-medieval religion in a more positive light than did their colleagues, like Johan Huizinga, who wrote before 1960.[22] According to Huizinga, in fifteenth-century France and Holland faith and piety were very much alive but not well, because they had been corrupted by a materialistic, vengeful, and formalistic late-medieval culture. "The people usually lived in the lackadaisical corruption of an entirely externalized religion. . . . The mind of the people, only incompletely Christianized, had never quite lost its disgust for men who were not allowed to fight and had to be chaste!"[23] Such generalizations about late-medieval Christianity are now recognized as unsupportable. Faith was certainly a more serious matter for some people than for others, and disdain for the church and its privileges did lead to manifest anticlerical sentiment. Clergy, however, were also criticized because laypeople themselves held Christianity and its ideals in the highest regard and saw that clergy were not living up to their standards.[24]

One historian has suggested the following picture of how medieval Christianity changed over time.[25] By the year 1000, village people were reorganizing their lives around a network of Christian parishes. The church building was central and the sacraments began to pull the faithful together. "Their church, surrounded by its cemetery, became an essential place, the material cement of their solidarity, the sheltering refuge, the usual location of their gatherings. The village community regrouped itself around its dead, its guardian saints and their relics."[26] By the twelfth century, baptized believers in Western Europe were being subjected to tighter supervision by a clerical elite, but religious activity in the parishes continued apace in an expanded Latin Christendom. Secular clergy, who did not belong to religious orders, paid increasing attention to the pastoral care of their flocks in order to counteract the influence of new orders whose preachers were intruding on their domains. Suburban churches were founded as towns expanded and older parishes thrived without being overwhelmed by monastic reform or lamed by the costs of the Crusades.[27] People did not know that the height of the Middle Ages was passing into a later phase; Christian awareness and practice prospered.

Indeed, far from being in decline or full of "lackadaisical corruption," the fourteenth- and fifteenth-century church turned out plenty of Christians who eagerly embraced the regular offerings of parish life. They attended mass and received the sacraments; they visited convents and joined lay religious associations known as confraternities that organized devotions for the living and supported masses for the souls of the departed.[28] Through confraternities and on their own many laypeople contributed to the social, charitable, and cultural life of their parishes. They showed up for sermons, processions, mystery plays, and pilgrimages. They prayed and had prayers said for them. They left money and property to religious foundations and acquired indulgences to decrease their time in purgatory. They gave alms. They participated mainly in a "religion of doing, extroverted and festive," even though the examination of one's conscience was becoming more common.[29] If one focuses on piety in the parishes, local Christianity seems to have been alive and well through much of the Middle Ages. Europe was Christianized not only in breadth but also in depth.

Some historians have cast shadows over this rosy picture. In Spain at the end of the Middle Ages Christianity has been called a veneer under which "the religion of the people remained backward."[30] The Middle Ages were judged to be "churchly" rather than "Christian," because the clergy and their institutions played a prominent role in society while orthodox belief among the people remained superficial.[31] In his popular books, Jean Delumeau painted the late Middle Ages and early modern Europe in the dark hues of anxiety and fear, sin and guilt.[32]

These negative judgments, and more positive ones, are based on two variables. The first is the nature of the sources. If they are heavily peppered with examples of religious deviance, such as records of the Inquisition in southern France, then a more negative picture of Christian belief and practice emerges. Inquisitors may leave the impression of widespread heresy, although the people suspected of heresy were often respected by neighbors and thought to be quite orthodox. In early-fourteenth-century Montaillou, for example, "Cathars" considered themselves to be "good Christians,"[33] and earlier in the Lauragais suspected heretics were called "good men," "good women," believers, and friends of God.[34] Generalizations about religious mentality based on these sources are risky, but it is almost certainly wrong to use them as evidence that European society was riddled with heresy and paganism. The inquisition in the Lauragais uncovered no heretical network or conspiracy but rather the "mundane experience of a quiet sanctity" that was nevertheless transformed by the investigators.[35]

Delumeau selected motifs like contempt for the world and the dance of death on which to base his gloomy assessment of the late Middle Ages.[36] In contrast, one could point to the vivid, upbeat pictures of fifteenth-century life in a medieval housebook preserved at the Wolfegg castle in southern Germany. A panoply of late-medieval culture, from tournaments to technology and from recipes to romance, it is organized around several themes like the children of the planets. If this housebook were our only source of knowledge about medieval society, then neither Christianity nor the macabre would appear to exert much influence on fifteenth-century European life. Only one depiction of religious activity is contained in all sixty-three of its parchment leaves: among the merry children of Sol, shown in one corner, a woman gives alms to a beggar while three pious souls kneel before a crucifix (figure 3).[37]

Figure 3. Sol and His Children. *Medieval Housebook*, fol. 14r. South Germany, 15th century. Wolfegg castle.

The second variable affecting judgments about the depth of Christianity is the gap between religious professionals and the laity. The spiritual life of monks and mystics may be held up as exemplary, but the mundane life of the parish was a world away from the cloister. Many extant medieval texts belong to the genre of spirituality, but they reveal little about actual devotional practice outside the cloister. We do not yet know as much about the religious conviction of people who lived below the ivory towers and outside the ranks of nobility who supplied most of the upper clergy. Recent studies of individual parishes and dioceses, however, expose the vibrancy and importance of religious life. Late medieval parishioners were not waiting for the Reformation; they were part of a dynamic and creative community that gave order and purpose to their lives and centered their religious practice on the parish church with its Christian liturgy and cult of the saints.[38] Many laypeople had no desire to scale the heights of contemplation or to descend the steps of humility; but they did keep books, buy wax, raise funds, organize ales, attend mass, donate money for lights, altars, statues, private masses and prayers, join processions, and pursue such concrete duties and devotions without which real Christianity could not exist.

As the medieval housebook indicates, laity did not restrict themselves to such activities, but their piety was far more vital than it was perfunctory. Despite the variables that urge caution when drawing big conclusions, it is not rash to suggest that by the end of the fifteenth century the Christianization of Europe, judged by participation in Christian ritual and practice, was substantially achieved. Why then did many sixteenth-century reformers decry it as idolatrous and unchristian and label their predecessors as superstitious? What did they find deficient in the piety of late-medieval Christians that had to be changed? Before answering those questions, it is useful to consider how medieval theologians themselves wrote about superstition and piety.

Superstition and Piety

Over the centuries, the definition of superstition underwent a distinct evolution in Christian usage.[39] When early Christian apologists accused pagans of superstition, they meant idolatry, that is, worship of the gods in Greco-Roman religion. Only when state-sanctioned paganism began to disappear and Christianity was installed in its place did the notion of superstition as false belief and worship come to mean something different from historical pagan practices.[40] By the time of Thomas Aquinas (d. 1274),

superstition as idolatry was distinguished from two other kinds of superstition, which Thomas called divination and observation, that is, foretelling
the future and magic.[41] Thomas based this distinction on a passage from
Augustine and, like Augustine, he connected superstition to the activity
of demonic powers.[42] Thomas also made clear, however, that superstition
could now be present in Christian worship and practice. In answer to the
question of whether anything "superfluous" could be found in worship,
Thomas answered that everything which contradicted the essence of worship (giving glory to God and subjecting the mind and body to God)
was both superfluous and superstitious, because it consisted in externals
and did not pertain to the interior worship of God.[43] By the thirteenth
century, therefore, superstition was no longer the prerogative of a pre-
Christian cult; its forms had migrated to the Christian parish. Idolatry and
other kinds of superstition were associated more readily with Christian
worship than with pagan practice.

In the West, Carolingian theologians had already drawn a sharp line
between paganism and Christianity. In the debate over images, for example, Theodulph of Orleans did not trust people to make the distinction
between worship of gods and veneration of images, which John of Damascus was confidently asserting in the East.[44] Defending the veneration of
images against the charge of pagan idolatry, John furnished a fascinating
statement of the continuity among pagan, Jewish, and Christian practices
even while he was trying to prove the discontinuity:

> If you speak of pagan abuses, these abuses do not make our venera-
> tion of images loathsome. Blame the pagans who made images into
> gods! Just because the pagans used them in a foul way, that is no rea-
> son to object to our pious practice. Sorcerers and magicians use
> incantations; so also the Church prays over catechumens; the former
> conjure up demons, while the Church calls upon God to exorcise
> demons. Pagans sacrificed to demons; Israel offered blood and fat to
> God; the Church offers the bloodless sacrifice to God. Pagans make
> images into demons, and Israel made images into gods, for they said,
> "These are your gods, O Israel, who brought you up out of the land
> of Egypt." But we have set up our images of the true God, who
> became incarnate, and of His servants and friends, and with them we
> drive away the demonic hosts.[45]

This easy way of drawing parallels among pagans, Jews, and Christians
must have scared Theodulph and led him to paint a "stark contrast

between a world of profane objects and the small cluster of 'sacred things'" reserved for the clergy to mediate and interpret.[46] The range of authentic piety was restricted to clerical supervision, and superstition came to be identified with claims to access divine power that did not receive a clerical blessing.

In the thirteenth and fourteenth centuries, the prosecution of popular movements like Waldensians[47] and Cathars as heresy indicated that superstition was being defined from within Christendom. Remnants of outright paganism gradually faded from the awareness of laity and the target of Christianization became popular or folkloric beliefs attached to Christian teaching and ritual. Although medieval reformers saw this kind of superstition as a persistent problem that needed attention, it is a mistake to apply the label of superstition to late-medieval Christianity in general. When theologians and preachers inveighed against superstition, their admonitions did not imply that all laity and clergy held such beliefs or engaged in such activities. Nor were superstitions incompatible with regular churchgoing, living in the cloister, or giving alms to the poor. For that matter, although medieval theologians like Thomas Aquinas offered theoretical definitions of superstition, the distinction between superstition and orthodox practice is difficult for modern historians to make.[48] It can only be made on theological grounds and by observing how superstition was defined by the writers who criticized it.

In the late Middle Ages, those criticisms were still sharp and specific. A good example is the memorandum on superstitions associated with hearing mass that was written by the Parisian chancellor and theologian Jean Gerson (d. 1429).[49] He regarded it as presumptuous and superstitious to assert that a person would not die, or go blind, or starve on the day on which that person had devoutly attended mass. Such notions, he had reason to suspect, induced people to expect worldly advantages from going to church and brought ridicule on the sacrament.[50] Gerson dismissed other notions as mere illusions, for example, the belief that people would stop aging during the time spent at mass. If these notions were found to have a credible authority behind them, Gerson recommended withholding that information because people were prone to believe such "curiosities and wizardry" and were quick to applaud preachers who said such things.[51]

Gerson gave special attention to "false and presumptuous and superstitious" notions surrounding the intercession of saints. People should never be taught to expect healing from prayer to a saint. On the contrary, a pious prayer implored a saint to intercede with God, and if that prayer promoted the salvation of the petitioner and did not place an obstacle in the way, then it would be heard! The number of prayers made no difference, nor did the form or order in which they were offered. Saints would not be influenced by such external forms, but only by a pious mind and heart and comparable devotion.[52] Gerson's admonition exemplified Thomas's definition of superstition as external supplements that were superfluous to true worship and to interior devotion. Nevertheless, one can hardly imagine advice that would have flouted more directly the expanded role of multiple prayers in popular late-medieval forms of devotion like the rosary.

Another memorandum by Gerson attacked superstitions tied to specific holy days and explored their origins with scholastic organization and efficiency.[53] In this case superstitions were related to the cycle of nature or to the calendar: if the feast day of St. Paul brought with it clear skies, then the harvest would be good, but snow or rain foreshadowed scarcity, while fog meant that animals would die. The day of Holy Innocents (December 28) was not propitious for beginning any task at all.[54] Gerson admitted it would be tedious to discuss all those things which induced people "to make causes out of things which were not causes and to claim as experience what had not been experienced." Among the reasons he did offer for this human tendency, however, was an unusual reference to the early days of Christianization. Such notions could derive from the "leftover practice of Gentiles, pagans and other heathen as they were encountered at the beginning of conversion."[55] The remedy for these misguided souls was to trust the experts and especially those who rightly observed and taught the law of God.[56]

At the beginning of the sixteenth century, an Augustinian monk and professor of theology at Erfurt, Johannes von Paltz (d. 1511), reported on superstitions connected with extreme unction from his experience as an indulgence preacher in Germany. Instead of desiring the sacrament as a salutary preparation for death, people feared they would be certain to die once they received it. Paltz also heard that a spouse who recovered unexpectedly after having received the sacrament was required to postpone for one year the resumption of sexual relations. If a woman was pregnant when she received the final anointing, her life was thought to be even more at risk if she lived to give birth. Paltz sought to counter these and similar notions by attributing them to the devil, and he preached that, contrary to popular fears, extreme unction gave even the worst sinner a chance to escape the devil's snares.[57]

According to Paltz, superstition appeared in four guises: pilgrimages to unapproved sites, magic, astrology, and alchemy. Not only were common folk guilty of such behavior, but also high officials in both church and state.[58] Paltz was especially critical of people who ran off on pilgrimages after abandoning their jobs or their families. He was careful about whom he accused of consulting soothsayers, but he criticized prelates for not taking more assertive measures against the devil who was behind the practice of all magic. Although no obvious "servants of idols" were known to him, he did believe some were always lurking. People who consulted soothsayers merely to recover an object they had lost were false Christians because they were showing preference for worldly over eternal goods.[59] Even churchgoing came in for criticism. Since Paltz believed that meditation on the passion of Christ would bring special comfort to sinners, he urged them to listen to a complete sermon on Good Friday rather than running from one church to another.[60]

In Paltz's eyes, the antithesis of superstition was genuine Christian piety. What defined that piety in the late Middle Ages? Paltz's exhortation to stay put for a complete Good Friday sermon indicates that one important component was the passion of Christ. It served Paltz and theologians like Johannes von Staupitz (d. 1524) as the primary channel of divine mercy, and they emphasized the passion to such an extent that humanity's role in the process of salvation was reduced to a minimum.[61] Instead of demonstrating true contrition for their sins before absolution could be granted, people needed to feel only some regret or simply to appreciate the infinite value of Christ's own suffering. Conscientious preachers like Stephan Fridolin (d. 1498), a monk of the Franciscan observance who provided pastoral care to nuns in the convent of St. Clare at Nuremberg, ranked God's mercy above his punishing righteousness. He taught that salvation depended completely on the suffering of Christ, which by itself without the threat of judgment was able to produce sufficient contrition for sin and turn people to God.[62] God's judgment was not ignored by these preachers, but divine compassion was emphasized within a theological framework that attempted to balance dread and solace.[63]

Paltz and Staupitz inherited a specific Augustinian theology of piety in which the passion of Christ played a significant role. That theology can be traced to three members of the order who lived at Erfurt in the early fourteenth century: Jordan of Quedlinburg (d. c. 1380), Henry of Friemar (d. 1349), and Hermann of Schildesche (d. 1357). Henry was the author of a widely circulated commentary on the Ten Commandments and Hermann wrote a handbook for clergy that was popular in the later Middle Ages. Jordan's *Meditations on the Passion of Christ* and his exposition of the Lord's Prayer were important contributions to late-medieval devotional literature. These authors understood their audience to be all Christians, and their works belonged to an Augustinian campaign to Christianize their world through the order's platform of spiritual knowledge.[64] This knowledge formed the core of an Augustinian theology of piety that was built upon love of God and love of neighbor. The educational and pastoral activity of the Augustinians attempted to instill this love in such a way that believers would come to know the compassion of God and be channels through which that compassion reached others.

Love and compassion formed only one basis of late-medieval piety, however. Also familiar to laypeople was the emphasis on divine judgment and on the divine justice that had to be satisfied by the performance of meritorious works of love and devotion.[65] The Augustinian theology of piety, for example, stressed the debt that believers owed to God. Through the passion of Christ, God's gracious gift, the faithful were taught how much they owed and the impossibility of paying off the debt. They must strive to pay it, nonetheless, by doing good works to others lest they lose the grace already bestowed upon them. Since they were in constant battle with the devil, however, even the elect could not be certain of salvation, and they needed the help of the saints. In addition to the merits of Christ's passion, the suffering of the saints supplied additional help and ready access to the ear of God that Christ the judge might be too distant to provide. Superstition could creep into late-medieval piety from both directions—seeking God's grace through the passion of Christ and its representation through the mass, or doing penance and loving others through the good works that might repay the debt owed to God and to the neighbor. In both cases the uncertainty of salvation could tempt the faithful to try additional ways of obtaining divine favor that theologians regarded as superfluous and superstitious.

In late-medieval piety, divine judgment coexisted with compassion and human merit with the suffering of Christ. According to medieval authors, the product of this piety was a believer who eschewed all forms of superstition and demonstrated a faith formed by love. These model Christians, who approximated the ideal of monastic perfection, were portrayed by Denis the Carthusian (Denys Rickel, d. 1471) in terms of a biblical text that enjoined the imitation of Christ (1 John 2:6): "Whoever says, 'I abide in him,' ought to walk just as he walked." According to Denis, all people who said they were Christian should walk as Christ walked; and since Christ was said to be without sin or guile and kept his father's commandments, every one of the faithful was obligated "to avoid sin which . . . [was] transgression of the divine law and disobedience of the heavenly commandments." A model to emulate was Job, who had claimed: "My heart does not reproach me for any of my days" (Job 27:6).[66]

Like other theologians, however, Denis did not expect all Christians to embody this ideal. Although they were held to follow Christ by avoiding mortal sins, they could not escape venial sins. His expectations remained high nonetheless, especially when it came to the need for Christians to impress Muslims: "Just as the law of Christ was superior to all laws, thus Christians ought to be more virtuous, more perfect, and more exemplary than everyone else in the world. Their superiority requires their daily lives to be rightly ordered, internally and externally, in word and in deed: in their clothing, in what they eat and drink, when they sleep and when they go out, in every way in which they make use of created things and of earthly possessions." To a certain extent Denis, who belonged to a strict monastic order, was following a monastic missionary strategy from an earlier period. Citing the "venerable fathers" John Cassian (d. c. 432) and John Climacus (d. 649), Denis argued that no one deserved to be called a Christian whose way of life did not compel an unbeliever to recognize the [divine] lawgiver who established that life as divine, wise, and just.[67] After Europe was officially Christianized, Denis was still holding Christian piety to a standard that would convince non-Christians to adopt the faith.

Even with their limitations, the high expectations placed on Christian piety by Denis and other monastic commentators make it difficult to ascertain the depth and character of devotion on the eve of the Reformation. Historians do, however, appear to agree on one feature of that devotion: late-medieval piety should no longer be appraised as merely external or formal[68] but as heartfelt and rewarding. In the mind of preachers like Paltz, Staupitz, and Fridolin, piety required devout intentions as well as external conformity with the church's teaching. Piety was both an interior and an exterior matter, not only for preachers and theologians, but also for laity. It would be presumptuous for historians to assume that activities like attending mass, invoking saints, acquiring indulgences, or praying rosaries were practiced as mere externals without corresponding inner devotion. One could go through the motions, perhaps, but it is impossible to say that an act of ritual observance had no inner effect at all. Affective stances like penitence were inculcated by devotion to central figures of late-medieval piety such as the "blessed sinner" Mary Magdalen. She was conflated with other biblical Marys, like the woman who dried the feet of Jesus with her hair (Lk 7:37–50), and thus celebrated as the symbol of genuine repentance.[69] True, some actions like the acquisition of indulgences were criticized because they did not enhance faith.[70] Others, however, like praying rosaries with indulgences attached, were the vehicles used by many laypeople to express and to intensify their personal belief.[71] Lay fraternities and pilgrimages tightened the bond between the interior and exterior elements of devotion. By sponsoring worship and caring for the needs of one another, members of lay fraternities embodied the social ideal of charity and took seriously their obligation to one another.[72] Corpus Christi fraternities created loyalties by promising intercession and support in times of crisis and by organizing shared religious experience during prayer and festivals.[73]

Nor should one dismiss as external the piety of Christians in the late fifteenth century who traveled from their parish of St. James at Rymättylä in southern Finland to Santiago de Compostela on the northwest coast of Spain. Such long pilgrimages were not uncommon. St. James was also popular in Denmark, where twenty-three churches and five fountains bear his name and where there is widespread evidence of the "pilgrim-shell," the symbol of St. James preserved in several different forms, including the souvenir brought back from Spain.[74] In one of Erasmus's colloquies, a pilgrim who has just returned from Compostela reveals that he was fulfilling a vow to his mother-in-law after her daughter had given birth to a healthy baby boy. When asked how the saint responded, the pilgrim acknowledged that St. James did not speak but seemed to smile and nod his head and gave him some of the famous shells.[75] Like this fictional traveler, real pilgrims would scarcely have undertaken their journeys without conviction about its value for their own well-being, earthly and eternal. In the parish church at Rymättylä an imposing traditional fresco of the last judgment dominates the wall over the altar. Sitting on a rainbow, Christ holds in his right hand the lily of grace and in his left the sword of justice. On the left the damned are swallowed by the jaws of hell, while on the right the redeemed are led by St. Peter into heaven. In all likelihood, this complementary presentation of dread and solace moved more than one parishioner to undertake the long and perilous journey to Spain.

The fear of hell and hope of heaven moved late-medieval Christians to engage in concrete acts of piety, but seldom if ever were the acts treated solely as formal or individual obligations. Believers were convinced that they lived in a communion of saints with the departed and that they could ease the pains of their loved ones in purgatory. Their worship and piety formed a "cult of the living in the service of the dead,"[76] and that cult brought them benefits, especially through the intercession of saints. Late-medieval churches were filled with saints, and it was the case elsewhere as in England that laity "looked to the saints not primarily as exemplars or soul-friends, but as powerful helpers and healers in time of need, whether bodily need or the last spiritual extremity of death and the pains of Purgatory."[77] The veneration and intercession of saints contained a mixture of superstitious, folkloric, and Christian elements; the same can be said for prayers, pilgrimages, indulgences, and other types of medieval piety. Excess and superstition connected with pilgrimages were chided by reformers, but Eamon Duffy is right to call this piety lay Christianity instead of superstition and to consider it the devotional mainstream and not the devotional underground![78] For medieval people it was Christianity as it had been inculturated in Europe and become the religion of a new European Christendom.

This mainstream was fed by the currents of weekly liturgies and festivals surging through local parishes, like the popular eucharistic feast of Corpus Christi, which received impetus in the thirteenth century from the beguine community of pious women in Liège.[79] The Eucharist could also be abused by heresy and superstition, but it was still the centerpiece of the lively devotion of late-medieval Christian people. Despite occasional criticism, the priests and bishops who presided over them shared for the most part in the same devotion. Sixteenth-century reformers, however, saw this piety as something more harmful than Christianity mixed with a dash of superstition. Like Gerson they condemned what they identified as superstitions,[80] but Protestants also went further and labeled some of the piety idolatrous and unchristian. Hence sixteenth-century Christianization was not equivalent to medieval reform, but it entailed a more sweeping renewal of Christendom than medieval preachers and theologians had deemed necessary. The Reformation was the product of a Christian Middle Ages, but for most reformers that Christianity was in many ways seriously deficient.

Reformation Ideals

Despite the success of medieval Christianization, early-sixteenth-century reformers did not think their society was Christian enough. In 1520 Martin Luther issued the following lament:

> Who then can comprehend the riches and glory of the Christian life?
> It can do all things and has all things and lacks nothing. It is lord over
> sin, death, and hell, and yet at the same time it serves, ministers to,
> and benefits everyone. But alas in our day this life is unknown
> throughout the world; it is neither preached about nor sought after;
> we are altogether ignorant of our own name and do not know why
> we are Christian or bear the name of Christians. Surely we are named
> after Christ, not because he is absent from us, but because we believe
> in him and are Christs one to another and do to our neighbors as
> Christ does to us. But in our day we are taught by human doctrines
> to seek nothing but merits, rewards and the things that are ours; of
> Christ we have made a taskmaster far harsher than Moses.[81]

The leaders of sixteenth-century Protestant communities knew that
Europe had been gradually Christianized in the preceding centuries, but,
as Luther's lament shows, they concluded that the process had either failed
or was incomplete. Most of them did not think their culture was completely pagan or unchristian. Although reformers used hyperbole to that
effect, they recognized that essential elements of the faith—the Bible,
creeds, rituals—had been handed down to them in a church that was in
some sense Christian. Later in his career, Luther acknowledged that tradition when it was challenged by the radical wing of the Reformation: "We
confess, however, that under the papacy much that is Christian, in fact, all
that is Christian was present and that from there it came to us."[82] Nevertheless, Protestant reformers were also convinced that Christianity as
taught, believed, and practiced in their day remained so distorted that it
had to be overhauled in order for European cities and countries, women
and men, to become Christian by their standards. In other words, they
would not Christianize as before, i.e., convert pagans to Christian belief
and ritual, but convince people who had already been baptized to believe
and practice the faith in a way judged by Protestants to be more valid. In
this sense they also wanted to Christianize Europe.

Luther's lament over late-medieval religion suggested the kind of
Christians he envisioned and why he thought so few could be found. In
Christian Freedom, the treatise from which the lament is taken, he drew a
template of Christian life that resembled an ellipse with two foci: faith and
love. Genuine Christians were those who both believed in Christ and
acted as Christs to one another. In his mind, few believers of this kind
could be found, because the ideal was hard to realize and because significant obstacles were present: "merits, rewards, and the things that are

ours." These obstacles were not mainly theoretical, although a theology of merit and reward underlay them. The actual hindrances belonged to the practices of late-medieval piety that were thought to gain the salvation of those who engaged in them (penance, indulgences, saints, the mass, pilgrimages). In place of this piety, Luther proposed substituting a way of life that redirected the activity of believers toward the welfare of the community:

> The Apostle has prescribed [Phil 2:1–4] this rule for the life of Christians, namely, that we should devote all our works to the welfare of others, since we have such abundant riches in faith that all other works and our whole life are a surplus with which to do good for the neighbor by a voluntary benevolence.[83]

The passage quoted above summarizes the theology that underlay Luther's vision of the newly Christianized life and would become normative for Lutheran doctrine: justification by faith alone instead of by faith and meritorious works. It demonstrates that for Luther justification was never just a theoretical construct but a practical guide for maintaining the right attitude toward works. The acts of piety and charity performed by Christians were not necessary to their own salvation because they needed nothing beyond faith. For themselves those acts were superfluous and Christians could, therefore, "by a voluntary benevolence" devote those same acts "to the welfare of others." This theology was Luther's answer to the historical judgment that Christianization had not worked because believers were so focused on the potential merit and reward to be gained from their actions that they overlooked the unique basis of salvation: the work and presence of Christ himself. If they focused on Christ alone as the source of salvation, then in Luther's scheme believers would be free to direct their charity to others. The goal of this theology was not unlike that of medieval reform: believers who were more fervent in faith and charity. The differences lay in the kind of works that qualified for this new earnestness and in the motivation that produced it. Ideally for the early reformers, no actions were viewed as legitimate if they were considered meritorious or if they undermined the role of Christ as the sole agent of redemption. Faith was not deemed a human supplement to the atoning work of Christ but a divinely granted vehicle through which the benefits of that atonement were received.

Although he did not initially intend for it to happen, Luther's agenda for Christianization would break with that of his medieval predecessors and become part of a Reformation that turned into a permanent rupture between the Roman Church and the various Protestant and Radical movements that developed their own agendas for a new campaign of Christianization. As a result of this rupture, the sixteenth-century Reformation yielded a restructuring of Christianity in Europe that was broader than the alteration that followed the Hussite Revolution in fifteenth-century Bohemia. That remarkable upsurge of Czech nationalism and reform, which was inspired by the preaching and martyrdom of Jan Hus (d. 1415) and fueled by his followers, has been called by some historians the "first reformation."[84] The claim of priority for Bohemian reform acknowledges its integrity and dissuades other historians from reducing Hus to a proto-Protestant or to a forerunner of the Reformation.[85]

Despite the significance of Hus for Luther and other Protestants who invoked his cause, defenders of the Reformation's uniqueness have used theological weapons against the notion that it was closely aligned with the Hussite movement. There were to be sure theological differences between Hus and Luther,[86] but if the Reformation vision is used as a criterion, the Czech movement certainly anticipated the sixteenth-century goal of Christianization. Writing from prison in Constance during June of 1415, Hus articulated a vision of Christendom under the headship of Christ that recalls Luther's lament a century later:

> Now faithful Christendom exists without a pope, a mere man, having Christ Jesus for its head, who directs it the best; for its heart, which vivifies it, granting the life of grace; for the fountain which irrigates it by the seven gifts of the Holy Spirit; for the channel in which flow all the streams of graces; for the all-sufficient and unfailing refuge to which I, a wretch, run, firmly hoping that it will not fail me in directing, vivifying, and aiding me; but will liberate me from the sins of the present miserable life, and reward me with infinite joy.[87]

The Hussite movement had its specific agendas for the reform of Christendom that were based on biblical teaching and practice. Following Hus, it focused on the necessity of obeying the law of God, called for clerical reform, and demanded the giving of the chalice to the laity so that during the Eucharist they could receive both elements (hence the name "Utraquists" for the mainstream of Hussite reform). Hus also questioned the system of indulgences and papal authority to the extent that, although theological differences between Hus and sixteenth-century Protestants can be discerned, their vision and their agendas were clearly similar.

Nevertheless, to associate Hussite reform with the Reformation need not take away from the distinctiveness of either movement. They were different both in scope and in outcome. Unlike evangelical movements of the early sixteenth century, Hussite reform in the fifteenth century did not ignite a European-wide Reformation; and instead of producing new confessional churches, by the sixteenth century the mainstream of Czech reform was itself leading to one of those confessions. The Hussite movement had divided into radical Taborites and Utraquists, and many of the latter together with the Bohemian Brethren embraced the Czech Confession of 1577, a stance that cost them dearly in the 1620s when they were forced to convert to Catholicism or to emigrate. The Hussite movement did eventually contribute to the restructuring of Christianity, and in this perspective Czech reform is best understood not as a first reformation but as the late medieval movement that best anticipated the Reformation vision in which its own descendants participated.

In the sixteenth century, Protestants and dissenters like the Anabaptists were not the only groups to envision a more Christian society. Partly in reaction to the growing breech, the Roman Church developed its own agendas for reforming the clergy and educating the laity that aimed at more informed expressions of the faith. This process was already labeled Christianization by the French historian Jean Delumeau, who used it for the attempt by the Catholic reformation to bring genuine Christianity for the first time to rural France.[88] As he described it, the rural missionaries found that "the intellectual and psychological climate of the people was characterized by a profound unfamiliarity with the basics of Christianity, and by a persistent pagan mentality with the occasional vestiges of pre-Christian ceremonial."[89] Catholic missionaries, therefore, relied on better-trained clergy, who no longer identified closely with the populace, to teach it orthodox Christianity for the first time. According to Delumeau, both Catholic and Protestant reformations converged in their efforts to Christianize the masses and to spiritualize religion.[90]

There are two problems with Delumeau's use of Christianization to describe the Catholic Reformation. First, although Delumeau was right to find similarity between Catholics and Protestants, especially in their desire to make the belief and practice of people more consciously Christian, it was not the goal of either reformation to spiritualize religion in the sense of internalizing piety at the expense of ritual. Both Catholics and Protestants wanted to purify ritual, to be sure, but neither thought that religion could survive without it and they divided to a large degree over the issue of how much ritual to abolish. To them Christianization did not mean the spiritualization of religion but, rather, the realignment of internal attitudes with orthodox Christian practice.

The second problem with Delumeau's use of Christianization was his portrayal of late-medieval people as so full of superstition, anxiety, and guilt that they appeared to be unchristian.[91] The Reformation as Christianization, however, does not require such a negative portrayal of the Middle Ages. Even though Protestant reformers used descriptors like idolatrous and pagan for polemical reasons, most of them knew they were not bringing orthodox Christianity to areas where it had never existed or to people who were scarcely better than pagan. These people were practicing with enthusiasm the traditional Christianity that had permeated their culture. Reformers were not planting the faith for the first time but attempting to re-root it according to a different theology and model of piety. Instead of assuaging anxiety and guilt through channels of mercy like the penitential system and the intercession of saints, the believers addressed by reformers were directed to corporate absolution, the sermon, a reduced number of sacraments, catechetical instruction, personal devotion, and acts of charity that were not to be considered meritorious. Whether this direction reduced anxiety or not, it was not the replacement of paganism with Christianity but an attempt to replace one Christian system of faith and practice with another that had been altered more by Protestants and dissenters than by Catholics.

Where it germinated in the minds of reformers, the Reformation vision was a certain religious mentality, that is, a set of convictions about how Christianity should best be defined, believed, and practiced. How did this mentality develop? The first generation of Protestant reformers—Martin Luther, Huldrych Zwingli, Philipp Melanchthon, Urbanus Rhegius, Martin Bucer, Thomas Cranmer—were well-educated priests, monks, and humanists who had developed high ideals during the course of their training. To one degree or another they were all theologians, whether they taught in a university like Luther and Melanchthon, or served in ecclesiastical positions like Zwingli, Rhegius, Bucer, and Cranmer. Scarcely a generation later, John Calvin would produce the first version of the *Institutes* before assuming any pastoral or teaching office. The Reformation, however, was not only a quarrel over academic theology but also over religious practice. Like their predecessors at the new University of Wittenberg (1502), the initial agenda of Luther and his colleagues was to strengthen the faculty and the curriculum in the direction of biblical humanism.[92] Nevertheless, the Reformation in Germany did not ignite over curricular reform or medieval scholasticism, but over the offer of a papal indulgence and the claims made for it. In Zurich, the Reformation began in defiance of rules governing the Lenten fast, in Strasbourg over the requirement of clergy to remain celibate, and in England over the right of a layperson, albeit the ruler, to divorce and remarry. The debates over these issues were also theological, but the underlying concern was how clergy and laity should practice the faith.

During these debates, Protestant reformers developed strong theological convictions about the nature of Christian freedom and its consequences. These convictions were often cast as ideals, such as that described in Luther's treatise quoted at the beginning of this section, but they generated real conflicts with the Roman hierarchy when reformers persisted in their challenges. These challenges eventually confronted the sacramental system, the cult of saints, monastic vows, and clerical authority as soon as Protestants contrasted the practice around them more intently with descriptions of early Christianity in the Bible and in patristic texts. Meanwhile, Catholic reformers were calling for improvement of the same system by founding new orders, attempting to make the clergy more accountable, and cleansing the traditional rituals of superstition. They also used biblical and patristic texts to justify their reforms. The visions of both Protestant and Catholic reformers were inspired by the ancient texts of the faith.

Comparable texts had motivated communities of the New Devout that dotted the landscape of northern Europe by 1500. The Brothers and Sisters of the Common Life were not new monastic orders but stood rather between them and the lay movements of the Reformation. Indeed, since they did not occupy any medieval estate, they had to possess a spiritual disposition which could accept that humble status and find the presence of God both in solitude and in their life together.[93] They voluntarily held all property in common, studied and meditated on the Bible, taught children and adults, and copied texts. They produced popular devotional books like *The Imitation of Christ* by Thomas à Kempis (d. 1471) and the *Rose Garden of Spiritual Exercises* (1491) by John Mombaer. Prominent theologians and scholars were associated with the Brethren. Gabriel Biel (d. 1495), whose works were studied by the young Martin Luther, served as the prior of several houses in southwestern Germany before and after he taught theology at the University of Tübingen. Though critical of the education he obtained from the Brethren, the prominent humanist Erasmus of Rotterdam (d. 1536) lived as a youth in one of their hostels and received instruction from a Brother. The Reformation cannot be traced directly to the influence of the New Devout, but their vision of pious living and learning was shaped by the same ideals of monasticism and humanism that contributed to the Reformation.

The Monastic Precedent

Medieval humanism is usually seen as a precursor of the Reformation, while monasticism is identified as one of its major targets. There are good reasons, however, for believing that monasticism, broadly understood as all women and men in religious orders, made a positive contribution to the vision of sixteenth-century reformers. In the late Middle Ages, religious communities were undergoing reforms of their own without any hint of the Reformation to come. In a remarkable show of religious vitality they were founding new houses, recalling their members to a stricter observance of the old rules, and deepening their personal devotion.[94] Of special interest is the Observant movement within the mendicant orders. Three of the "most dynamic religious figures" between 1490 and 1520 were all Observant friars: Girolamo Savonarola (d. 1498), a Dominican; Francisco Ximinez de Cisneros (d. 1517), a Franciscan; and Martin Luther (d. 1546), an Augustinian.[95] All three reformers were shaped by the commitment of Observants to a stricter and more intense life than non-Observants, or conventuals, were practicing.[96] The Observant movement reached its peak in the fifteenth century and was especially widespread in the Franciscan and Augustinian orders.

The list of sixteenth-century Protestant reformers who had been monks is long. Martin Bucer had been a Dominican, and John Eberlin von Günzburg was a former Franciscan.[97] The radical author of the *Schleitheim Articles*, Michael Sattler, was a former Benedictine monk and his wife was identified as a Beguine. Ambrosius Blarer, reformer in Constance, was a former Benedictine,[98] and the humanist John Oecolampadius entered a Bridgettine monastery for two years before deciding for the evangelical movement and becoming the reformer of Basel. Many of the monks in Germany who became Lutheran reformers had been Augustinians: Martin Luther, Andrew Osiander, John Lang, Wenzel Linck, and Stephan Agricola. As the list indicates, the Augustinian Hermits were important mediators of the early evangelical message in Germany, and almost half of their houses, including newly established ones like Wittenberg, were in the regions of Thuringia and Saxony.[99]

Luther's home cloister in Erfurt belonged to the German congregation of Observant Augustinian houses, and in 1511 he undertook a journey to Rome on behalf of seven of these houses to oppose a reform plan supported by Johann von Staupitz, vicar-general of the German congregation and his future mentor. Backed by the general of the order, Staupitz wanted to merge the Observant houses with the non-Observant Augustinian province of Saxony and Thuringia. Luther gave up his opposition to the plan and moved from Erfurt to the Augustinian cloister in Wittenberg, where he succeeded Staupitz in the chair of biblical theology at the university. Staupitz soon gave up the office of vicar-general and concentrated his efforts on preaching, pastoral care, and theological study.[100] Earlier in his life, Staupitz had taught that the Christian life was preserved by the word of God alone, especially by teaching it to children before they could make decisions to the contrary. Let the preachers stop preaching for six years, warned Staupitz, and you will see what I mean.[101] *Mutatis mutandis* this attitude also expressed the goal of many sixteenth-century reformers and catechists. Staupitz finally decided not to support the Protestant movement, but he left an indelible personal and pastoral mark on Luther,[102] and his advocacy of monastic reform constituted an important legacy to the Reformation.[103]

Beyond the specifics of Augustinian practice, other ties between monasticism and the Reformation, both Catholic and Protestant, are discernible. The ties with Catholic reform are direct in spite of the fact that many new orders were founded in the sixteenth century. Those new foundations did not presuppose a criticism of the medieval orders such as Erasmus leveled at monks he viewed as ignorant and lacking in sincerity. Reform within the old houses continued alongside the formation of new orders, and ideals of monastic reform were applied to the church as a whole. The Capuchins, founded in 1528, grew out of the Franciscans, and the reform of the Camaldolese Order in 1511 by two devout humanist monks, Vincenzo Querini (d. 1524) and Tommaso Giustiniani (d. 1528), informed the proposal for a broad reform of Christendom sent by them to Pope Leo X in 1513.[104] On the Protestant side, Oecolampadius wrote that he left the cloister and found Christianity, but he admitted that Christianity had survived intact in the monastery and that the interior life of a monk was still attractive.[105] Luther's struggle with the validity of vows and his unhurried retreat from the cloister suggest the persistence of a monastic identity that had been formed over fifteen years in the monastery before he was excommunicated. Thereafter, he continued to live in the

Augustinian house at Wittenberg, first as a celibate man until he married in June of 1525, and then as a spouse and parent until his death in 1546. By that time he had spent almost thirty-five years in the same monastic complex.[106]

Positive references to monastic attitudes and practice appear in Luther's writings alongside the better-known polemic. Not only did he insist that he had been the best monk he could be, but he also adapted the tools of monastic spirituality for the study of Scripture and recommended them in place of his own writings. *Oratio, meditatio, tentatio*—praying and meditating on the text with attentive regularity were augmented by resort to the Bible in conflict, testing, and controversy. At those times Luther believed that Scripture would open itself to the seeker in ways that were especially rich and consoling.[107] In the lectures on Genesis from the last decade of his life, Luther held up Abraham as the true monk because he knew how to live in the world without being of the world. The mendicant orders were just the opposite, he alleged. Despite their commitment to begging and poverty they lived as if their priority were the accumulation of worldly wealth and property.[108] As the ideal monk, Abraham represented for Luther what all Christians ought to think: their truest home was not the earth that God had created for them to enjoy while they were pilgrims, but the spiritual kingdom that would conduct them to their eternal home with God. Alongside its affirmation of earthly joys, duties, and sorrows, the Reformation's portrait of the Christian life retained from the monastic ideal an element of detachment from the world that was urged on all believers. Luther did not simply give up the monastic ideal; he applied much of it to Christians in general, including the evangelical counsels derived from the Sermon on the Mount.[109]

This tendency to apply a monastic ideal to all believers was not unprecedented. It belonged to the idea of reform that was embedded in the history of monasticism, and many medieval attempts to inspire a more devout life for the laity may be read in this fashion.[110] Monastic orders were always reforming themselves, reaching back to old traditions and experimenting with new ways. At no time was this truer than in the twelfth century, named by Giles Constable a time of reformation in its own right. Reformation (*reformare, reformatio*) was the word used for religious change, and religion itself was primarily "a way of life . . . not a system of belief." From 1100 to 1160 the heart of reform was an attempt to "monasticize first the clergy, by imposing on them a way of life previously reserved for monks, and then the entire world."[111] This goal had been embraced by the papal reform movement associated with Gregory VII

(1073–1085), and it was reaffirmed under his successors Victor III and Urban II, both of whom were Benedictine monks. Encounters with stricter forms of eremitical monasticism in central Italy during the early eleventh century paved the way for the papacy to think of reform in monastic terms.[112] One of these hermits, Dominic of Sora, established a dozen churches and monasteries,[113] while another, Romuald, who founded the Camaldolese Order, reportedly wanted to turn the whole world into a hermitage.[114] According to James of Vitry, "all the faithful of Christ serving the Lord under the rule of the Gospel and ordained under the one highest and supreme abbot" should be called regulars, that is, people who live by a rule.[115]

By the twelfth century, the ideals of monasticism were being stretched to fit innovative forms of the religious life. In contrast to austere hermits and strict orders like the Cistercians who fled to the wilderness, Benedictine monasticism showed how material prosperity and spiritual well-being, interaction with the world and separation from it, could exist side by side.[116] Its communal form of the monastic life became a model in which human friendship and charity toward others formed essential parts of a full Christian life.[117] Preaching and pastoral work were also fitted, sometimes awkwardly, into the new religious ideal alongside withdrawal from the world, especially by the Franciscans, Dominicans, and Augustinians, which were founded in the thirteenth century. The formation of mendicant orders and the subsequent rise of semireligious lay groups—Brothers and Sisters of the Common Life, Beghards, Beguines, confraternities—were part of a late-medieval process called "religionization" by Eric Saak.[118] These "micro-religions," as Saak names them, sought to apply the ideals of the religious life to specific communities of clergy and laity that possessed their own theology and ideals of piety. Religionization corresponded to the late-medieval tendency to expand the concept of "religious" from those who chose the monastic life to other believers who applied aspects of the monastic ideal to their existence without legally institutionalizing their communities. Saak distinguishes religionization from Christianization because it was not the general conversion of Europe that was sought, but the continuous Christianizing of believers by catechizing them in distinct communities.[119] Religionization, therefore, corresponds to what this essay is calling the ongoing Christianization of Europe, a process that intensified during the late Middle Ages and then entered a decisive second stage in the sixteenth century. It captures one aspect of this intensification, namely, its unfolding in religious communities that were no longer restricted to monasticism, but religionization does not account for the majority of believers who were not members of these communities. It does, however, illustrate the extent to which monastic ideals expanded their influence during the late-medieval period and were positioned to shape the Reformation.

These attempts to accommodate monasticism to life in the world did not shield monks and nuns from rebuke and criticism. If all Christians were to become religious, then the religious had to be held to a higher standard. In 1493 the Tübingen professor Konrad Summenhart wrote for the provincial chapter of Benedictines at Hirsau a sharp tract which denounced ten errors of the monks. Summenhart castigated them not only for worldliness in general, but also for the lavishness of the cloister and its furnishings, the elaborate decoration of churches, the neglect of biblical study, handing over possessions of the cloister to relatives, excess in food and drink, and tolerating monks who still owned private property.[120] The abbey at Hirsau had enjoyed several decades of prosperity and expansion, but that did not prevent the monks from requesting a critique from Summenhart that was aimed in part at their own order. Both inside and outside the cloister, the integrity of religious life was vigorously debated as the Reformation began.

Alongside this debate, medieval monasticism anticipated the Reformation through its theology. Monastic theology as taught in the twelfth century by nonscholastic experts like Bernard of Clairvaux (d. 1153) continued to exist in the fifteenth century and its goals blended with those of sixteenth-century reformers.[121] Unlike scholastic theology, which emphasized the logical analysis of religious topics in academic debate, monastic theology encouraged the study of sacred texts in order to promote religious life and to enhance the experience of God. For the Carthusian Nicholas Kempf, the cloister was the only place where a genuine theologian could take to heart what one learned with the intellect and practice it with security and direction.[122] Conrad Zenn, an earnest Augustinian who wrote on behalf of the regular observance that was adopted in his house at Nuremberg, believed that reform entailed more than the removal of specific abuses. It presupposed a deeply spiritual attitude toward monastic existence as perfect Christian living in the presence of God.[123] That attitude by no means belittled theology or the acquisition of knowledge, nor did the spiritual knowledge desired by the Augustinians exclude theology in the form of scholasticism. The two often met in the lives of gifted monks like Martin Luther who learned scholastic theology while living in the cloister. Nevertheless, if monastic theology is defined by the Augustinian criterion of seeking knowledge for the sake of loving God and neighbor, then the goal of Reformation theology was closer to monastic than it was to scholastic theology. By concentrating on the application of theology to piety and insisting that believers informed by spiritual knowledge could live more faithful lives, reformers were drawing on the tradition of monastic theology even while the Protestants among them rejected the structure of monasticism and applied its ideal to life outside the cloister. For that reason it is possible to say: "In its dynamic utopias the early Reformation was a new monasticism."[124]

The Humanist Dilemma

Medieval humanism was also a vital source of the Reformation vision. Enhancement of the Christian life had been the goal of many scholars who participated in the rebirth of learning that permeated the intellectual culture of late-medieval Europe. By returning to the classics, the Bible, and patristic sources and making these texts more reliable and accessible, humanists hoped to change the study of theology and to improve both education and behavior. In Cranach's depiction of the Reformation, Philipp Melanchthon (1497–1560) is shown drawing water from the well of ancient sources (*ad fontes*) while a colleague pours it on the new vines (figure 4). Many humanists were also masters of rhetoric who gave new life to composition and to preaching. Although they may have criticized the scholastic method and certain features of monasticism, some of them had taken vows and they envisioned a religious life that was not entirely different from the goal of monastic reformers.

The Italian humanists of the early Renaissance—Francesco Petrarch (d. 1374), Coluccio Salutati (d. 1406), and Lorenzo Valla (d. 1407)—all believed that "the problem of the religious life was internal and subjective, concerned with the relations of the individual, of all individuals, to God."[125] Influenced by his study of Platonic philosophy, the Florentine scholar Marsilio Ficino (d. 1499) presented the Christian religion as a way of living that was shaped by awareness of the divine goal that the presence of God brought to the soul.[126] The importance attributed by these humanists to the internal sources of religious life was honored by both Catholic and Protestant reform,[127] but the early humanist attempt to define the relationship among the laity, the secular clergy, and the religious (monks and nuns) anticipated the Reformation as well. The question was similar to the issue debated in the sixteenth century: Was the clerical or monastic life closer to perfection than the life of the laity and should the former be considered superior to the latter? Petrarch and

Figure 4. Lucas Cranach the Younger. *The Vineyard of the Lord* (1556). Detail: Philipp Melanchthon and a colleague drawing water for the vineyard. Stadtkirche, Wittenberg.

Salutati both affirmed the advantages of the religious life, while Valla was the sharpest critic of monasticism.[128] Three generations later, humanists and Protestants would sound more like Valla than like Petrarch or Salutati, but the Reformation embraced both points of view in its attempt to enhance the Christian life.

The importance of humanism for the Reformation has been repeatedly documented for major Protestant reformers and for leading Catholics like Ignatius Loyola and the early Jesuits. It can also be found in textual scholarship and printing, the new interest in biblical languages, the rush to educate clergy and laity of all ages, the civic virtue and loyalty that supported a reformation of the cities, and the assault on popular superstition and clerical abuse. All of these influences can be found among Protestants and Catholics, yet humanists had to make a religious choice that was part of a process that Erika Rummel called the confessionalization of humanism.[129] By and large, those Swiss and German humanists who found themselves in a younger generation by 1520 (like Philipp Melanchthon, born in 1497) decided for the Protestant movement, while those humanists from an older generation (like Erasmus, born in the 1460s) decided to remain loyal to Rome and became important early supporters of Catholic reform. Rummel has illustrated how typical humanist ideals and convictions, such as education and open debate, were used by Protestants and Catholics in order to further their causes. Humanists made their commitments to one side or the other, however, on the basis of a principle they shared: Christian faith and practice needed to be deepened and purified. Like monasticism, humanism anticipated the Reformation vision by advocating reform of the religious life. As reformers, however, humanists would adopt different agendas for achieving that reform and would apply the skills of education and debate to those agendas.

The ambivalent attitude of Erasmus toward monasticism indicates how difficult it was for humanists to decide for or against the Protestant Reformation. Erasmus is well known for his criticism of monks and canons (priests who were members of clerical chapters)—criticism that won him applause from humanists like Bernhard Adelmann, himself a devout canon in Augsburg.[130] Commenting on Erasmus's depiction of monastic life as a kind of idleness,[131] Adelmann reported to his humanist friend in Nuremberg, Willibald Pirckheimer: "In this book [Erasmus] detests the laziness and the multitude of monks and clerics. I fear he admonishes these brethren to the point that they will try to hinder his work. You would scarcely believe how they hate him. . . ."[132] In *The Praise of Folly* Erasmus's early criticism of monasticism was sharpened by satire,[133] and its themes were popular in Italy.[134] Nonetheless, Erasmus was aware that criticizing monks and priests when they fell short was easier than praising or imitating them when they did their duty and kept their vows: "People are more ready to criticise the clergy if they happen to be bad than they are to emulate them when they are good. So it is that monks who really are pious do not stimulate people to follow their example because they seem to be only practising what they preach, whereas if they are not everyone is terribly shocked."[135]

Erasmus may have spoken from experience. He was an Augustinian canon at Steyn from 1488 to 1493, and he remained a member of that order for the rest of his life. In 1517, after presenting the facts of his illegitimate birth, he was granted a dispensation from the requirements of residing at Steyn and of wearing the full religious habit. Like Protestants, Erasmus was both attracted by the monastic ideal and repelled by examples of monastic practice around him.[136] One of his earliest works, written soon after he entered the house at Steyn but not published until 1521, was a defense of the monastic life under the traditional title *Contempt of the World*. Writing to his friend at Steyn, Servatius Rogerus, in 1514, Erasmus argued: "How much more consonant with Christ's teaching it would be to regard the entire Christian world as a single household, a single monastery as it were, and to think of all men as one's fellow-canons and brethren, to regard the sacrament of baptism as the supreme religious obligation, and to consider not where one lives but how one lives."[137] This argument may justify the refusal of Erasmus to restrict his life to the monastery, but it also expresses his monastic ideal and the extent of its application to all believers. Four years later, he would ask Paul Volz rhetorically: "Why do we so closely confine the professed service of Christ, which he wished to be as wide open as possible? If we are moved by splendid names, what else, I ask you, is a city than a great monastery?"[138]

Erasmus's pointed criticisms of monasticism should not be ignored. Dating mostly to a period before the outbreak of the Reformation, they belonged to his rejection of ceremonialism as the essence of piety and its replacement by the desire to love Christ and to follow him by loving the neighbor.[139] This stance had been advocated by medieval authors like Thomas à Kempis in the *Imitation of Christ*, and it was the interior compass that guided Erasmus's journey.[140] Monasticism, he believed, was intrinsically neither good nor bad; its value depended on whether it served the life of piety. This was the gist of his comment in the *Enchirid-*

ion of 1503 that began with the provocative declaration, "Monachatus non est pietas":

> Being a monk is not a state of holiness but a way of life, which may be beneficial or not according to each person's physical and mental constitution. I personally do not urge you to adopt it, nor yet do I urge you against it. I merely advise you to identify piety not with diet, or dress, or any visible thing, but with what I have taught you. Associate with those in whom you have seen Christ's true image.[141]

When Erasmus's provocation was attacked by the Spanish Franciscan Luis Carvajal as discrediting the evangelical life, Erasmus replied that if monasticism consisted in living according to the gospel, then all Christians had professed the rule of St. Francis and all were monks who lived according to the gospel.[142]

Erasmus was a typical reformer insofar as the ideals of monasticism and Christian humanism converged in his vision. Both learning and living were to be pursued with Christ in view. The study of letters should not be loved for the sake of knowledge alone, but in order to discern Christ more clearly and then to love him and to communicate this knowledge and delight to others.[143] Living by the gospel in the imitation of Christ was learned by hearing and reading the Bible in one's own tongue and acting on what one learned. It did not require the rejection of exterior piety, but God was more pleased with invisible piety than he was with visible forms of worship.[144] At this point, however, Erasmus and other humanists who would be reformers had to make a crucial decision. Was it possible to cultivate this invisible piety and still make use of visible forms such as the cult of saints? Against Huldrych Zwingli and other Protestant humanists, Erasmus decided that believers could also honor Christ through the saints, if it gave them joy, and that they should follow Christ in the saints by putting away their own vices and striving for saintly virtues. In one colloquy, Erasmus attacked Zwingli's policy of removing every trace of saints from the churches by having Mary plead helplessness and threaten to take her son Jesus with her:

> Although I am unarmed, you shall not cast me out unless you cast out the son I am holding in my arms together with me. For I shall not be parted from him. Either you cast him out together with me, or you let us both remain here—or do you prefer a church without Christ?[145]

All the same, Erasmus turned down a request to compose lives of the saints, preferring instead to let his scholarship cast light upon the "Lord of the saints."[146]

Erasmus decided that changing one's attitude was sufficient to realize both the humanist and monastic ideals of the Christian life. Although being a monk did not guarantee piety, neither did the abolition of monastic vows. Zwingli was a humanist who decided differently about monasticism, the cult of the saints, and the other issues that ultimately divided Protestants from Catholics. For him abolishing monastic vows did not guarantee piety, but he was convinced that one could not be a pious Christian *and* a monk. As he read the Bible and the early church theologians, the valid expressions of Christianity did not include monasticism as he had seen it practiced. If humanism did give priority to the internal dimension of the religious life, perhaps Erasmus remained more faithful to the vision of early humanism than Zwingli and his Protestant colleagues. At the same time, no reformer emphasized the humanist ideals of education and debate more than Zwingli. The decision of humanists for and against Protestant reforms rested on which vision of Christian life they extracted from ancient texts and judged to be authentic and desirable. To become Protestant, it was not possible to ignore practices judged to be unchristian; they had to be changed or abolished.

The goal of reform envisioned by Erasmus and other humanists was impressive. In place of reliance upon external forms they sought to instill genuine Christian piety into all believers by making available the earliest texts of the faith. For them a Christianized Europe would resemble a reformed monastery containing an excellent library that was assiduously used by believers going about their daily tasks in accord with the teaching of Christ. In their monastery saints might still be venerated, private masses and prayer vigils celebrated, daily hours observed, and even indulgences acquired. These activities would not, however, dominate the devotion of the people. Their piety would instead revolve around the teaching and learning of Scripture, reverence toward God in daily life, and charity toward their neighbors. It was a grand and noble vision which many Catholics could accept and to which many Protestants, owing to their own affinity with monastic and humanist ideals, could almost subscribe. Without this humanist vision, sixteenth-century reformers would not have conceived and debated their own.

To push European culture toward the realization of their vision, sixteenth-century reformers made maximal use of the resources of a reawakening society. The Reformation vision of a Christian Europe was nevertheless different from its medieval ancestors. The Reformation sought more than an intellectual and cultural awakening and strove to become more than another stage in the long tradition of monastic reform. For reformers both Catholic and Protestant, religious transformation and social change were more important than intellectual renewal, and the religious penetration of society as a whole took priority over the reinvigoration of its clerical and monastic sectors. The Reformation was a second step in the process of Christianizing the entire culture, an extensive attempt to rid Europe of superstition as medieval commentators had defined it and to produce a purified Christian culture according to the various agendas of Catholic, Protestant, and Radical reform.

Figure 5. Lucas Cranach the Younger. *The Vineyard of the Lord* (1556). Detail: Luther raking the vineyard. Stadtkirche, Wittenberg.

Chapter 2

Martin Luther's Agenda

A Christian Germany

Christianizing Christendom

Martin Luther's reforming agenda developed gradually during his early career as a teacher, but once it was full-grown, by the year 1522 when he returned to Wittenberg from exile at the Wartburg castle, he fixed his eyes on one goal and made decisions about specific reforms accordingly. That goal was to provide a religious environment in which believers would develop as fully as possible into the model Christians described by him in *Freedom of a Christian*: free through faith to serve others in love. The creation of these "real Christians" (to use his term)[1] took precedence over other agendas that interpreters have occasionally tried to impose on Luther in order to make him more palatable to modern religious values like freedom of conscience, church unity, specific interpretations of Scripture, or separation of church and state. For Luther, reforming Christendom meant that those concerns, in the way he understood them, were secondary to his primary goal and, insofar as they were valid at all, had to support its achievement.

Luther's single-mindedness partly explains his stances that still make modern observers uncomfortable. His refusal to compromise with Zwingli, for example, over the presence of Christ in the Lord's Supper (1529) arose not from a nonchalant attitude about religious unity but from his conviction that the full human presence of Christ in the sacrament was essential to the nurture of faith. His appeals to Protestant rulers after 1525 to establish and defend the evangelical churches were not declarations of secular supremacy but Luther's judgment at the time about the best way of guaranteeing the survival of the new Christendom. Luther's advocacy of an uncompromising stance by Protestants at the Diet of Augsburg in 1530 and at the Diet of Regensburg in 1541 was based not on stubbornness but on suspicion that the theology and practice on which the new Christendom was built would be undercut. His persistently harsh rejection of papists, Turks, and Jews, especially during the 1530s and 1540s, was a result of his fear, shared by others, that evangelical or Protestant Christendom, especially in its Lutheran form, was still at risk from these opponents of true Christianity. Luther's agenda does not account for all of his religious intolerance and polemical discourse. They were also features of the apostolic self-expression that developed out of his personal and religious experiences. As I contend later in this chapter, however, his claim to know what authentic Christianity was cannot be separated from his conviction that he above all others was called to lead a movement that would bring it to Germany at last.

Luther's early leadership of reform in Wittenberg and his defense of giving both wine and bread to the laity from that period illustrate how Luther's agenda worked. The defense, entitled *Receiving Both Kinds in the Sacrament*,[2] was published in April 1522, exactly one year after Luther had made his dramatic speech at Worms and was declared an outlaw in the Holy Roman Empire. It also appeared about one month after Luther returned to Wittenberg from exile at the Wartburg castle and preached eight sermons that criticized his colleague, Andrew Karlstadt, for pushing local reforms too far. The texts of these Wittenberg sermons are not as reliable as the widely distributed pamphlet, *Receiving Both Kinds*, but they have exercised more influence on modern conceptions of Luther's agenda. Since the sermons advocate the gradual implementation of changes, both historians and theologians have labeled Luther a conservative reformer and criticized or praised him according to their preferences. Historians who have rehabilitated the integrity and good intentions of Karlstadt have sometimes criticized Luther, while some theologians have celebrated Luther's conservatism and his opposition to "radicals" everywhere.

Both groups miss the point of Luther's agenda. His call to slow down the pace of reform in Wittenberg was motivated, not by the desire to make as few changes as possible, but by his conviction that reform was not exclusively an external matter. Luther had already voiced sharp criticism of indulgences, the mass, and monastic vows, and he was determined to make conspicuous changes of his own. As he saw it, however, some changes had been forced on people before they were ready. In the Wittenberg sermons, Luther stated a guiding principle whose radicality has often been missed. Christian devotion was marked by love as well as faith, and love obligated those believers who were ready to make changes to wait on those who were not, until the latter had been brought to the point where their consciences would not be violated: "Therefore, let us show love to our neighbors; if we do not do this, our work will not endure. We must have patience with them for a time, and not cast out those who are weak in faith; and [we must] do and omit to do many other things, so long as love requires it and it does no harm to our faith."[3] At stake for Luther was a new way of practicing Christianity that would arise spontaneously, express itself in the right relationship between faith and love, and replace those rituals that, in his experience, ran roughshod over consciences.

That new piety and its motivation were clearly described in the pamphlet *Receiving Both Kinds*. By Luther's day, the laity were required to confess to their parish priest at least once a year, perform the penance imposed upon them, and to attend mass at Easter but without receiving the wine of the sacrament. Luther preferred to set aside this "unchristian" regulation, dating from the Fourth Lateran Council (1215),[4] in favor of a free decision by all "that they may go to the altar not by compulsion but moved by their own consciences and the hunger of their souls."[5] The principle of communing only when one truly desired it was Luther's criterion for the authentic use of the sacrament and it took precedence over the number of elements received. To be sure, Luther argued that the reception of both elements by everyone was "right, Christian, and evangelical,"[6] but at the same time he acknowledged that many people were not ready for it. He thought they would receive both elements only because it was the new regulation, not because they sincerely desired the sacrament, and their consciences would still be vulnerable to guilt over breaking the old rule. To force people to receive both elements would gain nothing. "If it were ordered that this practice be used and if people were to become Christians merely because they received the sacrament in this way, then nothing would be easier than to be a Christian; even a sow could be a Christian."[7]

Although correct external practices like receiving both elements were important, the use of them was free and they were always secondary to faith and love. Luther's agenda was first to create "real Christians," as he called them, believers whose main concern should be whether or not they had become "different" people. Insisting that people define their religious status by obeying ecclesiastical rules, like the requirement of an annual confession and communion, rendered the sacrament a mere formality and created, in Luther's view, a society of virtual pagans:

Ask yourself whether you are showing love to your neighbors and are serving them. If you do not find these evidences of faith within yourself, if you are living the same as before, still packed full of unfaithfulness, hatred, envy, wrath, and unbelief, then, dear friend, by all means stay away from the sacrament until you have become a different person. Don't let yourself be driven to it by the crowd or custom or ordinance of the pope. Heavens, if this idea were really put across, it would mean that where thousands come to the sacrament now, scarcely hundreds would come, . . . and so we would at last become again a group of real Christians, whereas at present we are almost completely pagan and only Christian in name. Then we should be able to do what is now impossible for us, namely, separate from our number those in whom we see by their works that they have neither faith nor love.[8]

Luther's admonition to "stay away from the sacrament until you have become a different person" applied to the new evangelical community in Wittenberg. In his estimation they were still in "captivity in Babylon" but wanted to act as if they "had already arrived home." "Everyone wants to be called Christian," he said of those who wanted to require immediate changes, "and we have to permit it; but then they do not want to exercise faith and love."[9] Forcing the issue and creating sects was not the answer. Rather, "there is nothing else to do but to preach the gospel and to keep people away from the sacrament and all external rites until they feel and show themselves to be Christians and of their own accord press forward to faith, to love, and then to the external sacrament and similar things."[10]

Most interpretations of these passages have focused on the pace and not on the goal envisioned by Luther. The goal, however, was the heart of his agenda. Christianity as practiced around him looked subchristian to his eyes. In *Freedom of a Christian* he had written: "Any work that is not done solely for the purpose of keeping the body under control or of serving one's neighbor, as long as nothing is sought contrary to God, is not good or Christian. For this reason I greatly fear that few or no colleges, monasteries, altars, and offices of the church are really Christian in our day— nor the special fasts and prayers on certain saints' days."[11] In place of inappropriate reliance upon external ritual, Luther set as the goal of his teaching a stance that he called "proper faith and genuine love":

I have taught in such a way that my teaching would lead first and foremost to a knowledge of Christ, that is, to pure and proper faith and

genuine love, and thereby to freedom in all matters of external conduct such as eating, drinking, clothes, praying, fasting, monasteries,
sacrament, and whatever it may be. Such freedom is had and is used
in a salutary way only by those who have faith and love, that is, those
who are real Christians. On such people we can and should impose
no human law—nor permit anyone else to do so—which would bind
their conscience. But always we must first have the people who are
supposed to possess such liberty, that the wine may be stored and kept
in new vessels [Mt 9:17].[12]

Luther not only laid down a principle, but he also applied it directly to
the sacrament of the altar.[13] This procedure combined a gradual abolition
of the mass with a new emphasis on the words of institution. Masses "performed as sacrifices and good works" were "to be abolished." People
should no longer pay to have them said but, until they died of their own
accord, priests who celebrated them should not be dragged away from the
altar.[14] In the meantime preachers were to emphasize the words of institution. "For these words are a thousand times more important than the
elements of the sacrament; without them the sacrament is not a sacrament
but a mockery before God."[15] People should take however many elements
were offered, for "the law of love is far to be preferred above the institution of both kinds."[16] In fact, no mass at all should be celebrated except
when people were present and wanted it, whether once a week or once a
month, "for the sacrament should never be celebrated except at the insti-
gation and request of hungry souls, never because of duty, endowment,
custom, ordinance, or habit."[17] Private confession was not required, but
Luther advised people to make confession gladly before they went to the
Lord's Supper, or at least not to despise it.[18]

He recommended a similar way of reforming other practices. The worship of images was forbidden, and Luther wished there were no images on
the altars because idolatry was always a danger. Still, he thought it wiser
to retain them and to preach against the wrong use of images when they
were adored or placed in churches as a pious act.[19] Priests were free to
marry and monks and nuns were allowed to leave their cloisters, but they
should do so only after they had acquired a conscience strong enough to
withstand the accusations of the devil before they died.[20] No one had
to observe the fasting rules of the church, and Luther implied they were
the least damaging of all regulations.[21] Making people disobey them,
however, fundamentally distorted the evangelical piety that he was
attempting to teach: "We try to prove ourselves evangelical by receiving

the sacrament in both kinds and in our own hands, by pulling down images, by devouring meat, by abstaining from prayer and fasting, and that sort of thing. But nobody will lay hold of faith and love, which alone are essential, and in which alone there is any power."[22]

The goal of Luther's agenda was an ideal construct: a true or perfect Christian who would be motivated by nothing external but whose faith and love would arise spontaneously from an encounter with the divine word. This ideal construct was vividly presented in his essay on Christian freedom: "A Christian is the freest lord of all, subject to none; a Christian is the most dutiful servant of all, subject to all."[23] The freedom of Christians was the gift of faith and their duty was the expression of love. They were liberated from the practices of late-medieval religion as the means of meriting salvation, but they were not free from the divine commandments to love God and serve the neighbor. Luther's agenda involved, however, more than an ideal construct. To facilitate both faith and love, he had concrete changes in mind like those discussed in *Receiving Both Kinds*; and once they were implemented in evangelical towns and territories, the Reformation in Germany would begin in earnest.

Luther's concentration on faith and love indicates that the target of his reforming agenda was the people of Christendom rather than the medieval church. Luther was not originally aiming at structural reform but at the deeper infusion of an entire society with faith and love. This would happen first of all in people, not in institutions, and these people were initially the laity and clergy that Luther encountered around Wittenberg: parishioners and students who heard his lectures and sermons, fellow monks in the Augustinian order, priests in the parishes and in the clerical chapter of All Saints, colleagues at the university, local nobility at the ducal court of Saxony, and eventually members of his own household. Martin Luther did not see himself as a postmedieval man trying to reform the medieval church because it was full of corruption and abuse. He was a sixteenth-century monk, priest, and professor in Wittenberg, who wanted to make the theology and piety of his society more Christian than it was. The agenda developed by him during the years 1517 to 1522 was to Christianize Christendom.

An important clue to this agenda is found in one of Luther's earliest calls for reformation, casually referred to as his address to the German nobility. A different sense of his purpose, however, is disclosed by the full title: *Address to the Christian Nobility of the German Nation concerning the Improvement of the Christian Estate.*[24] The target of reform is the "Christian estate," that is, the status that is common to all baptized believers, whether they are laity and belong to the "worldly estate," or clergy and belong to the "spiritual estate." Using these traditional terms, Luther appeals to the nobility as Christian laity to carry out reforms since, in his view, the spiritual estate or the clergy, to whom the responsibility rightly belongs, has so far refused.[25] This refusal has led to the misery of Christendom,[26] and the guilt belongs to the "Romanists," who have built three walls around themselves in order to prevent reform, hastening thereby the downfall of Christendom.[27] Because he was in Saxony, Luther was indeed appealing to nobility in Germany, and he did make use of traditional German grievances against Rome. First and foremost, however, he was appealing to Christian nobility to do something about the abject state of Christendom.

Luther's attack on the first wall provides the most important key to his agenda. The "Romanists" insist that clergy, the spiritual estate, have authority over the laity, the worldly estate, and therefore civil authorities have no power to make the upper clergy reform. This claim is unnatural, even unchristian, argues Luther on the basis of 1 Corinthians 12:14–26, a text that admonishes each member of the body to help the other and to prevent its destruction.[28] Luther simply abolishes the distinction between the two estates and declares that all Christians, clergy and laity, belong to the same spiritual estate.[29] Therefore the laity, now just as spiritual and Christian as the clergy, have as much right and obligation to reform Christendom as do the clergy.

The theological name that has been given to this move by Luther is the priesthood of all believers; on the basis of biblical texts cited by the reformer, all Christians were said to belong to a common priesthood. Its significance for Luther's ecclesiology and doctrine of ministry has been much debated, but its original purpose was larger: to legitimize the reform of Christendom by lay Christians, that is, by civil authorities who were spiritually equal to clergy and possessed both the divine mandate and the power to accomplish reform. The doctrine has also been used to argue that the Reformation enhanced the dignity of secular work and contributed to the rise of democracy. Luther, however, was not making the argument that all Christians belonged to the same class of society, but rather that they belonged to the same spiritual or Christian estate. He was not advocating the secularization of society, but its Christianization: all believers would be considered equal and their common identity, the Christian estate or existence in Christendom, would be improved.[30] Instead of reducing the priesthood to the level of laity, Luther was raising the laity to the level of priests, not to take over their pastoral function, but to take seriously their Christian faith and responsibility.

It is true that Luther never intended to start a new church; but that statement can be misleading if it implies that his agenda was simply to reform the medieval church. As he pursued the goal of Christianization, Luther did not think in terms of medieval and modern, or Catholic and Protestant, churches, but in terms of Germany before and after the rule of the papacy: "All I seek to do," he wrote, "is to arouse and set to thinking those who have the ability and inclination to help the German nation to be free and Christian again after the wretched, heathenish, and unchristian rule of the pope."[31] Luther's agenda was more radical than church reform. In order to Christianize Germany, Luther became convinced that he had to liberate the church from "the papacy at Rome,"[32] which some of its defenders insisted was the head of the church. As a result, Luther expanded the notion of church so that it would be equivalent to the Christian estate or Christendom as defined in the *Address to the Christian Nobility*. This true church was a spiritual entity like the Christian estate itself. It was not tied to Rome but included "all those who live in true faith, hope, and love" wherever they gathered throughout the world.[33] The church was not invisible; it became visible every time an assembly of believers gathered for worship. But it was not simply physical either, because true Christendom could never be restricted to one human leader or organization like the Roman curia.

Through this lens Luther viewed the continuity and discontinuity between medieval and Reformation Christianity. Authentic Christianity did exist in Europe prior to the Reformation, but it existed within a Christendom that Luther regarded as subject to the papal antichrist. Nonetheless, under the pope, Christendom did not die out. The essentials of the faith—Scripture, genuine sacraments, the ministry, and the catechism—were passed on to the reformers and their communities in a reformed Christendom. If we rejected everything in the papal church, argued Luther,

> then we would cast out even Christendom from the temple of God and all that it contained of Christ. But when we oppose and reject the pope it is because he does not keep to these treasures of Christendom which he has inherited from the apostles. Instead, he makes additions of the devil and does not use these treasures for the improvement of the temple. Rather he works toward its destruction, in setting his commandments and ordinance above the ordinances of Christ.[34]

Luther was not speaking about continuity between institutions as if the essentials of Christianity had been transferred across the Reformation divide from the Roman Church to Protestant churches. He saw it this way: in spite of the papal tyranny that almost destroyed Christendom, the essentials of the faith had survived in order to serve the cause of a newly Christianized Europe. In his eyes there was both continuity and discontinuity, not between churches in their modern confessional forms, but between a captive Christendom, in which authentic Christianity had barely survived, and a liberated Christendom, in which the centrality of faith and love was being restored. For Luther, of course, the discontinuity was much greater than for most modern historians, who rightly judge the traditional religion of medieval Europe to have been Christian. This discrepancy, however, confronts us with the radicality of Luther's judgment on the Christendom of his day and with the audacity of his reforming vision.

Theology and Life

Luther's vision was radical because it did not stop with the revamping of theology but encompassed major changes in the structure and practice of Christianity. As a rule, Luther has been understood as a reformer of theology who by accident became a reformer of the church. There is some truth in this view. When he was professor of Bible at the University of Wittenberg, Luther's official assignment was to teach theology through the exposition of Scripture. Soon after his arrival in Wittenberg, he participated in the humanist critique of scholastic theology and organized debates like the disputation of September 4, 1517, in which Franz Günther defended Luther's theses on sin and grace against nominalism. By that time Luther was making liberal use of Augustine to understand Paul's epistle to the Romans (1515–1516),[35] and he was enthusiastic about reforming the curriculum that was replacing scholastic authors with the Bible and theologians of the early church:

> Our theology and St. Augustine are progressing well, and with God's help rule at our university. Aristotle is gradually falling from his throne, and his final doom is only a matter of time. It is amazing how the lectures on the *Sentences* are disdained. Indeed no one can expect to have any students if he does not want to teach this theology, that is, lecture on the Bible or on St. Augustine or another teacher of ecclesiastical eminence.[36]

Luther was not the only scholar with high curricular expectations. A former professor at the university, the Nuremberg humanist Christoph Scheurl, declared in 1518 that Wittenberg was divinely chosen for the liberation of Christian studies from the yoke of pagan philosophy.[37]

Historians have also treated Luther's Reformation discovery as a theological problem. Did Luther discover justification by faith before or after the ninety-five theses, and when did justification by faith become Reformation theology as opposed to a revision of late-medieval spirituality? Regardless of the answer, the issue was analyzed in theological terms. Either the discovery of a new theology was complete prior to the indulgence controversy or, in the view of many scholars, the events of the controversy stimulated Luther to draw conclusions that gave his theology full Reformation character. In the second case, the indulgence controversy made a better theologian of Luther. He was then able to stand up for the authority of Scripture (as he interpreted it) over the authority of the church and was ready to translate the New Testament and to apply his faith-centered theology to practical issues in a way that undergirded a conservative strategy of reform. As a result, so goes a companion argument, Luther's theology slowed down and tamed the tiger of radical reform that was implicit in the original evangelical message.[38]

For Luther there existed an inseparable connection between theology and life. That connection can be seen in both the account of his Reformation discovery and in the ninety-five theses. The account, which dates from 1545,[39] describes the discovery at two levels. First, there is the exegetical or theological level. At last Luther finds a satisfactory explanation of Paul's statement in Rom 1:16–17 that the righteousness of God is revealed in the gospel. True to his pattern of setting Paul against the scholastic theologians, Luther argues that the gospel can only reveal God's righteousness if that righteousness is a gift from God and not a standard by which God judges sinners. Later in the same account he reports that Augustine was familiar with this notion of a passive righteousness. In his early lectures, Luther often read Paul through the lens of Augustine, setting them both against the scholastic tradition of nominalist theology in which he had been trained.[40] In so doing, Luther joined the theological debate among medieval scholars who drew on Augustine's writings for support of their positions.

On a second level, Luther describes the discovery as a personal experience. The new insight into God's righteousness makes him think that he has "entered paradise through open gates."[41] This reaction is so exuberant because, as Luther reports, it is the antithesis of his experience as a monk. He tried to be a perfect monk, but no matter how strictly he obeyed the rule or how religiously he confessed, he still felt that he was an unworthy sinner who could not live up to the standard of God's righteousness. When he discovers that righteousness could be a gift instead of a demand, he undergoes a transformation that feels like going to heaven. It also transforms his life on earth. He calls into question traditional ways of living the faith that do not bring the same liberation, joy, or security that he experienced: monasticism, endowed masses and prayers, the penitential system with its indulgences, invoking the saints for help, pilgrimages to their shrines, compulsory almsgiving and fasting. Whether his discovery was sudden or gradual, whether it culminated before 1517 or thereafter, it was a discovery that affected both his intellect and his experience, his theology and his piety, his thought and his life. It forced him to reconsider the essence of Christian belief and practice.

The ninety-five theses were a radical consequence of that reconsideration. They denounced as unchristian the acquisition of indulgences without contrition and declared that true Christians did not need them: "Those who teach that contrition is not necessary on the part of those who intend to buy souls out of purgatory, or to buy confessional privileges, preach unchristian doctrine."[42] "Any truly repentant Christian has a right to full remission of penalty and guilt, even without indulgence letters."[43] "Any true Christian, whether living or dead, participates in all the blessings of Christ and his church; and this is granted by God, even without indulgence letters."[44] Luther had decided that showing mercy was better than acquiring indulgences. Therefore, "Christians are to be taught that whoever gives to the poor or lends to the needy does a better deed than the person who buys indulgences."[45] The point of the ninety-five theses could be summed up as follows: contrition and love are better than indulgences, and therefore believers should make repentance and its fruits the hallmark of their lives. The indulgence controversy impressed this point on Luther's agenda.

The papal right to issue indulgences was not the main target of Luther's criticism, but since the specific indulgence in question had been authorized by the pope, he found it irresistible to weave papal authority into the propositions for debate. In hindsight we see how this decision led more quickly to conflict with the Roman curia than his agenda might otherwise have done. In 1517 Luther was pretending to teach people the true and presumably Christian mind of the pope on indulgences;[46] within three years he was calling the pope antichrist and rejecting the pope and the "papists" as unchristian.[47] Others recognized more quickly than Luther that his attack could escalate into a full-blown conflict with the church hierarchy. Already in December 1517, the Augsburg humanist Bernhard Adelmann requested a copy of the theses from Willibald Pirckheimer in Nuremberg, adding that he wished the error of indulgences could be erased from the minds of the faithful because he knew of no other invention by which they were so deluded. After receiving a copy one month later, Adelmann expressed fear that Luther would be attacked and might succumb to those whose authority and advantage he had threatened.[48]

The attack came right away, but it failed to divert Luther from rethinking the shape of piety. He was forced to deal with the question of authority, but it never became his main agenda. Owing to the colorful encounters with Cajetan (1518) and Eck (1519), the conflict over authority has dominated the portrayal of the years 1518–1521. During this period, however, Luther spent most of his time reflecting on the Christian life and gradually working out its new contours for the laity. One of his earliest publications was an exposition of the penitential psalms,[49] and in late 1519 and 1520 he wrote several short studies or sermons on the sacraments.[50] Of the four major Reformation treatises that appeared in 1520, only his theological recasting of the sacraments, the *Babylonian Captivity of the Church*, appeared exclusively in Latin. The *Sermon on Good Works*, *Address to the Christian Nobility*, and *Freedom of a Christian* all appeared in German, the last simultaneously in Latin for Pope Leo X and the community of scholars.[51] In May of 1520 he published, also for laity, his short forms of the Ten Commandments, the Creed, and the Lord's Prayer.[52] By the summer of 1520, Luther had written about thirty works for the laity and they had appeared in 370 editions, on average over twelve editions per work. On the basis of this production, Heinz Dannenbauer claimed that Luther became the most popular religious author of his day and attributed Luther's success to the new model of piety offered in these writings.[53]

One publication from the year 1518 illustrates the early relationship between Luther's theology and his criticism of religious practice. Based on sermons delivered in 1516 and 1517, the *Ten Commandments Preached to the People at Wittenberg* concentrated on the first commandment and on the manifold ways in which Luther thought it was still being disobeyed.[54] The prohibition against "other Gods" (Ex 20:3) indicated that idolatry was the principal sin which people committed both outwardly and inwardly. Externally they were making idols out of trees, stones, animals, and stars; internally, they worshiped creatures by loving them and putting their faith in them. This idolatry rules everyone, argued Luther, until it is healed through grace and faith in Christ: "Faith in my word will make you free from other gods and a true worshiper of God."[55] In addition to this general analysis, however, Luther identified the sin of idolatry with specific forms of superstition borrowed in part from late medieval catalogues and divided into types that corresponded with three stages of life: those of adolescents, young adults, and older people.[56] Prominent and ordinary people, educated and uneducated folk of all ages, meddled in base types of magic and witchcraft and suffered the consequences of not taking seriously the power of evil. We live with false security, he exclaims, as if the devil were dead, starting bloody wars over our opinions and bringing lawsuits without end.[57] The accusation that magic and witchcraft were the devil's work was not novel, but Luther's association of the devil with superstition in general persisted throughout his career. In later writings, he saw the devil behind Christian practices that he rejected as magical and against God's will.[58]

Luther was particularly incensed by the way in which, he claimed, the cult of the saints and their relics implicated people in idolatry. He reserved special criticism for those people who prayed to the saints only for temporal and bodily benefits. These petitioners transformed the saints into idols, he argued, because they sought themselves and their own welfare in the saints and not the things that belong to God. Although Augustine conceded that it was better to seek earthly blessings from the saints than from the devil, Luther argued that such people deserved scant praise and should not be considered Christian even if God did sometimes answer the prayers of idolaters.[59] To make it clear that neither God nor saints ought to be worshiped primarily for temporal benefits, Luther challenged the claims made for specific saints "whose superstitious cult," he says, "is known to all."[60] The list included Anthony, Sebastian, Christopher, Lawrence, Vitus, Anna, Barbara, Apollonia, and Scholastica. The claims made for them were the chief appeal of late-medieval piety, and Luther was apparently already in trouble for calling them into question.[61] He fended off the criticism by recalling the issue at stake: obedience to the first commandment, or idolatry. "With the cult of the saints and their feast days, the Holy Spirit and the church mean for us to elevate our hearts to God and his works and to nourish our faith by contemplating the graces given to the saints."[62] At this early point, Luther's agenda was decisively influenced by his conclusion that the chief appeal of late-medieval religion was simultaneously the chief failure of Christian practice. "The only thing preached everywhere about the saints is how much they can do for our needs and not how much the merciful God was present in them."[63]

Luther continued the attack on idolatry and the cult of the saints in his lectures on the Psalms (1519–1521) that were delivered right up to his departure for Worms. Commenting on Psalm 16:6 ("The boundary lines have fallen for me in pleasant places"), Luther excluded the Roman hierarchy from the true people of God on that basis: "Only that which believes can be the church; consequently, the Roman pontiffs with their church are certainly idols and figments of the impious."[64] To his critical eyes, a new piety was essential because the old church, bereft of faith and ruled by idols, could hardly be called church anymore. The preachers offered nothing but little works from the lives of the saints. Faith would become extinct, and there would be nothing but pagan superstition where formerly there was the church of God; its substance would be lost while only the name of church would remain.[65]

For Luther, as for the Reformed tradition, the Reformation was a war against idols.[66] The charge of idolatry and godlessness was frequent and loud in the works that issued from the Wartburg during 1521 and early 1522. Criticizing people who approached Mary (and other saints) for help as if she were divine, Luther exclaimed that there was more idolatry in the world than ever before.[67] He also attacked the foundation of monastic vows as "godlessness, blasphemy, sacrilege, which has befallen [the monks] because they spurn Christ, their leader and light."[68] Vows made the monks virtually unchristian because their works were performed under the "pretext of the Christian name," contrary to the definition of being Christian, that is, "simply believing we are justified by the works of Christ without any works of our own."[69] Because the papacy had, in his opinion, so devastated the "Christian, spiritual priesthood" by dividing it from the laity, making ordination a sacrament, and turning the holy sacrament of the body of Christ into a sacrifice, Luther called it an "accursed, godless, and extreme idolatry which is enough to break the heart of a real Christian."[70] Comparing the church to the people of Israel and its infestation by various idols and their priests, Luther summed up the idolatry that had overwhelmed the church and ruined Christendom: "Oh miserable people that we are, to live in these last times so securely and unperturbed among all these Baalites, Bethelites, and Molechites, all of whom appear to be religious and Christian but who have nevertheless swallowed up the whole world and claim that they alone are the Christian church."[71]

Once the evangelical movement was well under way, Luther inveighed against practices that he thought smacked of idolatry. Writing in 1524 to an Austrian nobleman whose wife had died, Luther asked him to do away with the vigils and private masses for her soul because both were "unchristian practices which provoked God to anger."[72] In 1528 Luther noted that Isaiah reproached the people mainly for extensive idolatry that had gotten out of hand, "just as godly preachers do and have to do now and in every age."[73] Reminding the clergy assembled for the Diet at Augsburg (1530) what it was like, as he put it, "before my teaching began," he claimed: "If our gospel had accomplished nothing else than to redeem consciences from the shameful outrage and idolatry of indulgences, one would still have to acknowledge that it was God's Word and power."[74] After listing the ways in which the indulgence traffic had corrupted Christendom, Luther concluded: "In short, who wants to relate all the outrages that the indulgence alone brought on, as a truly mighty idol, in all the chapters, monasteries, churches, chapels, cells, altars, pictures, panels, yes, in almost all houses and chambers and wherever there was money?"[75] Later in the exhortation, Luther produced a remarkable list of parish practices and customs that had been or could have been changed, although he acknowledged that they need not have been discarded if they had been left as "child's play" and not promoted as necessary to faith.[76] In the lectures on Genesis (1535–1545), Luther renewed his denunciation of saints as idols, specifically St. James of Compostela and St. Benno of Meissen.[77] He repeated his charge that the pope's conversion of the Lord's Supper into horrible idolatry was an example of the way in which Satan had set up idolatrous forms of worship and traditions.[78]

Luther was not the only one who understood the agenda of reform to be the abolition of idols from the Christian life. In Wittenberg, Philipp Melanchthon worried about the idolatrous handling of consecrated elements that were left over after the sacrament.[79] In Lower Saxony, the superintendent of the clergy, Urbanus Rhegius, urged magistrates to remove any images that could be venerated by the uneducated and superstitious crowd so that idolatry might be avoided.[80] During the Lutheran reformation in Denmark, many admonitions addressed to the parishes and their priests were concerned with idols. They demanded that images be removed from the churches after they had been removed from the hearts of people and that all but one altar should be eliminated.[81] In Württemberg, Johannes Brenz instructed the city council of Schwäbisch Hall that the first commandment required them to abolish all public forms of idolatry:

Since, therefore, papist masses and statues to which people make pilgrimages are public idolatry, and since the religion of the Turks and the Jews are manifestly impieties against Christ, no godly magistrate ought to tolerate them in his jurisdiction. Clearly, whoever tolerates such things when he is able to abolish them pollutes himself with the impiety of others.[82]

Such harsh judgments were a matter of conviction, and one Catholic opponent, the English humanist Thomas More (d. 1535), charged that Lutherans themselves were so full of impiety that they surpassed even the Turks. In his *Response to Luther* (1523), More wrote that nothing was more deceptive and violent than the tactics used by the Lutherans and that this violence was nowhere more evident than in their rejection of the saints:

Never have the images of the saints been mistreated with such insult as these scoundrels, who do not fear not only to tear them away from their most holy shrines, to cast them aside when torn away, to trample them down when cast aside, but also to abuse them trampled down and trodden underfoot by every kind of mockery and insult.[83]

Even Turks, he claimed, venerated the mother of God, while Lutherans could barely stand her name.

For Luther, idolatry was so reprehensible because it was the antithesis of faith. In the lectures on Galatians (1531), he argued that faith alone attributed glory to God, but the self-righteous, who did not have faith, deposed God from his throne and set themselves up in his place.[84] This idolatry happened not only in the mind but also in the everyday practice of religion. It was a corrupt theology that also corrupted life in all its dimensions, including the practice of religion:

Now you see for yourself that all those who do not trust God at all times and do not see God's favor and grace and good will toward them in everything they do and everything they suffer, in their living or in their dying, but seek his favor in other things or even in themselves, do not keep this [first] commandment. Rather they practice idolatry, even if they were to do the works of all the rest of the commandments and had in addition all the prayers, fasting, obedience, patience, chastity, and innocence of all the saints combined. For the chief work is not there, the work without which all the others are nothing but mere sham, show, and pretense with nothing behind them.[85]

The Apostle and His Movement

Luther's agenda was part of a larger Wittenberg reform movement supported in the beginning by faculty colleagues like Karlstadt and then by others who either came to Wittenberg—for example, Philipp Melanchthon (d. 1560), Justus Jonas (d. 1555), and John Bugenhagen (d. 1558)—or who ended up in other towns as evangelical preachers—for example, Wenzel Linck (d. 1547), John Lang (d. 1548), and Urbanus Rhegius (d. 1541). It was Luther, however, who had been put on trial in Rome and who by late 1521 began to think of the movement as his own. What was the source of this claim to ownership and of its persistence against heavy opposition? One source was certainly his professorial duty to lecture on the Bible. Luther understood that he had been called to teach the correct meaning of Scripture even when it questioned practices promoted by the clergy. His early criticism was hardly novel, but his comments took a more radical turn in 1518 when he began to insist that Scripture was a supreme authority that trumped canon law and "ruled even over the pope."[86] His claim to have Scripture on his side invited charges that he was setting his opinion over against the accumulated wisdom of the church's tradition and its teachers. Luther's Catholic opponents argued that Christ had given to the church and not to individuals the right to interpret Scripture and to determine its truth.[87] According to John Eck, who debated this point with Luther at Leipzig, Scripture was not authentic "without the authority of the church."[88] Luther had opened himself to the heretical accusation of singularity.

Luther was singular indeed, but his singularity exceeded the claim that he could interpret Scripture better than his Catholic opponents. He also came to believe that the evangelical movement belonged to him and that he and his agenda were subject to the authority of none but Christ. The most critical factor behind this claim was the apostolic identity that Luther assumed in 1521. Luther had by this time begun to think like a prophet: because the last day was at hand, he believed Christendom was facing its last opportunity to rid itself of idolatry and to convert to the true faith. Conversion was not just an interim solution for individuals, however; it led to the creation of evangelical churches that needed preachers to teach and to supervise new forms of worship and practice. Evangelical clergy had to be trained and sent to towns throughout Germany, and this sense of urgency led Luther to think of himself not only as a prophet but also as an apostle and a missionary. Although he had lectured on three of Paul's letters and appropriated his theology, Luther now began to identify with the ministry of Paul. This apostolic identity not only enhanced his zeal for the mission to Christianize Germany but it also elevated his sense of ownership and authority.

Luther's claim to exclusive authority over the movement was audacious, and it prevented in part the coalescence of evangelical growth into a unified movement. He was not alone responsible, but the apostolic claims made for his Christianizing agenda increased the diversity of the Reformation and became an essential part of the story. As early as 1522, those claims were making him insufferable to opponents and difficult even for colleagues. Sometimes he refused to negotiate points of evangelical disagreement like the presence of Christ in the Lord's Supper. When he did debate them, in writing or in person, for example, with the Swiss reformers at Marburg in 1529, he insisted that he was right and accused his opponents of having a different spirit.[89] The more opposition he faced, the more tempted he was to identify himself and his movement with true Christianity. He lumped into one category all those whom he judged to be enemies of the gospel: Turks, Jews, papists, and sacramentarians, the last category including Protestants and dissenters who rejected infant baptism or the bodily presence of Christ in the sacrament. He regarded them as agents of the devil who, in the last days of the world, had unleashed a final assault upon Christendom. The harshness of this polemical attitude and the language in which it was couched alienated some of his contemporaries and later readers as well.

Sundry reasons have been suggested for Luther's harshness and audacity: his maladies, his anger and disappointment, his personality, or his apocalyptic vision. The most important reason, however, his apostolic identity, was disclosed by Luther in a letter in which he dedicated the treatise on monastic vows (1521) to his father Hans. With his father's help, argued Luther, he had been able to shake off the identity of a monk and adopt a different calling. Hans had been right to resist his son's desire to become a monk, even though Hans had never tried to remove Luther from the cloister. God, however, had finished the job that his father had begun. Now that monastic life and the papacy were behind him, he realized he was called to serve Christ in a way more committed and genuinely religious than being a monk. Luther felt liberated and bound at the same time, describing himself as "a new creature, not of the pope but of Christ." Echoing the *Freedom of a Christian*, he went on: "Although [Christ] has made me the servant of all, I am nevertheless subject to no one except to him alone. He is . . . my immediate bishop, abbot, prior, lord, father and teacher; I know no other."[90] Just as a monk had to obey the abbot alone, Luther was now obligated to obey no one but Christ. He had developed a powerful sense of being accountable to Christ alone, and instead of leading him to respect and to engage his critics, this accountability prompted him to dismiss his opponents and their views. Time and again Luther exhibited an exaggerated sense of personal entitlement to leadership of the movement.

How did this sense of entitlement develop? Any answer to this question is hypothetical, but one explanation fits the content of his reforming agenda. Luther was not born to rebel against authority, nor was he made to rebel because he had problems with his parents, as suggested by Erik Erikson. As history, Erikson's famous *Young Man Luther* is seriously flawed.[91] Instead of rebellion, Luther's experience was one of liberation. Luther felt he had been freed by Christ from scholastic theology, from the cloister, and finally from the papacy. The freedom of a Christian about which he wrote was his own experience, and this freedom enabled him to resist efforts to persuade him to recant. Once liberated, however, he also felt bound to serve the one who had liberated him and gradually to lead the movement that, in his opinion, Christ had given into his hands. To his father Luther wrote: "I hope that [Christ] has snatched one son from you in order that through me he might begin to help many other children of his; and I am convinced that you will not only willingly allow this, as you ought, but also rejoice at it with great joy!"[92]

Luther's apostolic identity and the experience on which it was based had three important consequences for Luther's agenda. In the first place, reform took on the character of a divine mission and he became its charismatic apostle. His devotional writings in particular challenged readers to become Christian in a way that was similar to his own experience. He described freedom in faith and love not as a doctrine to be learned but as a new identity to be assumed; and he was able to write about it so engagingly and describe the theological implications so sharply because it had happened to him—a human being and a trained theologian. He also regarded this liberation and its impact on life as more than a theory; it was a divine reality that had overtaken him and should now infuse the rest of Christendom.

Second, the conviction of being accountable to Christ alone reinforced both the christocentric dimension of his Reformation discovery and the Christianizing character of the agenda that accompanied it. The opposite of idolatry was not just faith in God but faith in Christ, who was the only Savior and provided exclusive access to the Father. For that reason, Christianizing Germany meant more to Luther than pushing traditional Christianity into corners of the empire where it had not yet arrived. It meant changing Christianity in order to make Christ central to its faith and practice and thus to intensify the specifically Christian character of European religion. Although he was discarding a medieval monastic identity and leaving his Augustinian superiors behind, Luther was adopting Christ as his new abbot and reaching for the old ideal of turning the world into a monastery. He wanted to bring Germany, and more of Europe if possible, into the same subjection to Christ that he had experienced for himself.

Third, Luther believed he had risked more than anyone else for the evangelical movement, and he was determined to assert his leadership against those who had suffered less. For example, he told Thomas Müntzer, a former ally turned sharp critic: "We know what faith is, and love, and the cross; and we can learn no greater thing on earth than faith and love. Hence we can know and judge what doctrine is true and not true, and whether it is in accordance with the faith or not." He then declared rights to the Reformation. Müntzer and his followers, said Luther, "enjoy and use the fruits of our victory; they have done no battle for it and risked no bloodshed to attain it. But I had to win it for them and, until now, at the risk of my body and my life."[93] Serving Christ alone, as he understood himself to be doing, placed him above colleagues and opponents alike and convinced him that the evangelical movement belonged, at the human level, to him.

In Luther's mind, therefore, the Reformation became a missionary movement that was under his leadership. As his own vocation crystallized during exile in 1521, he identified closely with Paul and chose the apostolic mission recounted in Acts as an early Christian paradigm for the reform that was beginning in Wittenberg. From the Wartburg, Luther wrote to Philipp Melanchthon, comparing Wittenberg to Antioch and his colleagues to early Christian missionaries: "You lecture, Amsdorf lectures; Jonas will lecture; do you want the kingdom of God to be proclaimed only in your town? Do not others also need the gospel? Will your Antioch not release a Silas or a Paul or a Barnabas for some other work of the Spirit?"[94] He would not be disturbed, claimed Luther, if the Lord opened a door for the word at Erfurt or Cologne or anywhere else, since there was a surplus of preachers in Wittenberg and a big harvest everywhere else.[95]

Others were thinking this way as well. The earliest Reformation pamphleteers addressed the towns in which they had formerly served exactly as the apostle Paul had addressed his epistles.[96] These preachers echoed Luther's notion that the 1520s were a *kairos* for Germany, the last chance for Christianity to take root:

> For you know that God's word and grace is like a passing shower of rain which does not return where it has once been. It has been with the Jews, but when it's gone it's gone, and now they have nothing. Paul brought it to the Greeks; but again when it's gone it's gone, and now they have the Turk; Rome and the Latins also had it; but when it's gone it's gone, and now they have the pope. And you Germans need not think that you will have it forever, for ingratitude and contempt will not make it stay. Therefore, seize it and hold it fast, whoever can; for lazy hands are bound to have a lean year.[97]

Luther's theology of history was keyed to his reforming agenda. "God's word and grace," as he called genuine Christianity in this passage, comes and goes, and it must be seized when it is available. Now was the time for Germany to grasp it, and not only Germany but all of Europe that wanted to be liberated from the unchristian rule of the pope. In 1540 he encouraged Marguerite of Navarre, the evangelically minded sister of King Francis I, to spread the gospel as widely as possible in her kingdom so that it might truly live up to its name of a "most Christian France."[98]

For Luther to regard the Reformation as a missionary movement did not mean that one day an unbelieving world would be fully converted. He explicitly rejected that view in 1523. The majority would always persecute Christians because the cross was the truest mark of the church. The gospel had to be preached continually in order to bring people to faith, for "the kingdom of Christ was always in the process of becoming, never a finished event."[99] The mission was urgent, however, because the last days were at hand and reformers were convinced that idolatry had almost ruined the current state of Christendom. Even though only a few believed, the kingdom would extend its presence throughout the earth. Luther and his colleagues, however, regarded themselves as apostles whose work began at home: they were not being called to convert the heathen but to reconvert the faithful.

The New Piety

Reconversion meant that people had to be weaned from the old practices that encouraged idolatry and persuaded to accept a new order of piety that would guide their worship and daily life. In the words of Erika Kohler, who examined in detail Luther's attention to traditional Christianity, "the Reformation caused a reordering of the way Christians lived and worshiped."[100] Reformers understood this quite well, especially the clergy among them whose renunciation of celibacy and other vows had radically changed their lives. They realized that the Reformation had to be a "ritual process,"[101] in which revising the practice of religion would be just as important as restating the faith. Their charge that traditional Christianity was less than fully Christian stemmed from their observation of that practice as well as from their study of theology. Late-medieval writers like Johannes von Paltz and Jean Gerson had already set precedents for keeping both piety and theology in sharp focus.[102]

As far as worship was concerned, Luther offered his first revision of the mass in 1523 and then published the *German Mass* in 1526. He also prepared new orders for baptism, marriage, and other liturgical occasions; he translated and composed a number of chants and hymns.[103] The 1523 *Order of Mass and Communion* was a shift of strategy for Luther. Until that point he had used only books and sermons, he said, to call people away from their impious opinions about ceremonies. Although he still hoped that hearts would be enlightened, he believed that some action now had to be taken in order for scandals to be removed from the kingdom of Christ. Embodied in the new order of mass, that action was designed not only to move hearts with words, but "also to apply the hands" and to produce tangible results.[104] Nevertheless, Luther was offering these guidelines to the same people he described in *Freedom of a Christian*, insisting that these rites were the rites of "Christians, that is, children of the free woman [Gal 4:31], who would keep them spontaneously and voluntarily and who could change them as often and as much as they desired."[105] In his view, believers using these rites were liberated servants who should always take the middle road between despising ceremonies and treating them as laws.[106]

Luther's introduction to the *German Mass* of 1526 envisioned an ideal community of people who seriously desired to be Christian and gathered in one house without need for much liturgy or many chants.[107] This picture was influenced by the depiction of believers in biblical texts dear to the monastic tradition, such as Acts 2:44–47 and 4:32–37. Like the template of Christianity offered in *Freedom of a Christian*, it was an ideal portrait that represented Luther's ultimate goal. At the same time, Luther was working concretely to disengage people from the old rites and to create ways of expressing the faith in real communities.[108] Consequently, he not only produced orders of worship but in the 1520s also began to ponder how believers could come to terms with the economic, domestic, and political spheres in which they actually lived. Luther's agenda expressed itself most concretely in these social and political proposals.

It is easier to understand these proposals, however, if we study more closely Luther's use of the word piety. It is an unusual word to associate with him or his agenda. Piety connotes activity, both in attitude and in behavior,[109] and it has been tainted in some circles by pejorative associations with the eighteenth-century movements referred to collectively as Pietism. Some scholars also associate it with "human religion" in contrast to divine activity that was presumably more central to Luther's theology.[110] According to Walter Sparn, however, Luther's translation of the Bible was the first to bring the German words for pious and piety, *fromm* and *Frömmigkeit*, into robust religious usage.[111] Their most striking occurrence in Luther's works, a description of the Christian life, has been obscured in English translation because *Frömmigkeit* was translated not as piety but as righteousness:

> This life, therefore, is not righteousness but growth in righteousness, not health but healing, not being but becoming, not rest but exercise. We are not what we shall be, but we are growing toward it; the process is not yet finished, but it is going on. This is not the end, but it is the road. All does not yet gleam in glory, but all is being purified.[112]

Righteousness and piety meant the same thing for Luther: the fully reconciled relationship to God through faith that manifested itself in love even though sin continued to offer resistance.[113] That relationship had both a passive and an active component. Most scholars have emphasized the passive dimension because Luther spoke of discovering a passive righteousness. The term *Frömmigkeit* (piety), however, also appealed to Luther because it expressed the dynamic character of the Christian life. From the biblical texts that he knew well and taught on a regular basis he adopted an eschatological view of that life: it was fully pious in relationship to God but not yet fully pious in daily living. This simultaneity of righteousness and sin, the famous *simul iustus et peccator*, did not mean that Christian life was static. Believers were being purified and growing toward the consummation they would finally enjoy. Although Luther's agenda aimed at the creation of the ideal believer described in *Freedom of a Christian*, he was neither a starry-eyed optimist nor a gloomy pessimist about the new Christians he hoped to see produced by evangelical reforms.[114] They did not "yet gleam in glory," but they were being purified nonetheless.

During the early 1520s, Luther applied this distinctive view of piety to Christian life in the world. In *Temporal Authority* (1523), for example, he asked whether Christians, whose life was governed by the gospel and the Sermon on the Mount, should obey civil law or hold political office. To answer the question he constructed a model that would serve his vision and enable him to apply it to other subjects. This model is often called his doctrine of two kingdoms, two regiments, or two governments, but Luther never referred to it as *his* teaching. In fact, the impetus for thinking in these terms came from his colleague Philipp Melanchthon, who provided the stimulation in a letter that he sent to Luther at the Wartburg in 1521.[115] Melanchthon observed the absence of direct political guidelines in the gospel, that is, in those passages of Scripture which, in Luther's words, dealt with heavenly and divine things, not with mundane affairs like politics. Luther agreed, but he argued that the power of the sword was not evil and that it was divinely instituted in other passages of Scripture such as Romans 13:1 and 1 Peter 2:13–14.[116] Hence Christians could be involved in politics and should obey civil law.

In *Temporal Authority* Luther used this distinction between heavenly and earthly matters to build the model of two kingdoms. It reflected not only his judgment of late-medieval society as subchristian but also the ideals of his reform agenda. Within Christendom he distinguished between genuine Christians, who were few in number, and the majority, whom he considered spurious or even unchristian. Genuine Christians were produced by the Holy Spirit in the kingdom of God and needed no commandments or civil authority. Spurious Christians belonged to the kingdom of the world and were ruled by the earthly sword that prevented unbelievers from doing evil. For the world to be ruled by the gospel, that is, for the ideal of Luther's agenda to be realized, society had to be filled with real Christians. That was not likely to happen, however, and therefore the sword was necessary, "for the world and the masses are and always will be unchristian, even if they are all baptized and Christian in name."[117] Despite this, Luther believed the Sermon on the Mount applied to all Christians and not just to those who had withdrawn from the world and sought perfection in monasteries and convents.[118] Those believers who sought revenge or who sued others in court to protect their property and honor were nothing but pagans under the name of Christians.[119] Consequently, believers who took seriously the new piety would not use civil authority for themselves but for the sake of protecting others and seeking justice for them.

Christians could, however, he argued, be magistrates even though magistrates did not have to be Christian in order to govern justly. Civil authority was an office created by God and Christians could fill it, but the spiritual kingdom was no longer to be equated with a Christendom governed necessarily by Christian rulers. For Luther government and family were not in themselves Christian but were the good designs of God, and believers should not shun them but serve others through them. Scholars have argued that Luther's view of Christians in politics was different from that of urban reformers like Zwingli and from the views of Erasmus and Melanchthon,[120] but the difference was mostly abstract. It may be true that Calvin thought more people could be Christian than Luther allowed,[121] but in practice it made little difference. When it came time to organize new churches in evangelical territories, Luther was just as adamant as Melanchthon, Zwingli, and Calvin that Christian laity obey the law and evangelical rulers protect the church. These theologians all preferred a reformed Christendom under Christian rulers and all of them encouraged believers to be more Christian than their ancestors.

Luther also applied his reform agenda and the model of two kingdoms to the structures of marriage, education, and business. It may seem as if he intended to secularize marriage instead of making it more Christian. His second treatise on the subject, *The Estate of Marriage* (1522), is dramatically different from the *Sermon on the Estate of Marriage*, published in 1519. In the earlier piece, marriage retained a sacramental quality and served the traditional functions of producing children and curbing lust, but by 1522 Luther had altered his view. Marriage was now, he argued, "an outward, bodily thing, like any other worldly undertaking." He protested against the restrictions of canon law and argued that Christians could marry non-Christians since there were plenty of Christians who in their secret unbelief were worse than "any Jew, heathen, Turk, or heretic."[122]

Luther did not, however, abandon the notion that Christians would behave in marriage differently from non-Christians. Matthew 19 forced him to admit adultery as a ground of divorce, but Luther said this remedy "did not apply to Christians, who are supposed to live in the spiritual government."[123] In other words, a true Christian would not divorce an adulterous spouse or hold grudges, but offer forgiveness and seek reconciliation.

Luther also asserted it was unchristian to condone prostitution. In 1539 he wrote that people who wished to be Christian would keep houses of prostitution out of their towns while those who tolerated such houses were no better than pagans.[124] Luther shared the view of his contemporaries that "the estate of marriage [had] fallen into awful disrepute."[125] To counteract this trend, it was necessary to "conduct ourselves in a Christian manner" and "hold fast first of all to this, that man and woman are the work of God." While Christian faith should not, in Luther's view, romanticize family life, it should regard marriage as a divine institution in which all the unpleasant duties were "adorned with divine approval as with the costliest gold and jewels."[126]

Although Luther denied that marriage was a sacrament and placed it above celibacy, he still claimed that Christians should treat it as holy. In this sense, he pursued the same goal as the medieval church: to Christianize marriage and lift it above the lowest cultural denominator. Joel Harrington was right to emphasize the long-range continuity between the medieval church and the Reformation: both wanted to make what they regarded as pagan customs of marriage into a Christian institution.[127] The reformers, however, judged that the methods of the medieval church had failed and they now sought to Christianize marriage by desacramentalizing it and elevating it over celibacy. Under these new terms, Luther and other Protestants hoped, marriages would lead to a stronger Christian society.

Business matters would also be treated differently by believers. Luther agreed with Paul that greed was idolatry (Eph 5:5) and that Christians were therefore prohibited from exploiting their neighbors.[128] In *Trade and Usury* (1524), he identified four Christian ways of exchanging goods with others: letting others steal your property; giving freely to others; lending, "expecting nothing in return" (Lk 6:35); selling only for cash and not giving credit.[129] How then would the world's business be transacted? In answer, Luther fell back on the model of two kingdoms: there were so few real Christians that the world would never be governed in Christian fashion. Instead, civil government had to keep non-Christians in check and ensure that all debts were paid.[130] Meanwhile, while he believed that some real Christians existed, others, whom he called "weak and immature" because they sued for justice, had to be taught better. "We ought to tell them . . . that such conduct is neither Christian nor praiseworthy but human and earthly, more of a hindrance to salvation than a help."[131] Luther's thought was far from utopian, but he did believe that medieval

Christianity, with its sharp distinction between the religious and the secular life, had settled for a less charitable society than believers could help to create.

According to Luther's timetable, this was the last chance to act, and as a result he advocated Christian schools for the training of teachers and preachers who could meet the crisis with "Christian determination."[132] By Christian schools, he meant schools that would undo the training he and others had received in the monasteries and universities of their youth. These new schools would teach "true Christianity," preparing the young for service both in the church and in the civil realm. "We ought to know how essential and beneficial it is—and pleasing to God—that a prince, lord, council member, or other person in a position of authority be educated and qualified to carry out their office as Christians should."[133] To meet the budget for such public schools, Luther had already admonished communities to act out of Christian love and not merely civic duty, and redirect the wealth of clerical chapters and monasteries to poor relief, evangelical preaching, and education.[134]

This admonition to the councils of German cities was an expression of Luther's nationalism, his humanism, and his eschatology. But it was also more than that. It was a plan for developing religious and civic leaders who would promote the piety of his reform agenda. In the spiritual kingdom believers would be taught a new notion of faith and how it saved them; and in the earthly kingdom they would be challenged to put that faith into practice, not in the old religious rituals but in secular structures of human life created by God. Faith was nurtured by new forms of singing and worship. The abstract ideal of love for the neighbor was concretized by teachings that affirmed the world and encouraged specifically Christian forms of engagement. This Christianizing agenda, hoped Luther, would not only draw out real Christians but also lead others to practice their faith more intentionally in the courthouses, homes, shops, and churches of their world.

Workers in the Vineyard

Cranach the Younger's depiction of the Reformation as recultivating the vineyard is an apt portrayal of Luther's program to Christianize Europe. As he saw it, the medieval church had planted the faith in the soil of pagan Europe but, after the faith had germinated, the bad husbandry of the papal church had neglected the field. Christianity had withered almost beyond recognition, and now the faith, in its genuine form, had to be replanted and cultivated. New growth might appear slowly and the reaper might come at any time. But, whenever the harvest was gathered, Luther hoped that God would find, if not a perfect crop, at least a more bountiful Christendom than ever before. Notwithstanding his conviction that the end was near, Luther sounded like a contented vintner when, three years before his death, he reported on the result of recultivation in Saxony: "I do not leave our churches in poor shape; they flourish in pure and sound teaching, and they grow day by day through many excellent and sincere pastors."[135]

Despite the important limitations noted in the Introduction to this book, viewing Luther's agenda in these terms helps to correct some misconceptions of his work. The first misconception was propagated by Luther himself every time he contrasted the reform of life unfavorably with the reform of doctrine. Comparing himself to John Wycliffe and John Hus in 1533, Luther said:

> Doctrine and life must be distinguished. Life is bad among us, as it is among the papists, but we do not fight about life and condemn the papists on that account. Wyclif and Hus did not know this and attacked the papacy for its life. I don't scold myself into becoming good, but I fight over the word and whether our adversaries teach it in its purity. That doctrine should be attacked—this has never happened. This is my calling.[136]

When Luther said he did not fight about life, however, he was not contrasting teaching and practice but rather teaching and morals, and specifically the teaching of the Roman Church and the moral behavior of its upper clergy. For Luther life had a moral or behavioral component; the good works that believers were called to do by keeping the commandments entailed behavior that benefited others. The reformation of life, however, involved more than the improvement of personal conduct. It replaced idolatrous ritual with evangelical forms of worship and piety: going to church, using the catechisms, praying regularly through Christ instead of invoking saints, devoting assets and time to assisting others in place of fasting, pilgrimages, and the like. To live out one's faith also meant for Luther to behave ethically in politics, marriage, and business where believers confronted complex issues of social and public justice.

The notion that Luther cared more about theology than ethics and expected less of believers than did other reformers has been especially prominent in American scholarship.[137] Just as Luther's concept of life should not be restricted to moral behavior, however, his concept of doctrine should not be equated with propositional or systematic theology. The word doctrine means teaching, and for Luther it meant teaching what was essential for Christian faith *and* living. In teaching that every believer ought to imitate Christ by serving others,[138] Luther was proposing doctrine that had an immediate impact on life. The right kind of good works, he proposed, did not presume to merit salvation but flowed from the faith by which one was saved. To judge by the energy that reformers devoted to explaining it, the concept of spontaneous, non-meritorious charity was apparently difficult for some preachers and laity to comprehend—not surprisingly since passages of Scripture that seemed to support merit and reward were cited in opposition to the reformers by Catholic theologians. John Eck alone listed over forty such passages in his handbook of sources that could be used against Luther "and other enemies of the church."[139]

Luther's agenda also corrects a misconception about his disagreement with Erasmus that contributed to the shape of the Protestant movement. This well-known controversy over freedom of the will is usually presented as a purely theological or philosophical disagreement in which, for Luther, the doctrine of justification by faith was at stake. Justification by faith was indeed at stake, but both Erasmus and Luther knew that the debate concerned what believers had to know in order to live a pious or godly life.

Erasmus had argued in his *Diatribe concerning Free Will* (1524) that Christian piety required believers to strive with all their might, use the remedy of penitence, ask for God's mercy, and never despair of pardon from a merciful God. They should attribute evil to themselves and goodness to God and believe that whatever befell them, whether happy or sad, was sent by God for their salvation because a just God could do no wrong to anyone. It was not necessary to pry into the secret working of God and ask about God's foreknowledge, or the role of the human will in salvation, or the extent to which necessity controlled human action.[140] In his reply to Luther's attack on this position as "devoid of Christ,"[141] Erasmus presented himself as a teacher of "ordinary people" and advised that Christians should submit themselves wholly to the will of God. He asked whose books taught the name of Jesus Christ more than his own, and he defended his position as orthodox.[142]

For Luther, the bondage of the will in matters of salvation belonged to the nature or essence of Christianity (*forma Christianismi*), and he named it the "cardinal issue between us, the point on which everything in this controversy turns."[143] Luther did not take this stance because it was philosophically necessary or indispensable for a correct body of doctrine but because he believed it was required for living the faith: "It therefore behooves us to be very certain about the distinction between God's power and our own, God's work and our own, if we want to live a godly life."[144] His disagreement with Erasmus involved both doctrine and life because both men thought that genuine piety could be produced only by a correct understanding of how God was active.[145] To Erasmus, insisting that the human will played no role whatsoever in piety would undermine human striving and encourage indifference. If God did everything, he asked, why should evildoers bother to improve their lives?[146] To Luther, granting the will any influence at the moment of conversion would lead people to think they could merit salvation on the basis of their efforts and increase the attraction of the very rituals he was calling into question.

This difference of opinion was certainly theological, but the crucial difference lay not in the doctrine of God or the natures of Christ but in the work of the Holy Spirit, that is, how the saving work of Christ was transferred to the lives of believers. Despite the influence of humanism on Luther's agenda and despite the fact that both Luther and humanists of the sixteenth century desired a more Christian society, he and Erasmus disagreed about the point at which theology intersected life. Erasmus thought believers could set themselves on the road to piety by reading the Gospels and imitating Christ, while Luther believed the human will first had to be turned around by the Spirit and then held on the path of faith and love.

Although the older Luther expressed contentment with the recultivation of Germany, at times he betrayed a deep disappointment that more fruit was not being produced. The vineyard to be recultivated was a large property, and even if he did not expect a perfect harvest before the last day, he had hoped for more healthy plants than he was able to see from his window in Wittenberg. It is helpful to remember that his disappointment was more structural than personal in the sense that a project as big as the Reformation could never completely succeed.[147] Luther bit off more than he could chew. In spite of repeated affirmations that believers were not perfect and remained sinners, his agenda was formulated in idealistic terms and doomed never to be perfectly accomplished. Not even a robust eschatology could stave off his disappointment. In his mind, the imminence of final judgment should have shaken people out of their complacency and made them more devout.

The Reformation was much bigger than Luther, however, and as he declined, other reformers were already at work enlarging the vineyard and cultivating acreage of their own. Luther's agenda was hardly set before it was challenged by a host of competitors whose vision of the Reformation extended not only beyond Germany but beyond Europe as well.

Figure 6. Lucas Cranach the Younger. *The Vineyard of the Lord* (1556). Detail: Reformers recultivating the vineyard. Stadtkirche, Wittenberg.

Chapter 3

The Urban Agenda

A Christian Society

The City and Beyond

While Luther and his colleagues were pursuing their agenda to the north, other reformers were attempting to Christianize the cities of southern Germany and Switzerland. Although these "city reformers"—Huldrych Zwingli, Martin Bucer, and John Calvin, among others—were influenced to a certain extent by the Reformation in Wittenberg, they developed agendas that were tailored to their particular contexts. The evangelical movement was never homogeneous; in the early 1520s when the Reformation began in Zurich and Strasbourg, however, differences among Protestants were just emerging. The awareness of belonging to different Protestant confessions was still forming in the 1530s when Calvin first joined the campaign of William Farel in Geneva. Strasbourg adopted a confessional Lutheran stance late in the sixteenth century, but during the early years Martin Bucer and his colleagues had refused to identify fully with either Zwingli or Luther. Although they were influenced by Luther and by a common evangelical cause, the city reformers were soon pushing the Reformation in new directions.

Zurich, Strasbourg, and Geneva were independent centers of the early Reformation and served as a platform for its spread far beyond their borders. They also represented, in the early stages at least, a distinct kind of reform, the urban or city Reformation, that historians have long recognized and debated. The classic statement of this distinctiveness was supplied by Bernd Moeller in his 1962 essay "Imperial Cities and the Reformation."[1] Moeller based his thesis on a late-medieval corporate identity that led these towns to see themselves as Christian communes.

69

That spirit facilitated the work of Zwingli, Bucer, and their colleagues, who adapted their theology to the civic context and won their cities in southern Germany for the Reformation. In spite of many adjustments made by Moeller and others to the notion of an urban reformation, it tends to be seen as more populist and socially progressive than the allegedly conservative Lutheran reformation in northern Germany.[2]

The notion of a progressive and far-reaching urban reformation was challenged by Heiko Oberman, who argued that Calvin's agenda for the Reformation was different from that of city reformers like Zwingli and Bucer. According to Oberman,[3] Calvin was able to see that the city reformation had failed in both Zurich and Strasbourg. Instead of becoming Christian communes subject to a reformed church, these cities made compromises with politicians that disappointed reformers like Leo Jud in Zurich.[4] Calvin determined to succeed where he thought the urban reformation had failed. In Geneva he would provide "an alternative to a Magisterial Reformation doomed to obey secular authority."[5] He did not regard himself as a city reformer but as "an officer directing a European army."[6] His target was the reform of Europe, not just Geneva, and his reformation is best described, according to Oberman, as a reformation of refugees, namely, Protestants from France and other countries who found refuge in Geneva but were eager to restore true Christianity to France, England, and the rest of Europe. By refusing to capitulate to the councils of Geneva and insisting on a purified church with authority to excommunicate, Calvin rejected the ideal of local civic unity that had guided Zwingli and the young Bucer. Instead, the Genevan reformer braced an army of refugees, new generations of Protestants, for the opposition they were certain to face throughout much of Europe.

Upon closer examination, however, it is difficult to find a significant difference between this program of reform and the visions of Zwingli and Bucer or, for that matter, Luther.[7] All four reformers had basically the same goal: to bring Christianity to a European culture they regarded as seriously deficient in true religion. Since they worked in different corners of the vineyard, so to speak, they tailored their agendas to local circumstances without abandoning their vision of recultivating the entire property. Calvin began his work later in the process and his ambition was larger; he wanted to convert large Catholic areas like France, and his followers wanted to complete the reformation started by Lutherans in some parts of Germany. One should recall, however, that Zwingli always had the Swiss Confederation and Europe in his sights[8] and that his successor, Heinrich Bullinger (d. 1575), expanded the orbit of the Zurich Reformation to other parts of Europe through his extensive and effective international correspondence.[9] Bucer was working for the kingdom of Christ outside Strasbourg even before he moved to England and wrote there his famous treatise of the same name.[10] Luther's ongoing exchange with non-German correspondents extended his reformation horizon beyond Germany, and the impact of Wittenberg was felt strongly in Scandinavia. In all four cases the mentality remained a missionary one: to convert not only Wittenberg, Zurich, Strasbourg, and Geneva, but also to make the rest of Europe more Christian than it had been. The Wittenberg movement was only a beginning. Without the distinctive visions and momentum generated by Zurich, Strasbourg, and Geneva, the campaign of Christianization would have changed much less of European religion than it did.

Zurich

In Zurich the Reformation began in 1522 with public defiance of the church's regulations on fasting during the season of Lent. To be sure, the deliberate eating of sausages took place in the private house of the printer Christopher Froschauer, but about a dozen people were present and each of them, except for Zwingli, received a small piece of sausage that was distributed in a manner reminiscent of the Last Supper.[11] The violations quickly became public knowledge and the council began to investigate the matter after more people broke the rules and the debate over fasting intensified. About two weeks later, Zwingli preached a sermon that defended the violators and published an expanded version of the sermon under the title: *The Choice and Freedom of Foods*.[12] It was his first Reformation treatise, and in it Zwingli told his readers: "You know your liberty too little."[13]

This was not his first attack on medieval piety. In three years of preaching at Zurich, Zwingli had already voiced criticism of the religion that surrounded him.[14] He had denounced the monastic negligence witnessed at Einsiedeln (a monastery and shrine which he had served as chaplain), the veneration of Mary and the saints, the festival of Corpus Christi, and the system of tithing. During the summer of 1522, Zwingli was involved in further disputes over the veneration of saints and monasticism,[15] and his supporters, future Anabaptists like Conrad Grebel and Klaus Hottinger, interrupted a sermon by an Augustinian monk.[16] In July, Zwingli could contain himself no longer after listening to four sermons by the Franciscan Francis Lambert of Avignon. When Lambert began to preach on Mary and the saints, Zwingli stood up and called out: "Brother, you are mistaken." At the insistence of Zwingli's opponents, a debate was arranged between him and Lambert that led the Franciscan to revise his views.[17] Shortly thereafter, Lambert joined the evangelical movement and served the Reformation in Strasbourg and in Hesse, teaching theology at Marburg from 1527 until his death in 1530.

The Reformation in Zurich, therefore, like the Reformation in Wittenberg, began with criticisms of late-medieval piety that escalated into a debate between reformers and ecclesiastical officials over the issue of authority. What motivated Zwingli to make these criticisms from the pulpit and in writing? How did his Reformation agenda take shape and how did it relate to Luther's development as a reformer and to the process of reform in Wittenberg?

Historians have typically emphasized the differences between Zwingli and Luther. These differences became primary factors in the formation of separate Reformed and Lutheran confessions, and confessionally oriented scholars of the nineteenth century often returned to these differences in order to defend their churches. For example, the Lutheran professor of legal theory and church law, Friedrich Julius Stahl (d. 1861), initiated his attack on the Prussian Union in 1859 with a chapter on Luther and Zwingli.[18] According to Stahl, their thought was governed by two fundamentally different principles: for Luther it was justification by faith alone, for Zwingli it was salvation from God alone without the mediation of any church functions. In Stahl's opinion, these different principles were not merely divergent theological emphases, but they led to different reformations and undergirded different confessions, one of which was obviously superior to the other. Luther's reform was the only original evangelical reformation. Insofar as Zwingli's reformation was original at all, claimed Stahl, it was not evangelical, and insofar as it was evangelical, it was not original.[19]

Contrasts between Luther and Zwingli have also been drawn by modern scholars. Gottfried Locher, for example, believed they started at different points: Luther began with a purely religious question while Zwingli was motivated by conditions of social and political urgency.[20] Locher included Calvin in this contrast. The reformer of Geneva viewed human beings as disobedient individualists and called them to order and to salvation under the glory of Christ.[21] Locher's contrast serves as a reminder that the theologies of Luther, Zwingli, and Calvin were not identical and that their different agendas should be respected. Their differences, however, should not be allowed to erase the similarities that witness to a shared Reformation vision. In his early biography of Zwingli, Oswald Myconius claimed that the young preacher exhorted his flock at Zurich to buy and read the books of Luther, although Zwingli himself refrained from doing so. Zwingli's strategy was to let people see for themselves that Luther was teaching the same things he was preaching and that both reformers were drawing from Scripture.[22] This claim by Myconius allowed him to preserve both the independence of Zwingli, asserted by the reformer himself, and his similarity to Luther. This similarity was rooted in a common concern summed up by Locher as the bottom line of Zwingli's message: the distinction between worship of God and the worship of idols, true worship or idolatry.[23]

Like Martin Luther, Ulrich Zwingli was a child of medieval Christianity. Although we have limited information about the years before 1519, his life seems to have been entirely normal for a bright child who was sent away from home to acquire a good education. His training in Latin, the classics, and the liberal arts was formally completed when he received the Master of Arts degree from the University of Basel in 1506. Around age fourteen Zwingli had a brush with monasticism in Bern. Because of his good voice, the Dominicans wanted him to join their order, but Zwingli's father and uncle, so the story goes, whisked him away and sent him to the University of Vienna. After further study in Basel, he was ordained in Constance in 1506 and became a pastor in Glarus not far from his alpine homeland. After ten years he moved to the famous Marian shrine at Einsiedeln, serving as a priest at the abbey and providing pastoral care to both inhabitants and pilgrims. From here he was called to the post at Zurich, where he took up his duties on New Year's Day 1519, his thirty-fifth birthday.

Among the early reformers, Zwingli had the most experience as a pastor, and on this count he was very different from Luther, who had fewer encounters with laity during his twelve years of monastic life prior to 1517. The differences usually noted, however, involve humanism and theological training. Zwingli had more formal training as a humanist scholar than Luther and he was an explicit admirer of Erasmus's philosophy of Christ. According to Fritz Büsser, the Zurich reformation owed its distinct character to Zwingli's humanism, especially to his leading role in a "Swiss humanist literary republic" that worked for the renewal of both Switzerland and Christendom.[24] The contrast with Luther's academic interests should not be exaggerated, however. Although the young Zwingli may have admired the theology of Erasmus more than Luther did, the reform in Wittenberg was heavily influenced by Melanchthon's humanist scholarship and by Luther's own humanist inclinations.[25]

Zwingli's theological training, however, was quite different from Luther's. According to Berndt Hamm, the distinctive influence on Zwingli's theology was not humanism but the *via antiqua*, the school of medieval theology that was allied with philosophical realism. At Basel Zwingli had probably been taught a synthesis of Thomas Aquinas (d. 1274) and Duns Scotus (d. 1308).[26] From this synthesis Zwingli derived two points that influenced his theology: the simplicity of the divine being and the sovereignty of the divine will.[27] These points supported his sharp distinction between spirit and flesh and his abhorrence of identifying God, who belonged to the realm of the spirit, with material objects. Consequently, Zwingli was quick to criticize any attribution of divine power to sacred objects, whether statues of saints or the bread and wine of the Lord's Supper. On the presence of Christ in the sacrament he thus disagreed strongly with Luther, whose training in the nominalist tradition inclined him to take the words of institution ("This is my body, . . .") literally and to insist that God was obligated by these words to be present in the sacrament.

Despite their different conceptions of divine freedom, both Zwingli and Luther agreed that human freedom in Christ was the heart of the gospel and that this freedom should be defended against all church regulations regarded as unbiblical.[28] Together with his successor in Zurich, Heinrich Bullinger, and the reformer of Basel, John Oecolampadius, Zwingli allowed room for adiaphora, that is, for rituals that were neither condemned nor explicitly commanded in Scripture. In some cases Zwingli and Luther disagreed about adiaphora, for example, to what extent the liturgy of the mass should be retained and whether or not pictures and statues of saints should be allowed in the churches. Nonetheless, the Swiss and the Wittenberg reformers agreed on the doctrine of justification and its implications for Christian practice.[29] Believers were justified by faith, not by adhering to church regulations like those which governed fasting and indulgences. For Zwingli as for Luther, faith expressed itself in self-disciplined conduct and works of charity. The freedom granted by faith and its impact on the believer's life were for Zwingli at the heart of Christianity: "The Christian religion is nothing else than a firm hope in God through Jesus Christ and a blameless life expressed in the example of Christ insofar as Christ grants it."[30]

To recapture this heart and apply it to the crisis of his day was Zwingli's agenda. Like Luther he believed that true Christians were scarce and that most people were no better than heathen.[31] Zwingli drew his own harsh moral from the classical tale of the labyrinth in which Theseus killed the minotaur and found his way out by following the thread of Ariadne. In Zwingli's labyrinth, however, there was no thread, no guide even for believers:

> The world is so full of deceit that we have no more the image of Christ than the heathen. Yea we are worse; for the heathen do all deliberately, so that repentance and misery does not come over them. . . . Tell me what have we of Christians more than the name?[32]

In 1525, dedicating the *Commentary on True and False Religion* to King Francis I, Zwingli defended the Reformation "in view of the foully disordered state of this order we call the world,"[33] which was mired in idolatry: "For we have taken unto us strange gods, far more absurd than any heathen nations ever had. What heathen nation ever worshipped as God a man destined to die tomorrow, or rather today, as we worship the Roman pontiff? . . . Because of our sins, therefore, we failed to understand this abominable idolatry, and that for a long time."[34] Like Luther, Zwingli was not above exaggerating the unchristian character of medieval religion or the devotion paid to the pope.

The remedy for idolatry was to trust in the Creator instead of in creatures and, specifically, to trust in the work and merit of Christ instead of seeking other ways of redemption. This trust (*fiducia*) played a central role in Zwingli's theology,[35] and it was already operative in his first Reformation treatise. The main line of argument pitted the freedom brought by the gospel against the idolatry of trusting in a certain attitude toward food:

> Now the Gospel is nothing but the good news of the grace of God; on this we should rest our hearts, that is, we should know the grace of the Gospel to be so certain and ready, and trust it, so that we may establish our hearts in no other doctrine, and not trust to food, that is, to eating or abstaining from eating . . . this or that food.[36]

Abstaining from certain foods in a spirit of vainglory and self-exaltation was, he argued, a "turning toward true idolatry." Zwingli, therefore, urged believers to "consider these words [Ps 81:8–12] well, ponder them carefully, and you will see that God desires that we hearken to him alone! If now we are thoroughly imbued with him, no new god will be honored within our hearts, no human instead of God, no feeling of our own instead of God."[37]

The issue underlying Zwingli's call for the free choice of food was the same conflict that Luther saw between faith and idolatry: People who

underestimated the salvation, mercy, and freedom of Christ were unbelievers.[38] Their idolatry was self-centered and the opposite of charity: "If
you are so concerned about others, as to what they should not eat, why
will you not note their poverty and aid it? If you would have a Christian
heart, act to it then."[39] Idolatry also separated true from false piety in general: "It is false religion or piety when trust is put in any other than God.
They, then, who trust in any created thing whatsoever are not truly pious.
They are impious who embrace a human word as God's."[40]

The solution for such impiety was a campaign of Christianization that
would call Switzerland to place its trust in God alone. Warning the con-
federates in the canton of Schwyz against alliances with foreign powers
(1522), Zwingli argued that the strength and unity of the confederacy
would prevail only if the Swiss people reformed and acted like Christians:
"Real piety, by which is meant true worship and prayer to God, has disappeared among us, as St. Paul writes to the Romans [Rom 1:28–31]."[41]
Zwingli applied Paul's words to the "heathen" to "us": "From these words
of Paul we learn that all these evils which he enumerates arise when we
desert God, do not fully recognize him, do not look up to him, do not
place our whole trust in him, but on the contrary despise him and regard
him somewhat as we would an old sleeping dog."[42] In 1522, Zwingli urged
Bishop Hugo of Constance to take the "lead over all the bishops of Germany in right thinking upon Christianity," since "from the whole great
body of bishops scarcely one or two thus far have shown themselves fairly
on the side of revivified Christianity."[43] For Zwingli, the Reformation
message of freedom went hand in hand with the Christianization of Germany and Switzerland.

On Zwingli's road to Reformation, as on Luther's, theological reflection and the critique of religious practice were inseparable. The contra-
diction between biblical theology and contemporary piety led both
reformers to demand the dismantling of devotional practices they
regarded as unchristian and idolatrous. The close connection between
theology and piety is stated in the *Sixty-seven Articles*, prepared for the first
Zurich disputation in 1523. After summarizing the gospel and affirming
that Christ was the "only way to salvation" and the head of his body,
Zwingli claimed that clerical or human ordinances were invalid because
"in the Gospel one learns that human doctrines and decrees do not aid in
salvation."[44] On the ground that they contradicted the work of Christ as
true mediator, he proceeded to reject the sacrificial character of the mass,
the intercession of saints, and regulations governing fasting, festivals, and
pilgrimages.

Implied in the articles of 1523 was the charge of idolatry against those practices, a charge made more explicit in subsequent comments on the veneration of saints and images. When the council was ready to decide about images and the mass after the second disputation of 1523, Zwingli argued for the abolition of all images or idols because God had forbidden them and because people had fallen into idolatry unawares.[45] This abolition would be a godly work because the money spent on images would henceforth be used for the poor, who were "a true image of God."[46] In the *Commentary on True and False Religion* (1525) Zwingli drew a sharp distinction between true worship and idolatry: "We worship a God who is invisible and who forbids us to make any representation of him, while they clothe their gods with any shape they please."[47] Even more emphatic was his statement in response to Valentin Compar (1525): those who sought from a creature, whoever it might be, what ought to be sought from the one true God were neither faithful nor Christian.[48]

Indeed, Zwingli sought to demonstrate that the reverence shown to statues of saints was the same reverence pagans paid to their idols.[49] Lighting candles and incense, naming the statues and praying to them, betrayed the idolatry involved: "Your god is the one to which you turn in need."[50] This declaration was almost identical to the definition given by Luther four years later in his explanation of the first commandment: "A 'god' is the term for that to which we are to look for all good and in which we are to find refuge in all need."[51] Like Zwingli, Luther continued with an extensive discussion of trust in God versus the idolatry found among pagans of old and under the papacy of his day. "Idolatry does not consist merely of erecting an image or of praying to it, but it is primarily a matter of the heart, which fixes its gaze upon other things and seeks help and consolation from creatures, saints, or devils."[52]

As much as they agreed on the need to replace idolatry with true faith and piety, Zwingli and Luther had one major disagreement, and it caused a rupture in the evangelical movement and overshadowed their common vision. This disagreement involved the mode of Christ's presence in the sacrament of the altar. The two reformers, their colleagues, and the Strasbourg reformers all agreed that the mass was not a sacrifice or a meritorious work, that wine and bread should be given to the laity, and that the spiritual partaking of the sacrament was necessary for the strengthening of faith. Zwingli and Luther did not agree, however, on whether the true body and blood of Christ were bodily or physically present in the bread and wine. Despite efforts by the Strasbourg reformers to reconcile the German and Swiss reformers on this issue, the disagreement was never overcome.[53]

Most interpretations make this difference between the reformers a theological one and base it either on their early training, as described above, or on their Christologies. Their disagreement on the presence of Christ, however, also had a common root: having rejected the sacrifice of the mass as idolatrous, both reformers were trying to position Christ, in a nonidolatrous way, at the center of eucharistic piety. Zwingli refused to accept a bodily presence of Christ in the elements because he was afraid that it supported a false piety which led people to venerate material objects: "We worship with embraces and kisses wood, stones, earth, dust, shoes, vestments, rings, hats, swords, belts. . . ."[54] The eucharistic community should instead concentrate on the cross as the genuine source of redemption and as the object of remembrance and thanksgiving.[55] Luther fiercely defended a bodily presence in the Supper, not because he was more medieval than Zwingli or a literal interpreter of Scripture in every case, but because he believed that the sacrament mediated forgiveness by bringing the believer into contact with the whole Christ, which included his human nature. Both reformers wanted to avoid idolatry by making sure that the Lord's Supper focused partakers on the saving death of Christ. They could not agree, however, on which theology and practice of the Lord's Supper placed Christ most effectively at the center of the meal.

The disagreement between Zwingli and Luther was not the first within the evangelical movement, but it was especially significant because it led to the formation of different Protestant confessions. A shared vision of Christianization did not lead to a unified evangelical movement. Reformers could agree that Europe needed to be Christianized anew, but they disagreed over what the new Christianity entailed and over the best way to convince people to accept it. In the case of Luther and Zwingli, the correct view of Christ's presence in the sacrament belonged to the essence of Christianity because it defined how people were connected to the saving act of Christ that was central to the religion. Modern ecumenically minded observers, who regard one another as Christians, can find ways to overcome the historical disagreement. Since Zwingli and Luther viewed late-medieval religion as unchristian, however, the stakes were higher for them. They made theological and practical decisions on the basis of which measures would best protect people from superstition. These measures would determine the survival or the death of Christianity, and when reformers disagreed, everything was at stake. For Luther, therefore, behind Zwingli the devil was throwing up opposition to the gospel, that is, to the revival of true Christianity as he defined it. Zwingli, in contrast, believed that Luther was leaving the door open to idolatry by allowing people to decide for themselves about fasting and the statues of saints. The vision of Christianization did not unite the reformers, but the intractability of their conflicts cannot be understood without appreciating the power of that vision for their reforming agendas.

Strasbourg

In Strasbourg, a large episcopal see and a free imperial city on the western edge of the Holy Roman Empire, the road to the Reformation was paved by Matthew Zell, a priest in the cathedral parish. Although he was not the first to do so,[56] in 1521 Zell began to preach in the spirit of Luther, to attack the immorality of the clergy, and to question cherished beliefs about Mary, purgatory, and the saints.[57] So popular were his sermons that the small chapel where he was preaching overflowed with listeners, and the parishioners asked if Zell could speak from the main pulpit in the nave of the cathedral, where more people could be accommodated. The request was denied, but the city council facilitated a compromise. A portable wooden pulpit was constructed and set in the nave when it was time for Zell to preach.[58]

In 1523 Zell was joined by two colleagues who assumed leadership of the evangelical movement. The older of the two, Wolfgang Capito (d. 1541), whom Zell had known in Freiburg, had earned doctorates in theology and law and occupied three pulpits before coming to Strasbourg first as provost at St. Thomas and then as pastor at New St. Peter.[59] The younger man, Martin Bucer (d. 1551), had entered the Dominican order at fifteen, but two years after hearing Luther present his theology at Heidelberg (1518) left the order, married a former nun, Elisabeth Silbereisen, and found refuge in Strasbourg in Zell's house. In 1524 Bucer became pastor at St. Aurelius, the parish of the gardeners' guild, after its members persisted in calling him despite the political liability of his status as a married former monk.[60] Zell, Capito, and Bucer, together with Caspar Hedio, who became the main preacher at the cathedral, led a cadre of laypeople and clergy who turned the Strasbourg evangelical movement into a lively and contentious specimen of the urban reformation.

As in Wittenberg and Zurich, changes in religious practice caused the evangelical movement to become a political issue in Strasbourg and forced the council to take a stand. The evangelical pastors began to flout mandatory celibacy of the clergy. Not only was Bucer a married ex-monk and priest when he arrived in Strasbourg, but then Anthony Firn, the pastor at St. Nicholas, announced that he would marry his concubine Katherine.

On this remarkable occasion, attended by some councilors and their wives, the sermon was preached by Matthew Zell, who by this time was planning to marry Katharina Schütz, the devout daughter of a solid Strasbourg family. After being converted to the Reformation message, Schütz had decided she was called to marry Zell and establish a partnership in the gospel. The ceremony was performed at the cathedral on December 3, 1523, by Martin Bucer, who gave both wine and bread to the couple at the mass that followed.[61] By January 1524, there were six married priests in Strasbourg, and when Bishop Wilhelm von Honstein ordered them to appear in episcopal court, the city council ignored his order and protected the pastors as citizens.

In Strasbourg, clerical marriage was serious Reformation business. Soon after the pastors were cited by the bishop, Katharina Schütz Zell sent him a sharp rebuke in which she pointed out that the Bible supported clerical marriage and could also teach him a thing or two about being a good bishop. The city council, caught between its desires to appease the bishop and to assert its independence, told Zell not to let his wife print the letter. Later that year, however, Schütz Zell published a booklet in which she defended her husband against slander and portrayed their marriage as harmonious and honorable.[62] Meanwhile, Bucer was seeking a wife for Capito. On April 28, 1524, Bucer wrote to Odile de Berckheim and invited her to consider marriage to Capito in order to counteract the "snare of the devil" called celibacy and to help pastors conform to Paul's exhortation (1 Tim 3:2) that a bishop have one wife.[63] Later that year Capito finally married Agnes Roettel, while Caspar Hedio married Margaret Drenss—against the will of her brother, who was a member of the council.[64] After Capito's first wife died, Bucer brokered a second marriage for him to Wibrandis Rosenblatt, the widow of the Basel reformer John Oecolampadius. In 1541, Rosenblatt then married Bucer after his wife and Capito had both fallen victim to the plague.[65] Married to three different reformers during her life, Rosenblatt, like Schütz Zell and other spouses, provided both symbolic and real support to the urban agenda.

These marriages were not so much acts of defiance as assertions of Christian freedom by the Strasbourg reformers. To Bucer's mind they were also an example of putting others first, which was expected in the kingdom of Christ. Bucer's agenda was guided by the principle of living for others instead of for oneself. It was the theme of his first Reformation treatise: *People Should Live for Others and Not for Themselves, and How They Can Reach That Goal* (1523).[66] Bucer appealed to civil authority to place the common good over personal advantage and to govern in such a way that God would be praised as ruler of all.[67] In order to establish the kingdom of Christ, he told Odile de Berckheim, we should risk our souls, honor, bodies, and possessions. Even those who had the gift to live without a spouse should go ahead and marry because it would stamp out demonic chastity and hypocrisy (the vow of celibacy), return honor to the divine state of matrimony, and blaze a trail for those weaker in faith who would not risk it on their own.[68]

Arguments for clerical marriage like those offered by Bucer did not convince everyone. Some women, like his wife, for example, and Katharina von Bora, had left the convent and married; but others, like Katherine Rem, a Dominican nun in the Augsburg convent of St. Katherine, defended the cloister and the monastic way of life with no-nonsense assurance. There is no evidence that Katherine had read Bucer's treatise, but in the same year (1523) she responded to the arguments of her brother Bernard, who had become Protestant and urged his sister to leave the convent. Bernard believed that Christian marriage was the answer to the natural lustfulness of women and that life in the convent was governed by human teachings and not the word of God. In reply, Katherine made her position clear: "You should not think that we are so foolish that we place our hope in the convent and in our own works. Rather we place our hope in God. He is the true Lord and rewarder of all things. Him do we serve more willingly in the convent than in the world, with the grace and help of God."[69] Bernard lamented that Katherine did not "yet know what a Christian life is and what a Christian person's duties are."[70] Nevertheless, Katherine was just one of many nuns in German cloisters who resisted the Reformation and made life hard for the authorities who tried to convert them. In the Duchy of Lüneburg, loyal nuns locked the doors of two convents to keep out evangelical preaching; at another they set slippers on fire and sang during sermons, and they refused to give food to the preachers sent to yet another convent.[71]

Within the Strasbourg clergy, Bucer soon emerged as the first among equals, and the desire to establish the kingdom of Christ remained the goal of his reforming work within the town and beyond its borders. Compared to other cities, the Reformation in Strasbourg was a drawn-out process. Ten years elapsed between the council's mandate to preach only the gospel (1524) and its ratification of a new church order for the city (1534). The mass was finally abolished in 1529, the same year that a matrimonial court was established and that Jacob Sturm, the chief magistrate of the city, began to forge a Protestant alliance, which became the Smalcald League.[72] Although the settlement of the 1530s gave the magistrates control of the church, the pastors still had to convince council members and other laypeople to follow their lead in making the Protestant city also a devoutly Christian one.[73] In order to accomplish this goal, the pastors met together weekly in the Church Assembly, a council of clergy designed to oversee the city's spiritual life. In 1541 Martin Bucer was installed as the Assembly's first president.

Long before this date Bucer and his colleagues had sought to realize the kingdom of God in Strasbourg through a system of discipline. Called by Bucer "the yoke of Christ," it combined excommunication, catechetical instruction, and confirmation into "an integrated system for religious instruction, religious oversight, and pastoral care."[74] Bucer hoped the city council would enforce such a system. He admonished the magistracy to do all it could to ensure that the citizenry would hallow God's name, expand his kingdom, and live according to his will.[75] Essentially, this meant that magistrates should control faith and morals in the city.[76] Ceding so much power to the civil authorities, however, led to a robust controversy between Bucer and another pastor, Anton Engelbrecht, who did not believe in forcing the new faith on people.[77] Although Engelbrecht was removed from his pastoral office, his protest was not entirely unsuccessful. Those articles which advocated enforcement of discipline by civil authorities did not become part of the church order ratified by the council in 1534. Nevertheless, as the council's agents, church wardens were authorized to check on the religious activity and conduct of the people and, if need be, to admonish people who dishonored the name of Christ to change their ways.[78]

Bucer was disappointed at the lack of civil enforcement, but he persisted in his effort to find a feasible system of discipline. He tried to require mandatory instruction of children and a yearly confession of faith by adults that would be supplemented by private meetings between clergy and laity prior to communion. His treatise *True Pastoral Care* (1538) emphasized the responsibility of the pastors for their people and based the need for penitential discipline on the obligation of shepherds to heal their sick and wounded sheep.[79] The council dragged its feet, however, and made only limited concessions to the clergy, not allowing them to exclude people from the sacrament and restricting their private consultation with parishioners. From the council's point of view, giving the clergy authority to impose public penance and excommunication threatened its own control over the city's religious life and risked subjecting it to the yoke of a new papacy. To Bucer, however, throwing off the papal yoke was only the first step in becoming Christian. One had to replace it with the yoke of Christ: "The gospel does not require that we destroy the pope's ordinances and not replace them with Christian ones."[80]

This standoff continued into the 1540s despite a second synod in 1539 and repeated urging by Bucer and his colleagues. Thoroughly discouraged, Bucer then proposed a new tactic: the creation of a Christian fellowship (*christliche Gemeinschaft*) in each parish. These fellowships would be the kernels of a voluntary system of discipline and oversight exercised by the pastors and newly elected elders. Participating parishioners made a public profession of faith and promised obedience to the pastors and elders who would visit them once a year and could require of them confession and absolution before communion. Other members of the parish would still receive pastoral services, but could be asked to abstain from the sacrament if they had led an unchristian life.[81]

For the pastors, the fellowships were structures through which they could apply, on a voluntary basis, the system of discipline they had long been seeking for the city. The structure was new but the motivation behind it was old. The fellowships were a final attempt to carry out their agenda of Christianizing Strasbourg. At first the council did not resist, although complaints were soon heard about the pastors' appropriation of the right to excommunicate. The council then insisted that the church wardens be more involved, but it did not balk until some of the fellowships became lay conventicles that seemed to threaten the council's authority. Bucer continued to defend them, but by 1548 the fellowships had begun to disappear. By that time Bucer and the council were preoccupied with a different threat to the Reformation. It came from outside the city in the form of the *Interim*, a compromise with the Catholic emperor that threatened to undo the Reformation and that led to Bucer's exile from Strasbourg in 1549.

Gottfried Hammann has identified several motives behind the creation of the fellowships that have their roots in Bucer's ecclesiology.[82] The fellowships illustrate more than Bucer's concept of the church, however; they represent the last attempt by Bucer to implement his agenda of turning Protestant Strasbourg into a Christian community. It is possible, as Hammann suggests, that the fellowships were a resurgence of the monastic ideal adapted to Reformed principles.[83] Since Bucer had no intention of establishing little churches of perfect Christians, he was not trying to reestablish monasticism in a structural sense. As a former Dominican monk, however, he knew that the goal of the mendicant orders was not primarily to take Christians out of the world but to make the world more Christian by their teaching and example. Bucer's fellowships had the same purpose. By their public profession of faith and their exemplary lives, its members were to inspire the city to take its reformed commitment more seriously and make the kingdom of Christ present in Strasbourg at last.

Although Bucer's strategy for Strasbourg did not succeed, he pursued his agenda elsewhere both before and after he left the city. In 1538 and 1539 Bucer composed for the territory of Hesse a system of discipline known as the Ziegenhain church order,[84] which contained provisions for a public confirmation ceremony and for public penance and excommunication, none of which ever became mandatory in Strasbourg. During the religious colloquies of 1540 and 1541 Bucer advocated a "bearable reformation" (*leidliche Reformation*) in Catholic areas of Germany that could be tolerated by Protestants and Catholics alike. He understood it to be a "Christian Reformation," in which Protestants would, in his words, free a little territory from the grasp of Satan and give it to Christ even if they could not topple Satan completely.[85] His hope was dashed by the failure of the colloquies and by the breakdown of the Reformation in Cologne for which Bucer, with the help of Philipp Melanchthon, wrote another ordinance that incorporated a system of discipline.[86]

The grandest presentation of Bucer's agenda was penned at the end of his life in England as a New Year's present to the young King Edward VI. When the *Interim* of 1548 forced him to leave Strasbourg, Bucer accepted an invitation to teach at Cambridge from Thomas Cranmer (1489–1556), Archbishop of Canterbury, with whom Bucer had corresponded for eighteen years. Before leaving for exile, Bucer and his colleague Paul Fagius spent their last days in Strasbourg in the house of Katharina Schütz Zell. Upon arriving in England and finally meeting Cranmer on April 25, 1549, Bucer and Fagius stayed with Cranmer at Lambeth Palace and then at his summer home in the south of England.[87] As Bucer assumed his duties at Cambridge that fall, he struggled with the new climate (he may have suffered from tuberculosis) and the new language while mourning the death of Fagius and the temporary absence of his wife and children. Inside of a year Bucer nevertheless managed to compose his design for the Reformation of England, *The Kingdom of Christ* (1550).

The theme of the work was not new. The kingdom of Christ was the substance of Bucer's Reformation agenda and it had appeared with frequency in his earlier writings.[88] Now he sounded the theme once more with enthusiasm and proposed an elaborate if abstract plan for its application to England. Its goal was to overcome the numerous superstitions that had dominated human hearts for so many centuries, to explain the mysteries of the kingdom to people as diligently as possible, and to exhort them "by holy persuasions to take on the yoke of Christ."[89] For Bucer this restoration was manifestly a missionary venture; indeed, he made it sound as if he had landed in the heart of heathenism. Since England had been for so long without "legitimate ministers" and "suitable heralds of the Gospel," he observed, Christ's religion had almost been obliterated among the people.[90] To reverse that situation, "evangelists who are appropriately learned and motivated for the Kingdom of Christ" must be sent to all the churches of the realm.[91] For the "experience of so many centuries" had shown that "Christ's religion entirely fails among the people when the Church's sacred ministry has been handed over to inept and unfaithful ministers."[92] After the ministers had instructed large assemblies of laypeople at least seven or eight times, Bucer was sure that God would give the king "a reformation of the churches complete and perfect in its numbers and parts." Apparently, Bucer expected a religious revival that would persuade the king's councilors and the people to receive Christ's kingdom "with prompt hearts and retain it with an abundant fruit of piety."[93]

Once received, the kingdom of Christ in England, Bucer wrote, would be established and upheld by laws just as the biblical covenant was preserved after it had been received by the Hebrews. The laws, fourteen in number, were actually specific proposals for carrying out Bucer's agenda, that is, to make of England a Christian commonwealth in a manner similar to his attempt to make of Strasbourg a Christian city. He relied on his experience in Strasbourg but he also benefited from the suggestions of new colleagues and tailored his laws to the specific situation in England. The first six laws illustrate the continuity between his work in Strasbourg and his proposal for England: mandatory instruction of children, keeping Sundays and the churches holy, reforming the offices of pastors and bishops, protecting ecclesiastical assets and using them in the right way, establishing a system of relief for the poor to be supervised by deacons, and regulating marriage. The last of these has drawn the most attention from scholars because of Bucer's liberal attitude toward divorce.[94] The long argument for reordering marriage and divorce, however, like the other thirteen laws, was part of Bucer's vision of life in a Christian society.

In 1551, not long after completing *The Kingdom of Christ*, Bucer died in England. His career as a reformer lasted almost thirty years but, like Zwingli and Luther, he never knew whether his vision would achieve success either in Strasbourg or in England. There were significant differences among these reformers, of course, but their agendas agreed on two points that were critical to the Reformation. First, they shared the view that the practice of Christianity was just as important as the new evangelical theology. According to Marc Lienhard, there existed a fundamental difference between Luther and Bucer that has been extended to Calvin and often used to contrast the Lutheran with the Reformed tradition: for Luther the most important concept was justification, for Bucer sanctification.[95] This contrast can only be detected, however, if one abstracts their theology from its context. When their historical agendas are kept in the foreground, it becomes evident that both reformers cared deeply about the fruits of faith and making them visible in daily life. Like Luther and Zwingli, Bucer was less concerned with systematizing theology than with shaping the Christian life according to evangelical teaching.[96] This practical bent enabled them to create new forms of worship and new institutions of education and charity, but it also kept their expectations high for the transformation of personal lives.

Second, all three reformers conceived of reformation as mission, a fact to which Walter Holsten called attention in 1953.[97] He analyzed a substantial body of literature on the subject, much of it critically, and then discussed the concepts of mission in the writings of Luther, Bucer, Zwingli, and Theodor Bibliander, a Hebrew scholar in Zurich who called for better knowledge of Islam and published a Latin translation of the Qur'an. While Holsten was writing on the Reformation *and* mission, however, he underestimated the extent to which the Reformation as a whole *was* mission. The reformers were acting on the premise that Europe had to be Christianized and that it was their calling to pursue this opportunity.

Both humanism and monasticism contributed to this missionary awareness. Humanist editions of early Christian sources reminded the reformers of religious ideals that made the piety around them seem inadequate and even idolatrous. The sense of mission in medieval monastic orders also lived on in evangelical preachers who installed the new form of Christianity in parishes they regarded as full of superstition. According to some historians, the Protestant Reformation was a missionary failure because it had no monks,[98] but its preachers, pamphlet writers, and printers assumed and modernized the old monastic task of spreading the faith. More dynamically than Holsten realized, piety and humanism, monasticism and mission interacted at the core of the Reformation, and nowhere would this be truer and more obvious than at Geneva.

Geneva

Bucer was forced to leave Strasbourg at the end of his career, but Calvin was forced to leave Geneva just two years after he began his reforming work. In 1538, along with William Farel, who had persuaded him to stay in the first place, Calvin was dismissed from the city. His proposed ordinance and catechism threatened the authority of the councils that governed the city. The reformers were accused of arrogating to themselves the right to excommunicate and violating the ban that had been placed on their preaching. In late April 1538, they were expelled and given three days to leave Geneva.

Farel went to Neuchâtel. Calvin intended to settle in Basel, but Bucer insisted that he come to Strasbourg. A French refugee himself, Calvin became a minister to the refugee community and adapted for his parish the liturgy, discipline, and organization of the Protestant churches in Strasbourg that were in place by the late 1530s. In the view of François Wendel, "Calvin organized in Strasbourg that first French parish which was to serve, in his mind, as a model for all the parishes which were afterwards created in the chief protestant centers of France."[99]

During his three years in Strasbourg, Calvin refined his view of reform. He had never intended to be a pastor or a reformer and apparently he was never ordained.[100] When he had arrived in Geneva the first time, he refused to "discharge any particular office,"[101] although gradually he was referred to as a pastor or preacher after first being called a reader. In Strasbourg he was not only a pastor but also a teacher in the school founded by Jean Sturm; he lectured on the Gospel of John and several epistles of Paul, including the book of Romans, on which he published a commentary in the fall of 1539. That same year the appearance of a second, expanded edition of the *Institutes of the Christian Religion* enhanced Calvin's reputation as a theologian. All these functions—pastor, exegete, theologian, reformer—belonged to the larger vocation that dominated his agenda: "Calvin in Strasbourg or Geneva was also a missionary, an envoy."[102] That agenda, not restricted to any one city, was to restore true Christianity to every place that he worked and particularly to the kingdom of France that he had been forced to flee. In his preface to the *Institutes*, Calvin addressed the "most Christian king of the French":

> My purpose was solely to transmit certain rudiments by which those who are touched with any zeal for religion might be shaped to true godliness. And I undertook this labor especially for our French

countrymen, very many of whom I knew to be hungering and thirsting for Christ; but I saw very few who had been duly imbued with
even a slight knowledge of him.[103]

In a revised preface to the 1559 edition, Calvin confessed simply: "God
has filled my mind with zeal to spread his kingdom and to further the
public good."[104]

Calvin's agenda had personal roots in his own refugee experience that
caused him to read the biblical story in a different way and "to discover
God as the first refugee, trekking with the people of Israel through the
desert."[105] During his late twenties (he turned thirty in Strasbourg),
Calvin the religious refugee was writing and working for a reformation of
other refugees, and this preparation enabled the mature Calvin to think
of himself as the spokesman for "all Christians in the European diaspora"
and not just for Genevans.[106]

His missionary and refugee mind-set was also shaped by the judgment
on European religion that he delivered in Strasbourg:

> [T]he light of divine truth had been extinguished, the word of God
> buried, the virtue of Christ left in profound oblivion, and the pastoral
> office subverted. Meanwhile, impiety so stalked abroad that almost
> no doctrine of religion was pure from admixture, no ceremony free
> from error, no part, however minute, of divine worship untarnished
> by superstition.[107]

As Calvin saw it, the vineyard of European Christianity was fundamentally ruined and needed replanting. Although that judgment is inconsistent with the records of the Genevan consistory, which indicate that most
Genevans were active participants in late-medieval religion,[108] unlike
modern historians and more like other reformers, Calvin regarded that
religion as subchristian at best and pagan at worst. After two years back in
Geneva, Calvin declared in a treatise on relics: "Indeed, people calling
themselves Christian have gone to such lengths as to exhibit the madness
of idolatry in a degree equal to that of the heathen of old."[109]

Calvin had returned to Geneva with a plan. He immediately asked that
order be established in the church and the guidelines set down in writing.[110] His most important demand was ecclesiastical discipline or the
right of excommunication, which he had tried to introduce in 1537.
According to at least one report, Calvin refused to return to Geneva unless
a consistory were established to exercise the discipline he desired. The

council was now in a cooperative mood. Prodded by the Bernese reformer Pierre Viret, it had already agreed to a consistory five months before Calvin returned. Moreover, on the day that Calvin left Strasbourg for Geneva, Bucer admonished the council by letter to listen to Calvin "in order to establish and to put in order the discipline and doctrine of Christ and the state of the church, according to his advice and counsel and that of other brothers."[111]

Much has been written about the way in which the consistory attempted to control morals in Calvin's Geneva. To focus exclusively on morals, however, is to miss the point of Calvin's insistence on discipline. Calvin was interested in morality not for its own sake but because moral conduct befitted the new Christianity that he was attempting to install. The reformer repeatedly complained about people who, "having nothing but the name and badge of Christ, yet wish to call themselves 'Christians.'"[112] This complaint extended to the way people dressed and presented themselves as well as to their behavior. A sermon published in 1561 dealt with the text: "[T]hat the women should dress themselves modestly and decently in suitable clothing, not with their hair braided, or with gold, pearls, or expensive clothes, but with good works, as is proper for women who profess reverence for God" (1 Tim 2:9–10). Calvin elaborated Paul's admonition as follows: "If women wish to call upon God purely, it is necessary for them, beyond the name of Christianity that they bear, to demonstrate also with effect through good works that they have been taught in the school of God."[113] Men and women were challenged to prove not only that the word of God came out of their mouth but that it had *also taken root* in them.[114] In the *Institutes* Calvin explained what it meant for the word to take root:

> For it [Christianity] is a doctrine not of the tongue but of life. It is not apprehended by the understanding and memory alone, as other disciplines are, but it is received only when it possesses the whole soul, and finds a seat and resting place in the inmost affection of the heart. Accordingly, either let them cease to boast of what they are not, in contempt of God; or let them show themselves not unworthy of Christ their teacher. We have given the first place to the doctrine in which our religion is contained, since our salvation begins with it. But it must enter our heart and pass into our daily living, and so transform us into itself that it may not be unfruitful for us.[115]

Christianity, Calvin believed, could never be reduced to a collection of rituals or doctrines; the content of the faith had to be internalized in such a way that it transformed people and their lives. This transformation required discipline and self-denial in a manner reminiscent of monasticism. Calvin rejected monasticism in its late-medieval form, but he also broadened the monastic ideal to include all Christians and applied the Sermon on the Mount to all believers.[116] Discussing self-denial as the sum of the Christian life, Calvin wrote: "Christians must surely be so disposed and minded that they feel within themselves it is with God they have to deal throughout their life. In this way, as they will refer all they have to God's decision and judgment, so will they refer their whole intention of mind scrupulously to God."[117] Ideally, therefore, discipline was the internal self-regulation of believers whose faith was working itself through their system and manifesting itself in a new way of life. The goal was to change the conduct of believers so that they acted like the Christians Calvin wanted them to be.

To attain this goal, however, Calvin knew that discipline had to be more than a self-regulating mechanism for individuals. His goal was to transform the citizenry into a Christian society by regulating people collectively and applying discipline so strictly that it would purge the church of nominal believers. When he defended the discipline of the church in book IV of the *Institutes*, he criticized those who called themselves Christians but whose conduct disgraced that name and weakened the church. As the sinews of the church, discipline held the members of the body together, each in its own place.[118] It prevented the defilement of the body by ensuring that those

> who lead a filthy and infamous life may not be called Christian, to the dishonor of God, as if his holy church were a conspiracy of wicked and abandoned people. For since the church itself is the body of Christ, it cannot be corrupted by such foul and decaying members without some disgrace falling upon its Head. Therefore, that there may be no such thing in the church to brand its most sacred name with disgrace, those whose wickedness brings infamy on the Christian name must be banished from its family.[119]

The consistory not only monitored behavior but also urged Genevans to participate in the Christianized Protestant culture. Genevans were obligated to attend church regularly and to present their children weekly for catechetical instruction. According to the *Ecclesiastical Ordinances* of 1541, they could not dissent publicly from the doctrine taught in Geneva.[120] A subsequent decree prohibited the use of certain saints' names at baptisms because they were the "names of idols." This 1546 decree was the result of a conflict between the pastors and a father who rejected the name Abraham, which had been proposed by the ministers, and insisted on calling his infant son Claude (the name of a popular saint). The council ruled out names "that had dominated the land" because their use could still lead to superstition and because these names recalled the idolatry from which "it has pleased God to deliver the land through his grace."[121] The consistory records demonstrate how people resisted giving up religious customs that were labeled papist. Genevans continued to call upon saints and the Virgin Mary, they prayed for the dead and fasted on Fridays, they read Books of Hours and even attended mass outside the city in the Catholic areas nearby.[122]

As the agent of Christianization in Geneva, the consistory tried to regulate marital behavior.[123] A marital ordinance was not officially adopted until 1561, but long before that the supervision of marriage was a prominent part of the consistory's work. In addition to monitoring the sexual behavior of all Genevans, the consistory guarded both people's entry into marriage and their exit from it. The engagement promises of young people, in contrast to canon law, required parental consent in order to be valid, and the consistory held couples to this regulation. The marital ordinance also prohibited the cohabitation of engaged couples before the "marriage had been blessed in church in a Christian manner."[124] One couple, an Italian man and a woman from Crete who said they had married in Venice, took advantage of this requirement, requesting the pastors to confirm their marriage now that they "had come to a Christian city where they wished to live according to the reformation of the gospel."[125] Divorces were permitted in cases of adultery and desertion, but they were not easily obtained. During the twenty-three years of Calvin's second term in Geneva (1541–1564) only twenty-six divorces were granted for adultery and only a few more for other causes.[126] Two notorious cases involved Calvin's brother and sister-in-law and a prominent Italian refugee who had converted to Protestantism but whose Catholic family had remained in Italy.[127] Both cases extended over years and illustrate the energy that was devoted by Calvin and the consistory to the reform of marriage.

The missionary mentality of Calvin and other reformers reopened questions such as restrictions on marriage between Christians and pagans. If, for example, Christians were not permitted to marry heathen during the first Christianization of Europe, could they marry or stay married to Catholics, judged to be idolatrous and subchristian, in the new campaign to Christianize the continent? In 1552 Calvin had to answer a "poor

Christian (i.e., Protestant) woman" in France with an idolatrous (i.e., Catholic) husband who still forced her to attend mass, to undertake pilgrimages, and to invoke the saints. She asked the pastors and magistrates in Geneva if she had to stay in the marriage or if the gospel gave her the freedom to leave and "to live to the glory of God."[128] Calvin expressed his sympathy but insisted that no text of Scripture, like the so-called Pauline privilege (1 Cor 7:15: "But if the unbelieving partner separates, let it be so"), supported her desire to divorce her husband, because she was the believing partner. Because he did not consider Catholics to be fully Christian, Calvin was able to apply a text that originally dealt with Christians and pagans to a marriage between a Protestant and a Catholic.

Although hesitant to allow Protestants to divorce Catholics, Calvin strongly advised against allowing them to marry in the first place. In 1549, he was specifically asked by Faustus Socinus (1539–1603) whether a Protestant should abstain from marriage with a papist as one would abstain from marriage with a Turk. Though he admitted that Catholics were "a little nearer" to Protestants than were Muslims, he argued that "papists" were still alien from Christ and that there was no marriage in the Lord "when one takes a spouse before that spouse has divorced the pope."[129]

The consistory, in its turn, tried to dissuade Genevans from marrying Catholics from outside the city. In 1542 Jane, the sister of Pierre Migerand, a member of the Council of Two Hundred, told the consistory that she had promised to marry a man, presumably a Catholic, from La Roche. She was admonished not to go "looking for her damnation" and not to "renounce Jesus Christ to go worship idols." The consistory advised the Council not to publish the banns in Geneva "because they should be published in La Roche in the papistry."[130] In its mind, Geneva was a Christian island in a sea of papal idolatry, and controlling marriage was an important religious shelter.

It fell mainly to the consistory, therefore, to expunge unchristian behavior and non-Protestant belief and practice from Geneva and to make the town into a Christian city. Some thought it succeeded. In the famous opinion of John Knox, by 1556 Geneva had become "the most perfect school of Christ that ever was in the earth since the days of the Apostles. In other places I confess Christ to be truly preached; but manners and religion so sincerely reformed, I have not yet seen in any other place."[131] Since Knox was writing after 1555, when Calvin and the consistory gained the right of excommunication, Calvin might have been more inclined to agree than he was before. Commenting in 1550, however, on the community of Christians portrayed in Acts 4:32–37, Calvin wrote: "If we compare our situation with what has been told by Saint Luke, we will see how far we are from Christianity."[132] Preaching on Micah in the early 1550s, he suggested that only 5 percent of Genevans were serious about God's word and that the rest seemed frozen, as if they had never heard it. In business he saw no sign of fair play and honesty, and sexual immorality seemed to be everywhere condoned.[133] On his deathbed, Calvin was still calling Geneva "a perverse and unhappy nation," telling his colleagues that "though there are good people in it the nation is perverse and wicked and you will have troubles when God shall have called me away."[134]

In order to explain his discontent, it is tempting to fall back on the old image of Calvin as the stern religious judge whom nobody could please. A more obvious and reliable explanation, however, is the idealistic nature of Calvin's agenda and the central role that Geneva played in accomplishing it. Like Luther, Bucer, and other reformers, Calvin tried to turn his town into a thoroughly Christian community and, although Knox thought it came closer to that ideal than any place he had seen, it was unlikely that the reformer in charge ever could have agreed. It was not Calvin's personality that prevented him from praising the Genevans, but his missionary mentality, which at times forced him, like Luther, into the role of disappointed idealist. If Geneva was to be a launching pad for the Christianization of Europe, then it also needed to be a laboratory in which the experiment of Christianization had visibly succeeded.

The agenda of Christianization also explains Calvin's refusal to tolerate beliefs judged to be heretical, such as the views of Michael Servetus, who was burned to death in Geneva in 1553. Servetus's writings were a direct challenge to the orthodoxy of Protestant and Catholic reformers alike. If the Reformation was claiming to build a society that was more Christian than medieval Europe had been, then Protestants could tolerate heretics even less than the Roman Church had done. Protestants had to prove they were more orthodox than the pope in order to defend themselves against charges of heresy and to establish their right to define true Christianity. From Zurich, Bullinger wrote to Calvin that the Servetus affair gave Geneva the opportunity "to wash us all clean from the suspicion of being heretics or of favoring heresy. . . ."[135] The missionary character of Calvin's agenda and the need to establish its credibility reinforced the hard line that Calvin took against his challengers. The same may be said for most other reformers as well.

The remaking of Geneva into an exemplary Christian city became more crucial, therefore, as it became a haven for Protestant refugees who would carry the campaign of Christianization to France, the Netherlands,

England, and Scotland. Although historians can distinguish between
Calvin and later Calvinism or between Geneva and "international"
Calvinism,[136] Calvin did not see it that way. He was not trying to Calvinize
France or to make Genevan Calvinism international, but to extend the
vineyard he had replanted in Geneva to the other fields of Europe. When
it came to France, Calvin offered a theological perspective of the persecution suffered by Reformed communities and their need to remain stead-
fast.[137] These gatherings of the elect were outposts of the kingdom of
Christ under attack by Satan, but they were also being sustained by the
Spirit until the persecution ended and the kingdom arrived in fullness.
These themes constituted a theology of history that informed Calvin's lectures on the Old Testament between 1555 and 1564, lectures that were
heard by a number of future preachers in France.[138] The same themes
undergirded his theology of mission and his dynamic conception of reformation. It was not the human restructuring of an institution, or even the
religious makeover of a city, but a cosmic clash not unlike Luther's vision.
In the face of demonic opposition, the kingdom of God that was founded,
protected, and ruled by Christ was expanding throughout Europe, and
Calvin expected God to bring it to completion.[139]

Since Calvin viewed the Reformation as God's mission, its success
could not be influenced or judged by human participants or observers.
Defending the Reformation to Emperor Charles V and the Diet of Speyer
in 1544, Calvin gave this rejoinder to the charge that no fruit had been
produced by reform: "The restoration of the church is the work of God,
and it no more depends on human hopes and opinions than does the resurrection of the dead or any other miracle of that description. . . . It is the
will of our Master that his gospel be preached. Let us obey his command,
and follow whithersoever he calls. What the success will be it is not ours
to inquire."[140] After this theological response based on 1 Corinthians
3:6–7, Calvin turned defiant and positive. With considerable optimism
about the results to that point, he declared it was false to say that no benefit had accrued from the reformers' agendas:

> I say nothing of the correction of external idolatry, and of numerous
> superstitions and errors; though that is not to be counted of no
> moment. But is there no fruit in this, that many who are truly pious
> feel their obligation to us, in that they have at length learned to wor-
> ship God with a pure heart, and to invoke him with a calm conscience,
> have been freed from perpetual torments, and furnished with true
> delight in Christ, so as to be able to confide in him? But if we are asked

for proofs which every eye can see, it has not fared so unhappily with us that we cannot point to numerous sources of rejoicing. How many who formerly led a vicious course of life have been so reformed as to seem converted into new people? How many whose past lives had been free from censure, nay, who were held in the highest estimation, have, instead of retrograding, been able to testify by their conduct that our ministry has proved neither barren nor unfruitful? Our enemies, no doubt, have it in their power to traduce and lacerate us by their calumnies, especially among the ignorant; but this they can never wrest from us, viz., that in those who have embraced our doctrine, greater innocence, integrity, and true holiness are found, than in all who among them are deemed of greatest excellence.[141]

Making a claim, even out of heartfelt conviction, did not make it so, however. This claim was impossible to quantify, even though Calvin believed every eye could see it confirmed. Moreover, because this passage appears in an obvious apology for the Reformation, one would hardly expect a declaration of its failure. Nevertheless, what it says about Calvin and his agenda is more important than the truth of its claim. Calvin confirms that he was indeed a missionary who wanted to turn nominal believers into real Christians. He not only wanted to abolish idolatry and superstition in public worship and piety; he also wanted to convert people's hearts and lives to a higher level of confidence and integrity. After his death in 1564, his agenda was vigorously pursued by his successor in Geneva, Theodore Beza (1519–1605), and by other Reformed leaders in the churches of Switzerland, France, Germany, Holland, England, Scotland, and Hungary.

Although Calvin downplayed the "correction of external idolatry" in his statement to Charles V, it was this correction of public worship and devotion that made Protestant agendas different from one another. The goal of Christianizing one city through the reform of ritual and the public exercise of discipline made Calvin's Geneva the exemplary expression of the urban Reformation agenda. That agenda and the pattern of urban reform were much the same, however, for those cities in Germany and Switzerland that became Lutheran and those that became Reformed. The division between Lutheran and Reformed lay not in their vision of Christianization or in the desirability of discipline but in the degree to which they believed worship and devotion had to be changed in order for theology and piety to be Christian. Lutherans kept, for example, the basic structure of the mass and frequent celebration of the Lord's Supper, liturgical vestments, the exorcism in baptism, and pictures and statues in the churches. Reformed churches replaced the altar with a table and the mass with a preaching service and a simpler meal celebrated less frequently, omitted exorcism and the use of traditional vestments, and removed statues and pictures from the churches.

Compared with the changes on which they agreed—the abolition of monasticism, clerical celibacy, the canon of the mass, the penitential system, pilgrimages, and the invocation of saints—the differences between Lutheran and Reformed seem small. If it was necessary to eliminate idolatry and to reinstate Christianity, however, in their minds no change was too small. Consequently, even though Lutheran and Reformed theologians agreed on the central message of Scripture, on the need to deepen devotion, and on the primary alterations in practice that had to be made in order to render their territory Christian, their specific agendas for change were enough to divide them. Reformed theologians identified more thorns and rocks in the vineyard than Lutherans did and insisted on their removal in order for the vineyard to be Christian. Other reformers would dissent more loudly still and insist on the removal of more debris. They were also committed to the Reformation vision of Christianization but no longer to a Christian Europe.

Chapter 4

The Radical Agendas

Christianization outside Christendom

Radical Reform

The German and Swiss reformers expected the civil authorities to sanction and uphold the changes they made. Even when princes and city councils refused to endorse every proposal or dragged their feet, the reformers sought their support and preached to them about their duty as Christian rulers. In his *Instruction of a Christian Prince* (1516), Erasmus had insisted that rulers were responsible for the moral and spiritual welfare of their subjects. Although Erasmus did not have Protestant state churches in mind, his ideal of a Christian ruler was adaptable to the political reality created by the rise of Protestant towns and territories independent of papal jurisdiction.[1] Christendom no longer depended on the alliance of civil rulers with the papacy; instead, the new Christendom relied on Protestant rulers who enforced the changes made within their jurisdictions. There was tension aplenty between the reformers and the civil authorities, to wit, between Bucer and the council in Strasbourg or between Calvin and the councils in Geneva, but none of these reformers, Luther included, seriously questioned the necessity of magisterial support, and none of them could have survived without it.

By and large, therefore, the Reformation was a magisterial reformation, and the vision of Christianization was pursued by reformers in cooperation with civil authorities. Still, loud dissent was voiced in many places. Before there were Separatists and Friends in Protestant England, various individuals and groups on the continent wanted to push the Reformation agenda beyond the new Protestant order and create a better Christianity, if necessary, without the support of civil rulers.

Early dissenters included Luther's colleague Andrew Karlstadt, who was squeezed out of the leadership in Wittenberg, and Thomas Müntzer, an early follower of Luther who prophesied that Christendom was giving way to the thousand-year reign of Christ. Karlstadt was hoping that Wittenberg would become a "Christian city" before Luther returned and—in Karlstadt's words—made a priority of sparing out of love the weak who were not yet ready for change.[2] After being rebuffed by the princes of Saxony, Müntzer went to central Germany and led a band of peasants to defeat in the revolution of 1525. The Zurich colleagues who pushed Zwingli to move more rapidly and who became Anabaptists were among the earliest dissenters, as were the disciples of Müntzer and other Anabaptists who formed fluid communities in southern Germany. Dissenters migrated to Austria and Moravia, and some of them organized communes that were eventually called Hutterite after Jakob Hutter, who served briefly as one of their leaders before his arrest and execution. The furrier Melchior Hoffman bequeathed his name to followers in northern Germany and Holland called Melchiorites. The most notorious Melchiorites took over the city of Münster and turned it into their version of the new Jerusalem before they were besieged and subdued in 1535. The survivors became the nucleus of a peaceful Anabaptist movement in the Netherlands and northern Germany under the leadership of Menno Simons; they gradually became known as Mennonites. Other dissenters had smaller followings or none at all: Caspar Schwenckfeld, a Silesian spiritualist; Sebastian Frank, a disaffected Lutheran and outspoken critic of all institutions; Michael Servetus, the physician and theologian who was burned in Geneva for opposing the doctrine of the Trinity; and Sebastian Castellio, an advocate of religious toleration who lived in Basel after crossing swords with Calvin.

These dissenters represented a significant minority of early sixteenth-century Christians known collectively as the radical reformation. This name owes its popularity and respectability to the historian George Williams, who bestowed it upon Anabaptists and others in his 1962 book of the same name. According to Williams, "this Radical Reformation was a loosely interrelated congeries of reformations and restitutions which, besides the Anabaptists of various types, included Spiritualists and spiritualizers of varying tendencies, and the Evangelical Rationalists, largely Italian in origin."[3] In order to distinguish it from a magisterial reformation, Williams proposed a religious definition of the movement: "The various exponents of the Radical Reformation not only opposed the Magisterial Reformation tactically and on principle but also clearly differentiated themselves from sixteenth-century Protestants, that is, the Lutherans and Reformed (Zwinglians and Calvinists), on what constituted both the experience and the conception of salvation, and on what constituted the true church and proper Christian deportment."[4] The tactical and principled opposition to a magisterial reformation entailed the separation of church and state, although Williams admitted that in "three or four instances . . . they were misled into thinking that regenerate magistrates from their own midst would prove more godly than Protestants and Catholics."[5]

By creating the term radical reformation and treating it so richly, Williams made it difficult to resist the notion that such a reformation actually existed. Not everyone was convinced, however. In 1965 Günter Vogler expressed skepticism that a radical reformation could be defined by religious criteria that were different from those of the Reformation as a whole.[6] Williams gradually retreated from a unifying theological criterion, first in comments made after the second edition of his work appeared,[7] and then in his introduction to the third edition, where he conceded that the term radical reformation was a catchall for those whose strategy to renew Christendom was rejected by the civil and religious authorities.[8]

If the term radical reformation is to be used, then it should be defined as that common dissent from the new religious order. Nevertheless, radical reformers shared the most basic feature of the Reformation that was, in the first instance, a massive expression of dissent—dissent from the way in which Christianity was taught, practiced, and structured in the late Middle Ages. From Martin Luther to Thomas Müntzer, from Calvin to Servetus, from Bucer to Hoffman, reformers more or less radical and the communities to which they belonged disagreed profoundly with the religion of their ancestors and replaced it with new forms of Christianity. The disagreements among Protestant and radical reformers were real and sometimes bloody, but they derived from a common rejection of Rome and a common desire for new forms of Christianity.[9] Many of these dissenters were labeled so quickly as pacifists, separatists, or spiritualists that their original connections with the Protestant reformers and their agendas are forgotten.

The image of radical dissenters as a homogeneous group of eager, nonresisting separatists has been undermined from at least two directions. In *Anabaptists and the Sword* James Stayer demonstrated that Anabaptists were by no means all pacifists.[10] By pointing out that a number of groups like the Hutterites planted their movements with the help of civil authorities, Hans-Jürgen Goertz showed that radicals were by no means all separatists.[11] Most historians now support the nonseparatist origins of the radical reformation. From the beginning radicals did not press for the formation of separate communities at all, but instead "strove in various ways for the Christianization of the entire society."[12] According to one model, dissenters began with the "idea of a radical reformation of all spheres of life," and the notion of a "separatist, pacifist Free Church" gained acceptance only after the militant wings of these movements were defeated by the authorities.[13] What made some dissenters radical was not pacifism or an innate tendency toward separatism, but their refusal to accept the limits on reform imposed by civil authorities at the risk of harassment, banishment, and execution. Consequently, they developed their own agendas for fulfilling the Reformation vision.

Radical Christianization

The radical dissenters of the sixteenth century wanted to Christianize their society. Their original intention was not to withdraw from public life and seek sanctuary in clandestine cells of true believers but to bring about a renewal of Christendom at large. Most dissenters belonged to early reform movements and pushed their leaders to make more far-reaching changes than their leaders or civil officials could accept. The conflicts that ensued led to their separation and repression and thwarted the realization of most radical programs.

The restitution of a pure, apostolic Christendom was, for example, the grand vision of Thomas Müntzer, who is usually remembered for leading a band of peasants to their destruction at Frankenhausen in 1525. His tragic end, however, was preceded by a short but passionate ministry during which Müntzer propagated one of the most demanding and radical agendas. Müntzer's goal was not the gradual transformation of small groups of believers but a complete overhaul of the entire Christian order that he regularly called "die christenheyt," or "die heylge christenheyt." Holy Christendom, he argued, had fallen from its original apostolic state, but could easily recover the spirit of wisdom and know the divine will by embracing the fear of God in fullness and purity.[14] If God did not intend for Christendom to become apostolic again, asked Müntzer, what purpose was served by preaching or by the visions of Scripture?[15] So long as "poor, miserable, pitiful, woebegone Christendom" did not recognize its wound, it was not to be helped.[16] It could be helped, however, by hearkening to "an earnest preacher," who would proclaim how God truly worked and would teach about real Christian faith, not the imaginary faith manifested by people no better than heathen when they called upon the saints in "open idolatry."[17]

Müntzer became that earnest preacher and devoted his short career to telling the hard truth of what he believed it meant to be Christian as he found it described in Scripture. True believers had to reject all idolatry, be ready to suffer persecution, demonstrate the effect of faith in their lives, root out the godless among them, and prepare the way for the kingdom of God. The most serious adversaries of this Christianity were the clergy whom Müntzer excoriated in his *Prague Manifesto* of 1521 and whom he continued to taunt and denounce after he returned to Germany. When he predicted that the apostolic church would be restored first in Bohemia, "and afterward everywhere," he was not making a theological announcement but, like an earnest preacher, heralding a new Christian society.[18] After he became a pastor at Allstedt in 1524, Müntzer was more specific. The core of a restored apostolic church became the league of elect believers whom Müntzer identified with his supporters. They were the wheat who would protect the gospel and help to expel the tares (Mt 13:24–30), namely, the unworthy clergy and laity who had supported the idolatrous veneration of the Virgin Mary at the Mallerbach chapel that went up in flames. Müntzer hoped the pious princes of Saxony would support the destruction of the godless and purify the church, but his famous sermon on Daniel 2 failed to persuade Duke John and he was forced to leave Allstedt.

Even before he joined the revolt of the peasants, whom he considered Christian brethren, Müntzer's agenda was not separation of the pious but exclusion of the godless. His league of the elect was modeled on the renewal of the covenant by King Josiah (2 Kings 23:2–5) and the destruction of the idolatrous worship of Baal. Müntzer had no intention of separating from Christendom and starting a new community in seclusion. Instead, he solicited the support of godly rulers and expected them to cleanse Christendom from its idolatry and turn it into the pure apostolic church portrayed in Scripture.[19] The time of harvest had come, and the tares were to be cast out while the wheat, filled with the Holy Spirit, greeted the new reign of Christ.[20] When the rulers refused, Müntzer himself took up the "sword of Gideon" at the head of common Christians, the "peasants,"[21] and prepared to destroy the godless in order to exclude them from the apostolic church that was arriving at last. Müntzer expected not only to win but also to see the fulfillment of his grand vision in a new Christian order.

Many leaders of the Revolution of 1525 expected a similar transformation of Christendom.[22] Peter Blickle, who proposed that designation for the Peasants' War, insisted that the traditional name was much too narrow. The so-called Peasants' War was in fact a social revolution that was more serious and comprehensive than a series of local uprisings. It was also a religious revolution. The *Twelve Articles of the Peasants* (1525) provided biblical support for the peasants' grievances and expressed their intention to conduct themselves in a Christian manner.[23] The Christian associations formed in South Germany and Austria envisioned a new social and political order based on the gospel and divine law.[24] Although Luther doubted that "so big a crowd" could all "be true Christians and have good intentions,"[25] the constitutions and related documents produced by the associations were blueprints for a new Christian society. "In the Tyrol, Salzburg, Württemberg, Alsace, on the upper Rhine, and in Upper Swabia, territorial and federal constitutions were to be drafted, guided by the principle that they should embody principles of the gospel and of godly law and thus lead to a Christianization of society."[26]

In most cases the goal was to bring about this new society by the peaceful negotiation of grievances and by structures of representative government. This intention was soon frustrated, however, by the violence that erupted and prompted reformers to contest the self-designation of these new associations as Christian. Martin Luther, for example, urged the authors of the *Twelve Articles* to "stop calling yourselves Christians and stop claiming that you have the Christian law on your side. For no matter how right you are, it is not right for a Christian to appeal to law, or to fight, but rather to suffer wrong and endure evil."[27] To be "genuine Christians," he wrote, they have to follow the example of Christ by committing the injustice to God and praying for their persecutors. "If you do not do this, then give up the name of Christian and the claim that Christian law is on your side, for then you are certainly not Christians but are opposing Christ and his law, his doctrine, and his example." "Christians do not fight for themselves with sword and musket, but with the cross and with suffering, just as Christ, our leader, does not bear a sword but hangs on the cross."[28]

The conflict between leaders of the revolution and Protestant reformers arose from their different conceptions of how to go about Christianization. For the revolutionaries of 1525, it meant using force, if necessary, to make concrete social and political changes that conformed to the Bible and that, in their judgment, were essential features of a just and Christian society. The authorities could be Protestant or Catholic; it made no difference. They could be resisted if they challenged the new Christian order being urged by the radicals. Like Luther, most Protestant reformers condemned violence and in particular rebellion against one's own ruler. They sought instead to persuade town magistrates and princes to adopt their reforms and to grant the evangelical movement political legitimacy. The line between radicals and magisterial reformers could become, however, a fine one. Protestant and Catholic rulers, with the support of reformers, did not hesitate to destroy peasant forces on the grounds that their revolution was a rebellion that threatened to destroy Christendom. Despite his strong pacifist leanings, Zwingli finally went into battle against the Catholic cantons, and Lutherans eventually resisted the advance of Emperor Charles V. Most radicals, however, were not social revolutionaries who condoned violence, and most Protestants regarded armed conflict as a last resort to preserve the new evangelical Christendom from chaos or destruction. Nevertheless, some radicals like Müntzer were willing to Christianize the society by force.

Force was not on the agenda of the Swiss and southern German Anabaptists, and neither was separation. Owing to the influence of the *Schleitheim Articles*, however, these earliest Anabaptists have been classified as separatists. The *Articles* expressed the consensus among Anabaptists who attended a conference at Schleitheim near the border between Germany and Switzerland in 1527. They were probably written by Michael Sattler, a former prior of the Benedictine abbey of St. Peter in the Black Forest. He worked as an Anabaptist missionary near Zurich and Strasbourg, and early in 1527 he met with Bucer and Capito to plead for the release of brethren imprisoned in their city. That same year, not long after the Schleitheim conference, both Sattler and his wife, Margaretha, a former Beguine sister, were arrested; two months later they were executed, Michael by burning and Margaretha by drowning. Sattler's memory was kept alive by the account of his trial and martyrdom. The *Schleitheim Articles* circulated in print and were the target of a refutation by Ulrich Zwingli in 1527.

The *Articles* utilized a sharp dualistic construction in order to justify the separation of Anabaptists from society. Calling themselves "children of the light" and "truly implanted members of Christ," the believers at Schleitheim rejected militant communities and invited others to retreat with them into conventicles of nonresisters, "who are separated from the world—and who should be separated in all that they do and do not do."[29] This separation required the avoidance of "everything which [was] not united with our God and Christ [as] the abomination which we should flee: . . . all popish and neo-popish works and divine services, assemblies, ecclesiastical processions, wine shops, the ties and obligations of lack of faith, and other things of this kind, which the world indeed regards highly but which are done in direct opposition to the commandments of God."[30] According to the Schleitheim template, there could be no compromise between a Christianized society and the world and, consequently, the emerging Protestant forms of Christendom ("neo-popish works") were also rejected. The contrast between the Schleitheim view of Christian community and that of Protestant Zurich was unmistakable on two points: the *Schleitheim Articles* forbade Christians from serving as magistrates or wielding the sword. Zwingli, however, insisted on a Christian magistrate and died himself on the field of battle.

Those followers of Zwingli who eventually broke with the reformer through the symbolic rite of rebaptism had not anticipated a separation. The first rebaptisms occurred in January 1525 after the dissenters, led by Conrad Grebel, failed to persuade Zwingli and the council to make quick and decisive changes to the mass and to the system of tithes. They insisted upon divine law contained in the Bible as the only legal basis for a new Christian order in the city, only to see that basis overridden by the council. Still they were slow to give up on the magistrates even when controversy erupted over infant baptism.[31] Only after the council insisted that infant baptism be upheld did the dissenters directly flout its authority with the rebaptisms that led to their expulsion. Although the *Hutterite Chronicle* reported that "therewith began the separation from the world and its evil works,"[32] their separate Christian existence only gradually became a reality through their expulsions and persecution, and separation first became a tenet at Schleitheim in 1527.[33]

The original agenda of the Anabaptists was therefore not separatist at all. The *Swiss Order*, an early document that may have preceded the *Schleitheim Articles*, did not call for separation but described a congregational structure that could have functioned in traditional parishes. It is difficult to ascertain which communities may have used the order, but in areas where Anabaptism enjoyed a popular reception there was no need for separate conventicles, and on occasion whole parishes became Anabaptist under the influence of a missionary or an apostle, as they were called. Near St. Gall in Switzerland, Hans Krüsi was able to win almost the entire parish of Tablat for Anabaptism. Its congregational worship included baptisms, readings from the Bible, and a simple commemoration of Jesus' death.[34] The strongest theologian of early Anabaptism, Balthasar Hubmaier, converted his parish of Waldshut in southwestern Germany first into a Protestant community and then a substantial segment of it into an Anabaptist congregation. After receiving baptism with sixty others on Easter Sunday, 1525, Hubmaier baptized about three hundred members of the parish. Still supported by the town, he involved Waldshut in the Revolution of 1525 and fled the town only after it was occupied by Austrian troops. Far from being a separatist, Hubmaier wanted believers' baptism to become part of the Reformation program as a whole, and he was the author of at least one document on which the commoners based their plan for a new Christian order.[35]

Some Anabaptists, therefore, who ended up on the fringes of official Christendom, found themselves living openly under the protection of a civil overlord. This was the case in Moravia, to which Hubmaier immigrated in 1526, establishing himself in Nikolsburg and winning over both the leading cleric in the area and the secular lord, Count Leonhart von Liechtenstein. In Nikolsburg, Hubmaier encountered Hans Hut, a loyal believer in Thomas Müntzer's vision of Christendom, who had undergone baptism at Augsburg in 1526. Hut was proclaiming that the new order, a "true Christendom," would arrive in 1528, and he had spread that message on missionary tours through southern Germany.[36] Hut's apocalyptic tidings, his rejection of civil authority, and his advocacy of common ownership threatened Hubmaier's conservative agenda, and Hut was imprisoned in spite of numerous sympathizers in Austria. Allegedly, Hut taught that "the Gospel should not be preached in churches but secretly and clandestinely in houses."[37] Yet his gospel posed a threat precisely because its content was not restricted to private Christianity but prophesied a different and very public social order.

Moravia is best known for the Hutterites, who did in fact start out as separatists. Under their first leader, Jakob Wiedemann, this group of German refugees in Nikolsburg resisted the parish-wide reformation started by Hubmaier and formed their own conventicles. When they were ordered to leave town, they pooled their possessions and headed for Austerlitz, where they were received kindly by the lords. The Hutterites proper emerged as a distinct group at the nearby town of Auspitz, where several small communitarian groups already existed and where Jakob Hutter was confirmed as their leader in 1533.[38] The early years were marked by schism and by persecution at the hands of the Catholic Hapsburg ruler in Austria, Ferdinand, but once the harassment ceased and they were able to lease land from the Moravian nobility, their communitarian experiment prospered. From small, separatist origins the Hutterites developed into a prominent, public form of communitarian Christianity with over thirty thousand people in seventy settlements. They had fulfilled the ideal envisioned by the Silesian Anabaptist Clemens Adler:

> Among genuine Christians all possessions are common. None should seek sole ownership of property. Each should contribute according

to his ability to the needs of the poor brothers or sisters. Where such [sharing] is not found among brothers and Christians, there is no genuine Christianity.[39]

The Hutterite insistence upon a community of goods as the mark of true Christianity was not shared by most Anabaptists. It was rejected as a violation of conscience, for example, by the Tyrolean Anabaptist Pilgram Marpeck, an independent lay theologian who lived in Strasbourg and Augsburg and traveled in Switzerland, Austria, and Moravia. He objected in similar fashion to the strict ban in use among the Swiss Brethren, arguing that it "destroyed the blossom before it was able to bear fruit."[40] For Marpeck, Christian community was produced by the "unconstraining Spirit," which stood against all forms of coercion, individual and collective. "The reordering Holy Spirit, willingly poured out by Christ in his cross, constitutes and is mediated by the new community, which patiently offers that Spirit to others without coercion."[41] Although Christians could not coerce faith, Marpeck did advocate obedience to civil authority for the purpose of keeping order and promoting public welfare. He organized and participated in Anabaptist meetings because they were the reordered communities that peacefully offered the hope of transformation. Marpeck did not withdraw from the world, however, but worked at civil jobs in the public sector. "He advocated not a monastic withdrawal from society, but a critical participation."[42]

The most notorious example of nonseparatist radical Christianization was the Melchiorite kingdom at Münster. Melchiorites were followers of the German lay preacher Melchior Hoffman, who predicted the return of Christ in 1533 and awaited his arrival from confinement in Strasbourg. There he was surrounded and influenced by a group of visionary prophets, the most important of whom were Lienhard and Ursula Jost and Barbara Rebstock.[43] Their vision of reform was more than a simple forecast, however; it was the most optimistic apocalyptic and missionary proposal of the Reformation. According to his *Ordinance of God* (1530), based on Matthew 28:16–20,

such a time has come that the proclamation of God's Word shall go out to all peoples as a witness and absolutely none shall be excepted; but rather to all tribes, pagans, tongues, and nations the gospel shall be revealed to their enlightenment. . . . And all those who hear this and do not stop up their ears but rather attend with alertness will inherit their salvation.[44]

This message was to be proclaimed by apostolic emissaries, who would gather those who did not "stop up their ears" into a flock of the elect and turn them into the Bride of Christ through believers' baptism.[45] The Bride of Christ was no shy newlywed, however. She was the legion of 144,000 elect who would reign on earth with Christ for a thousand years and survive the final tribulation (Rev 7:4; 20:4).

With the support of influential nobles like Ulrich von Dornum, Hoffman began to assemble this legion in East Friesland in 1530. In the sacristy of the Great Church in Emden, Hoffman reportedly baptized around three hundred people from all social classes.[46] East Friesland became the base for the spread of Melchiorites to Holland. After Hoffman's successor in Emden, the apostle Jan Volkerts, was banished, he went to Amsterdam and began to baptize followers. In 1531 Hoffman himself turned up in Amsterdam and joined Volkerts in baptizing about fifty people. When Volkerts surrendered to the authorities and was executed along with nine colleagues, Hoffman declared a moratorium on believers' baptism, but the Melchiorite movement expanded nonetheless, favored by the refusal of local magistrates to enforce the imperial mandates against Anabaptism. Apocalyptic expectations reached fever pitch in late 1533 as Hoffman's deadline for the return of Christ drew near, and leadership of the Dutch movement was taken over by Jan Matthijs, who claimed he had received the outpouring of the Holy Spirit predicted by Hoffman. Matthijs reinstated baptism as the powerful seal of the covenant that would protect believers from the eschatological tribulation to come.[47] The stage was now set for the Melchiorite takeover of Münster.

Situated in northwest Germany just to the east of Holland, Münster became Protestant in 1533 after the Catholic bishop and overlord, Franz von Waldeck, agreed to a treaty that allowed the city council to adopt a church order written by the leading evangelical preacher, Bernhard Rothmann (d. 1536). Soon thereafter, Rothmann fell under the influence of some radical preachers whom he had welcomed into the city, and all of them, together with the wealthy merchant, Bernd Knipperdolling, allowed themselves to be baptized by the first Melchiorites who arrived in Münster in January 1534. After the lieutenants of Jan Matthijs appeared the next week, many more people were baptized and Matthijs proclaimed Münster the site of the future new Jerusalem where the faithful should wait out the great tribulation. Hundreds now flocked to the city and Matthijs himself arrived in late February just as Bishop Franz was preparing a siege of the city. When a new city council that favored the Anabaptists was elected, all citizens who refused to be rebaptized, about two thousand, had to leave the town. Münster was now an Anabaptist city headed by Melchiorites who believed that the restitution of the kingdom of Israel (Acts 1:6) had begun and that the Anabaptist kingdom, headed by Jan of Leiden after the death of Matthijs, was the millennial kingdom of Christ on earth.

After more than a year of siege, Münster was taken by Bishop Franz with the help of Protestant and Catholic rulers who were shaken by the Anabaptist insurgents and their apocalyptic claims. Jan of Leiden, Knipperdolling, and Bernd Krechting (perhaps in place of Rothmann, who could not be found) were tortured and beheaded in the marketplace in January 1536, and their corpses were put in iron cages and hung from the tower of St. Lambert's Church as a warning to all would-be heretics and rebels.

The Münster Anabaptists were considered heirs of Thomas Müntzer and the Revolution of 1525,[48] and, although there was no historical connection, the association was not completely inappropriate. Neither Müntzer nor the commoners of 1525 imagined anything like the Münsterite kingdom with its despotism and polygamy; but Müntzer, Hut, Hoffman, Rothmann, and the Münster Melchiorites shared a chiliastic version of the Reformation desire to Christianize Europe by establishing with force, if necessary, the preconditions for the kingdom of God on earth. The Melchiorites pursued a militant agenda that differed from the pacifist model of the *Schleitheim Articles*, but they shared the radical vision of creating stricter Christian communities apart from alien magisterial control. They sought a new Christian order that was closer to perfection than the city reformations and nearer to the realized kingdom of God than Luther's anticipation of a divine intervention. To a greater degree these radical agendas also embodied the Reformation sense of mission, in part because of the chiliastic notions that were present and in part because their clandestine communities had to be connected and supported by traveling messengers.

In the end, radical agendas were threatening, not because their vision of a Christian society was completely different from mainline reform, but because they tried to force its fulfillment in ways that undermined the concept of Christendom. They pushed Christianization beyond limits that could be tolerated even by Protestant rulers. When their efforts to realize the vision were disallowed by civil authorities, radical dissenters were forced to pursue their goal outside the boundaries of Christendom, that is, outside the alliance of religious and civil authorities in their city or territory. Occasionally they received protection and support from secular overlords, and some radicals permitted use of the sword. Even when persecuted, their determination to embody a different Christian existence outside the old order gave these dissenters a radical profile of their own.

A New Monasticism

What made the radicals' demands intolerable to civil and religious authorities, especially where there was little threat of insurrection? Although
their refusal to submit to the new Protestant church orders was reason
enough for rulers to suspect them of political disloyalty, reformers
rejected them out of a deeper religious concern. That concern was raised
by the radical insistence upon strict accountability that required a demon-
strably different kind of behavior. In other words, reformers were threatened by the way in which dissenters demanded Christian perfection.

Some forms of perfection were more visible than others, like the common ownership of property, which was more widely entertained (if not
always practiced) than heretofore believed.[49] A strict system of discipline
that enforced the ban, the refusal to hold civil and military office, and
believers' baptism were concrete signs of perfection that set boundaries
around a separate community. One less quantifiable form of perfection
was the visible fruit of faith or moral improvement (*Besserung des Lebens*)
found to be lacking in so many believers. Sebastian Franck claimed that
the teaching of faith alone produced only deaf and unproductive people
who were unable to hear calls for improvement.[50] The mystical Anabaptist Hans Denck divided society into those who complained that the world
was full of evil and those who believed that God had never been more merciful, but in his eyes both groups fell short: "The majority of those who
now are happy, unfortunately, are happy without being improved—just as
the majority of those who complain are also not improved; and these two
groups always despise one another, each thinking that it is better, even
though neither is a bit better than the other, as their fruits demonstrate."[51]

In the south German city of Augsburg, home to a significant community of dissenters and a way station for Anabaptist apostles, the fruits of
faith were an explicit cause of controversy. Local leaders like Jacob
Dachser questioned the divine calling of reformers like Urbanus Rhegius
by claiming that their sermons had never enlightened or improved anyone.[52] Dachser gave up on the competing Lutheran and Zwinglian
preachers in Augsburg and summoned the "sisters and brothers" to a
"Christianity of obedience."[53] He wanted the fruits of faith to be more
visible than they were and he laid the blame at the feet of reformers. In
response, Rhegius enumerated ways in which faith manifested itself: spiritual fruits like love, joy, and peace, moderation in food and drink, restraint
in the practice of what offended the neighbor, and proper chastity that
required priests, monks, and nuns to renounce celibacy, take a spouse, and

support new families.[54] Rhegius claimed that such fruits were readily visible in Augsburg: "Although this is all clear as day and everyone knows
that it must have come from the grace of God because flesh and blood are
not capable of producing it, this Anabaptist nevertheless does not shrink
from making the malicious and outrageous charge that our preaching
bears no fruit."[55]

Rhegius was well aware, however, that Protestant reform in Augsburg
was producing uneven results. This awareness is transparent in his three-
fold criticism of the dissenters. First, contrary to Scripture, the Anabaptists
demanded that Christians be perfect even when they were still weak. Scripture, however, taught that "our life" was not a state of repose but a constant
exodus out of Egypt in which "we" constantly increased in faith, hope, and
love. The petitions of the Lord's Prayer—that sins be forgiven, God's will
be done, and God's kingdom come—demonstrated that Christian life in the
world was imperfect.[56] Second, he charged, Anabaptists would not be so
quick to judge if they knew what a real Christian was and how the children
of God, who were still contending with flesh and blood (1 Cor 15:50), were
mixed in with the crowd of unbelievers like roses among thorns.[57] Finally,
Rhegius suspected the Anabaptists of having a hidden requirement for perfection. He accused them of wanting to actualize a community of goods in
Augsburg and, whether that was the case or not, Rhegius wasted no time
in rendering his opinion: "God save us from your improvement."[58]

Rhegius's arguments elaborated his view of improvement more than
they convinced Dachser and other Anabaptists. Reform was to be pursued
in cooperation with civil authorities because so many people (*baptized* people) remained unaffected by the gospel and had to be restrained by the
sword.[59] Rhegius was pessimistic about the number of nominal believers
who could be persuaded to increase their faith, hope, and love. Few roses
bloomed among the thorns.

Rhegius's desire for more roses, along with his pessimism, was shared
by the dissenters in Augsburg, but they had different ways of demonstrating who was converted to Christianity. Dissenters urged serious
believers to leave the city's Protestant parishes and join the newly baptized
in a community that would hold them strictly accountable for their faith.
Although Rhegius claimed that the fruits of his preaching were visible, the
fruits contained in his list were much vaguer than believers' baptism,
refusing civil duties, and sharing one's property. Besides renouncing
Catholic forms of worship, the only concrete changes required by Rhegius
affected priests, monks, and nuns. He urged them to leave the clerical
chapters and cloisters in which they were sponsored by wealthy patrons

and to embark upon a less secure life by marrying and "making their living by the sweat of their brow." This renunciation of celibacy and communal living was a radical change for clergy, more radical perhaps than surrendering the old piety was for laity. Neither was radical enough for dissenters, however, who wanted to see more than married clergy and new forms of worship. For them accountability meant behavior that was different from the world around them and closer to perfection.

The meaning of perfection became a prominent issue among the separatist Mennonites.[60] In his *Fundamentboek* (1539–1540), Menno lamented: "Not all are Christians of whom it is boasted. But those who have the Spirit of Christ are true Christians, though I do not know where one might find very many."[61] His lament that true Christians were a minority did not mean that Menno envisioned a reformation only among small pockets of believers. In fact, Menno pled with magistrates for the end of persecution and, on a larger scale, for the conversion of the rulers themselves to "a pious, reasonable, yes, a God-fearing magistracy."[62] Nor did his early theology require the separation of true believers although it demanded the reform of conduct through genuine repentance. In their transitional state after Münster, the remnants of the Melchiorite movement still anticipated that the end could be near and therefore did not rush to institute practical guidelines for exercising discipline.[63]

As Menno and his followers evolved into a persecuted group of nonviolent Melchiorite Anabaptists, separation from the world became more pronounced and the ban and shunning became controversial means of imposing discipline and of promoting perfection. Under the influence of other elders, Menno urged an increasingly strict application of discipline. Some scholars regard Menno's insistence upon the ban as an anomaly while others see it as a consequence of Menno's early thought and of the need to cleanse the movement of revolutionaries.[64] As the imposition of church discipline, the ban has been connected to the penitential system of late-medieval Christianity, which Menno served as a priest.[65] It has also been explained as a reassertion of anticlerical sentiment in Menno's thought, which needed new targets once the external persecution of Mennonites waned. The eschatological battle with the church of the Antichrist had to be fought thenceforth against the enemy within.[66]

A strict penitential system was also an effective means of making believers take their faith and conduct seriously, especially for a community that was initially persecuted and remained suspect to the authorities. Besides, most reformers advocated some type of penitential or disciplinary system. Bucer's Christian fellowships and the consistory in Geneva are the best known, but church orders in Lutheran areas also authorized imposition of the ban. In Hamburg, for example, the church order adopted in 1529 declared:

> Open adulterers, whores, rowdies, regular drunkards, blasphemers and others who lead a shameful life and molest other people with their misconduct shall first be earnestly admonished by one or two preachers to change their life. If they will not do so, they are to be regarded as unchristian [*Unchristen*] and people who are damned, just as Christ teaches us by the judgment he renders in Matthew 18:15–20. They are not to be admitted to the sacrament, to their greater condemnation, until they publicly change their life, because they have publicly sinned. They can attend the sermon, however.[67]

To a certain degree, even shunning was advocated:

> At this time we cannot impose a more effective ban. Nor has Christ authorized anything further. He says: "Regard the person as a pagan and as damned" [Mt 18:17]. Beyond that, the person should be tolerated in the neighborhood and in the citizenry, in the realm of civil ordinances, for the sake of public peace, etc., but in such a way that Christians know they are dealing [only] with a fellow citizen and not with a Christian on those unavoidable occasions when they neither can nor should shun the person. On other occasions, insofar as it is possible and does not lead to discord, they should keep away from the person so that other people can tell that we have no intention of tolerating such people among us.[68]

Bugenhagen was worried about the perception of the new evangelical community in Hamburg, but more than civil reputation was at stake. The claim of the evangelical community to be authentic Christians also had to be validated, and this identity was defined as much by their public conduct as by their worship and their beliefs.

Since evangelical communities like the Lutherans in Hamburg remained under their civil jurisdictions, it was impossible to practice shunning absolutely (as the above text indicates), and additional punishment and discipline were entrusted to civil authorities who were not always willing to apply the law as severely as the pastors desired. The Hamburg order called for persistent offenders to be banished from the city, but they could be readmitted by the council if it was convinced they had amended their lives.[69] Nevertheless, the Christian claim and stability of these magisterial churches were supported by the civil authorities once new Protestant orders were approved.

In the case of Mennonites and other groups who did not live under comparable civil jurisdiction, their existence was insecure and their claim to be authentic Christians was validated by no one but themselves. The ban and shunning were applied and monitored by the elders, and the community was dependent on them for maintaining its identity, purity, and stability. The law was Scripture as they interpreted it, and it is not surprising that their leaders disagreed over how strictly that law had to be applied in order to preserve the Christian integrity of the community. Whether or not to shun one's own spouse or children who were banned, or to greet those who had been banned, or to do business with the "apostates" were decisions based on what action was necessary to retain and to express their Christian integrity:

> For a true Christian should always strive after that which is the best and the surest, and follow pure, unfeigned love, lest they abuse the freedom which they seem to have, to the injury and hindrance of their own souls, to the affliction and destruction of their beloved brethren, to the scornful boasting of the perverse, and to the shameful defamation of the holy Word and the afflicted church of Christ.[70]

Shunning and the ban were ultimately the ways in which these communities held people accountable and pursued their agenda of Christianization. Only by separating from the world could they avoid the indiscriminate mixing that would occur inevitably in places like Hamburg despite the condemnation of unchristian behavior by Protestant authorities.

Because of their desire for perfection and the separation it required, dissenters were compared to medieval monks and nuns. Urbanus Rhegius, for example, referred to Anabaptists in Augsburg as a "new monasticism" and warned against the rise of a new "baptizing order."[71] Claiming that mendicant monks were especially pestiferous because they considered begging a form of worship, Luther alleged that Anabaptists likewise refused to regard as Christian those who owned any property.[72] Challenging the Schleitheim article which placed the sword outside the perfection of Christ, Zwingli charged that Anabaptists "assume what the monks used to assume, viz., that they are in a state of perfection," and argued that civil magistrates and laws were necessary wherever the members of Christ had not arrived at perfection.[73]

Radical dissenters reminded reformers of monastic orders because their separation undermined the original vision of the Reformation: bringing a deeper and more serious Christianity to the populace as a whole instead of restricting it to exclusive communities. In that sense replanting the faith was an extension of the monastic ideal to the entire Christian society. When dissenters protested that such an extension diluted the vision, and when civil authorities refused to sanction their way of holding believers accountable, dissenters resorted to separate groups, the very thing that reformers had tried to eliminate and that now threatened to betray their broader vision. Dissenters began to reproduce precisely the two-tiered religious society that reformers were trying to abolish. The "new monasticism" was therefore condemned because it threatened to expose, in dramatic fashion, the Reformation as a failure. If Protestant reform was successfully replanting a kind of Christianity that fulfilled the vision of a more devoted populace, no one needed to abandon it in search of greater perfection. If all of Christendom was on the way to becoming a monastery, a "new baptizing order" was a grave obstacle and the last thing it needed.

Dissent and Toleration

Many but not all dissenters were members of Anabaptist assemblies. Instead of forming separate communities, independent dissenters proposed notions of Christianity that challenged two premises of the Reformation: the trinitarian basis of Christian faith and the claim that opposing ways of defining and practicing the faith could not be tolerated. Two important figures represent these challenges: Michael Servetus (c. 1511–1553) and Sebastian Castellio (1515–1563).

Servetus is best known for the antitrinitarian views that led to his execution in Geneva in 1553. As the most notorious dissenter of the sixteenth century, he was condemned by Catholics and Protestants alike and had to take cover behind aliases such as Michel de Villeneuve, which used the name of his birthplace in Spain. Although he worked primarily as an editor and a physician, he also studied law, mathematics, church history, theology, and philosophy. Well-versed in rabbinic and patristic sources in addition to Hebrew and Christian scripture, he used all of them to reconstruct a pre-trinitarian apostolic religion proposed by him as the true faith.[74] Servetus was not primarily a philosopher who opposed the doctrine of the Trinity on logical grounds. Instead, he was more like a reformer-historian, recovering the original Christianity that needed to be replanted in the Europe of his day. His agenda was concisely summarized by the title of his magnum opus, *The Restitution of Christianity*. By sending a copy to Calvin and then passing through Geneva, Servetus unleashed the sequence of events that led to his execution.

Servetus shared the desire of reformers to Christianize Europe, but the Christianity he hoped to replant was radically different from theirs because it rejected the doctrine of the Trinity adopted by the councils at Nicaea (325) and Constantinople (381). Servetus believed that by the fourth century, Christianity had been corrupted by the devil and its view of God fundamentally altered from its monotheistic basis in Judaism. He was not, however, denying the divinity of Jesus or replacing the notion of a triune God with a strictly unitarian theology. Quite the reverse was true. According to Servetus, the orthodox doctrine of the Trinity and contemporary Christianity did not take the divinity of Jesus seriously enough. Believers in his day were estranged, he maintained, from knowledge of the Son of God, and that estrangement prevented them from being saved.[75] Salvation depended on having the same divine nature as the Redeemer; consequently, believers had to be united with the true flesh of Christ that belonged to the substance of God.[76] Servetus sounded gnostic insofar as he appeared to deny the full humanity of Jesus. His theology, however, was radically christocentric, and by this implicit indictment of Protestant reformers, who prided themselves on recovering the centrality of Christ, he charged them with not being christocentric enough. For Servetus, the greatest blasphemy was to say "that God is, or acts, somewhere out of Christ."[77]

Servetus's theology was more complex than affirming the identity of Christ with God. Its goal, nonetheless, was to recover the integrity of early Christianity and to serve a missionary purpose that was not alien to the general Reformation vision. By reconstructing the Christian past in a way that was less abstractly trinitarian and potentially friendlier to monotheism, Servetus may have envisioned, like some early reformers, a more universal appeal of Christianity to Judaism and to Islam.[78] For Protestant reformers, however, Servetus's condemnation of the historic creeds and their trinitarian solution was a departure from the essence of Christianity itself. The Protestant claim that it was restoring authentic Christianity included an affirmation of the historic creeds as testimonies to the faith. This was a historical argument, of course, of the same order as the claims by Servetus and other dissenters who were defining Christianity according to pre-creedal sources alone. In fact, some Protestants, like Philipp Melanchthon, as well as moderate Catholics were debating the cutoff point after which ancient doctrine and practice would no longer be considered normative.[79] For Calvin, however, who had Servetus arrested in

Geneva, and for Heinrich Bullinger in Zurich, the rejection of Servetus's heresy protected the orthodoxy of the Reformation.

In Basel, Sebastian Castellio saw matters differently. In 1553, he had just been appointed professor of Greek at the university after working as a corrector for the publisher Oporinus. As a young man, Castellio had met Calvin in Strasbourg; he even took care of relatives and students of Calvin during the plague of 1541 while Calvin was attending the Diet of Regensburg. Recommended by Calvin—but not his first choice—for a new position as rector of the Collège de Rive, Castellio arrived in Geneva several months before Calvin to take up his new duties. It was not long, however, before conflict arose on several fronts between the reformer and his disciple. First, Calvin refused to admit him to the ministry because Castellio disagreed with the reformer on two theological matters; then, Castellio's mockery of the company of pastors for their cowardice during the plague sealed his fate. He was relieved of his duties in Geneva and finally found a new job in Basel, a cultural center known for its humanist scholarship and publishing trade.[80]

In 1553 the outcry in Basel against the execution of Servetus was so loud that Calvin asked the Geneva council for permission to publish a defense of the act. The reformer argued that Servetus's heresy had threatened the "order of piety" that was essential to a Christian commonwealth.[81] About a month after Calvin's defense appeared, Castellio published the work that made him a famous advocate of toleration: *Concerning Heretics Whether They Should Be Persecuted* (1554).[82] This small book was an anthology of texts, from early Christian authors and sixteenth-century writers, all of which opposed the execution of heretics. The longest contemporary passages were from Luther, Johannes Brenz (the reformer of Schwäbisch Hall), Erasmus, and Sebastian Franck. The main argument, however, was presented in the foreword by one Martin Bellius, who almost certainly gave the opinion of Castellio himself.[83]

This argument was not a plea for religious liberty in a secular state but an indictment of intolerance among Christians within Christendom. Instead of debating how to live in conformity with Scripture, he complained, believers were condemning one another because of doctrines about which they would never agree any more than Christians, Jews, and Muslims would agree on the identity of Jesus. Castellio was not a skeptic, however. He believed that religious conviction was a matter of conscience and that it could never be changed by force but only through argument and example.[84] The execution of heretics set the worst possible example and was the truest form of blasphemy, replacing idolatry as the worst kind of unchristian behavior. Instead of killing one another, Christians should show tolerance and patience; the surer of the truth they were, the less inclined they should be to condemn others.[85]

With this line of argument Castellio was proposing a reform agenda that recalled the Erasmian proposal to eschew useless debates over doctrine and to devote one's energy to the imitation of Christ. In reaction to the execution of Servetus, however, Castellio added to his proposal a call for the toleration of doctrinal disagreements that had arisen among Protestants and dissenters. He was also sensitive to the continuing challenge of Judaism and Islam, a challenge that had become more pertinent as Christian believers persecuted one another while claiming to recover the authentic faith. Castellio called, therefore, for the toleration of non-Christians as well, but always in the context of a society built upon a forbearing Christian way of life. He had seen some of this forbearance in Strasbourg, but no city actualized the degree of toleration envisioned by Castellio. Certainly not Basel. When the council discovered that the former Dutch Melchiorite, David Joris, had lived undetected in the city for twelve years, it disinterred his body and burned it at the stake while a shaken Castellio, who had known Joris, looked on.[86]

Although Servetus is best known as an opponent of trinitarian doctrine and Castellio as a champion of religious liberty, both dissenters also harbored the idea of a Christian culture. Servetus desired a restitution of early Christianity that relocated a divine Christ at the center of the godhead, where he would be more present to believers and more attractive to nonbelievers no longer alienated by a trinitarian deity. Castellio condemned religious intolerance as unchristian and offered toleration, teaching, and persuasion as ways to include disagreeing believers and even some nonbelievers in the same predominantly Christian society. During their careers both Servetus and Castellio had benefited from governmental support of the Reformation, but finally they refused to yield to theological pressure or to endorse religious intolerance. They rejected the reformers' agendas and insisted on their own designs for a recultivated Christendom. The Reformation had the best chance of succeeding, they thought, when it offered a christocentric message in a tolerant environment.

The End of Christendom

After it was forced into separation, radical dissent sowed the seeds of the end of Christendom—the eventual end of a state-supported Christian society—that most people in the sixteenth century could not yet see. The end of Christendom in that sense was certainly not the goal of most early reformers, and the new confessions of the sixteenth century left Christendom for the most part intact. Mainline reformers willingly cooperated with city councils and territorial rulers in order to have their agendas enacted for the society as a whole.[87]

In one sense, those agendas were indeed radical and utopian. They made an audacious claim: after more than a thousand years of planting the faith, the mission to Europe had gone awry and Christianity had to be recultivated in the devastated vineyard of European Christendom. From the beginning, all reformers sought to replant the faith with the help of civil authorities, either local communities, city councils, or princes. Karlstadt, Müntzer, and the Zurich radicals shared with Luther and Zwingli the vision of filling Christendom with more authentic faith and piety than it had contained. All of them hoped their agendas would be promoted by civil authorities and issue in a new Christian society.

When that turned out not to be the case, radical dissenters sought another way to infuse society with a truer Christianity, a way that would hold people more accountable, a way that led to separation and looked in some cases like a new monasticism. Not all dissenters, it is true, disdained civil authority. From Moravia to Münster and beyond, some dissenters benefited from political support or established it for themselves. Leaders like Peter Riedemann and Pilgram Marpeck maintained that radical Christianity and government were not irreconcilable. Nevertheless, the persecution of Anabaptists continued sporadically and they had to find refuge from the authorities.[88] Meanwhile, Protestant reformers were planting their new Christianity in corners of the vineyard that were coterminous with political boundaries. They regarded cooperation with city councils and princes, not as a retreat from radical or grassroots reform, but as the fruit of their earlier appeals to civil authorities to take over the reform of Christendom from the Roman bishops.

If all reform was radical in the beginning, did mainline reformers retreat from it when they cooperated with authorities to enact their agendas? Was radical reform the original Reformation? Peter Blickle has contended just that by defining the original agenda as a communal Christianity that gave authority to local communities of believers. He argued that Luther in particular retreated from this communal ideal after the Revolution of 1525, and that reformers who eventually entrusted change to the government betrayed that ideal.[89] The Peasants' War certainly prompted early reformers in Germany and Switzerland to cooperate more closely with civil authority, but it did not make these reformers suddenly magisterial. Their agendas were never strictly communal in the sense of being democratic, local, or anti-magisterial. Nor did they expect a voluntary grassroots reform movement to spring up in each parish. Reformers and dissenters alike intended to reform the whole society with the help of princes and city councils. The society-wide vision of reformers did not change; it was there from the beginning.

The case of Luther is an example. He never had an ideal ecclesiology built around the local community, not even in 1523 when he conceded to the Christian community of Leisnig "the right and power to judge all doctrine and to call, install, and to dismiss pastors."[90] In the title of this work, *That a Christian Assembly or Community Has the Right . . .*, the accent lay on the word Christian and not on the word community. Three years earlier, Luther had called on the Christian nobility of Germany to reform the *entire* Christian estate. In 1520 and 1523, Luther's point was not that local communities alone were the church, but that Christians in all social and political circumstances were spiritually equal and should reform Christendom by replanting the ancient faith. Luther's request to Elector John in 1526 to authorize a visitation of parishes in Saxony was not a departure from some early communal ideal but an application of the same society-wide ecclesiology that had informed his vision from the beginning. The church consisted of the faithful everywhere, for whom religious and civil authorities were obligated to provide the word of God. When religious authorities failed to do this—whether it was a local patron in the case of Leisnig or bishops in the case of the Saxon visitation—Luther argued that civil authorities should take the necessary steps to see that evangelical faith was preached throughout Christendom.[91]

Instead of viewing magisterial reform as the compromise of an original communal agenda, it is more accurate to say that the Reformation vision was pursued on two broad tracks after the radical dissenters were forced down the path of separation. One of these tracks, the magisterial, insisted on replanting the faith in cooperation with the authorities of Christendom, and this track produced new confessional churches. The other track—the radical reformation or radical dissent—was forced to implement its vision of Christianity in structures that were separate and only later tolerated by some officials as the utopian enthusiasm of the radicals began to fade.[92] Both tracks were authentic Reformation movements that pursued the project of Christianization through various agendas. Neither mainline reformers nor dissenters saw it that way of course. For them the different tracks were incompatible with each other. Only one track and one agenda, only one radical or one magisterial form of the faith could be true. Scripture and other authorities, if allowed, could support only one authentic form of the faith. In historical perspective, however, one can see that all of them attempted to bring to Europe a new form of Christianity which they claimed was both biblical and true.

By persisting with their agendas despite banishment and persecution, radical dissenters enlarged the Reformation vision. With hindsight one can see that the path of radical dissent pointed beyond Christendom in a way that magisterial reform did not. Like monasticism, radical dissent suggested that believers could be held strictly accountable only in small communities and even then with difficulty. It challenged the ideal of turning the world into a monastery and filling Christendom with true believers. Beyond a certain point—that is, beyond the external conformity enforced in confessional churches—society could not be peopled with committed Christians on a comprehensive scale. Because sixteenth-century Europe retained the structure of medieval Christendom and, for the most part, the vision of making it a more Christian society, the path of radical dissent seemed to be a dead end. It was, however, a prophetic path that pointed to the extension of the Reformation vision beyond Christendom.

Chapter 5

The Catholic Agenda

Christianization within Catholicism

Catholic Reform

Although traditional Christianity was alive and well prior to the Reformation, reform of the church had suffered a setback from restrictions placed by the papacy on the authority of church councils. A desire for renewal persisted nonetheless and reasserted itself in the Fifth Lateran Council (1512–1517), which met in Rome under Popes Julius II and Leo X. A proposal addressed to Leo X in 1513 by two devout humanists and reformers of the Camaldolese Order, Vincenzo Querini (d. 1524) and Tommaso Giustiniani (d. 1528), envisioned a broad program of Christianization that called for the conversion of Jews and Muslims, the reformation of the Roman Church, and the spread of Christianity over all the world.[1] The council, however, enacted less sweeping recommendations for regulating the clergy and improving their performance, teaching religion to young people, reforming the life of the cardinals, and reducing superstition. Reform of the priesthood and expansion of the religious life became persistent themes of Catholic renewal during the sixteenth century. In his *Constitutions* of 1542, the bishop of Verona, Gian Matteo Giberti, set down strict guidelines for clerical conduct. New orders for men and women appeared early in the century, for example, Theatines (1524), Capuchins (1528), the Society of Jesus (1540), and Ursulines (1544). At the Council of Trent (1545–1563) half of the decrees were about reform.[2]

Did these early developments constitute a reformation in its own right? For over half a century, historians have grappled with this question, mainly because the movement had come to be known as the Counter-Reformation. In the sixteenth century, the term Reformation was used by

Protestants and Catholics alike. By the end of the eighteenth century, however, German historians had commandeered the term for Protestant reform which centered on Luther and his followers.[3] A Lutheran legal historian from Göttingen, Johann Stephan Pütter (1725–1807), coined the label Counter-Reformation (*Gegenreformation*) for "the forced return of Lutherans to the practice of Catholicism in areas that had once been Lutheran."[4] Although Pütter's usage was narrower than later meanings, the precedent had been established for naming the rise of Protestantism "Reformation" and for calling the reaction of the Roman Church "Counter-Reformation." Leopold von Ranke (d. 1886) and Moriz Ritter (d. 1923) made this precedent into a pattern. Ranke's six-volume work designated the period between 1517 and 1555 as the Reformation,[5] while Ritter's three volumes traced German history through almost a century (1555–1648) that he called the period of the Counter-Reformation and the Thirty Years' War.[6]

This pattern was challenged in 1946 in a groundbreaking essay by the Catholic historian Hubert Jedin, best known for his four-volume history of the Council of Trent. Jedin argued that the changes which took place within sixteenth-century Catholicism were best captured by a pair of terms: Catholic Reform, for internal initiatives that extended late-medieval efforts to renew the church; and Counter-Reformation, for the reaction to Protestantism that included reforms mandated by Trent.[7] Over the last half-century, the use of Catholic Reform and Catholic Reformation has become more frequent because these terms are less polemical than Counter-Reformation and because they emphasize religious initiatives that were launched prior to Protestant reform. This point of view was already expressed in 1951 by H. Outram Evennett: "The Counter-Reformation was first and foremost a powerful religious movement . . . [which] eventually created a mature spirituality with clear characteristics of its own. . . ."[8] Evennett suggested that Protestant and Catholic reform were both outgrowths of the "reinvigoration of the religious urge" in sixteenth-century Europe.[9]

In the last twenty years, interest in the Catholic Reformation has exploded, and the search for the best name to capture it has intensified. Like the Reformation in general, the panorama of Catholic reform has been expanded and scrutinized. In 1984 Philip Hoffman followed the social consequences of the Counter-Reformation in Lyons all the way to 1789.[10] For a new survey in 1998, R. Po-chia Hsia decided to include Catholic expansion beyond Europe and selected a corresponding title, *The World of Catholic Renewal 1540–1770*.[11] Robert Bireley chose to omit the eighteenth century, but his reassessment of the Counter-Reformation began with 1450.[12] Meanwhile, the German historian Wolfgang Reinhard pushed for the recognition of Catholic reform as a process of confessionalization that was parallel to the same processes in the Protestant world.[13] In 1991 John O'Malley proposed the name Early Modern Catholicism, and he reargued the case in his recent survey of the entire enterprise.[14]

As O'Malley contends, names are crucial, and for that reason I have generally reserved the term Reformation for the broad campaign of Christianization shared by most reformers and to the restructuring of Christianity that resulted from it. Designating components of that restructuring process as Protestant, Radical, and Catholic reformations is also useful for contrasting different categories of sixteenth-century Christians and for giving integrity to the several agendas of Christianization. Those designations are especially important for the Radical and Catholic reformations, which were treated for so long mainly as reactions to Protestantism. The terms Radical Reformation and Catholic Reformation are so entrenched that I have also used those terms freely in this book. Nevertheless, I prefer to speak of Protestant, Radical, and Catholic reform movements and to reserve the term Reformation for the period as a whole in order not to lose sight of its religious purpose, overall vision, and unprecedented results. There were many kinds of reform, but only one confessional restructuring of Christianity in sixteenth-century Europe.

Assigning Catholic reform to one Reformation avoids casting Protestants and dissenters in the role of schismatics from the one true church that made a smooth transition from late-medieval Christianity to early modern Roman Catholicism. This was the stance of older Catholic historiography, and it could have been read into a title like *The Refashioning of Catholicism (1450–1700)* if Bireley had not presented such a strong ecumenical picture of Protestants and Catholics as "competing attempts to renew Christianity in the sixteenth century."[15] Prior to 1521, no reformer realized that some of the refashioning would occur outside the Roman Church and some of it inside, and despite his early criticism of the papacy not even Martin Luther could envision structures like the Protestant churches. Those reformers who turned out to be Protestants and dissenters thought that they, too, were "refashioning Catholicism," that is, they intended to refashion Roman Christianity of the late Middle Ages according to the catholic Christianity of the early church. The exclusion of these reformers from the Roman Church and their eventual identification as Protestants and dissenters did not change that intention. Moreover, with just as much dedication, Catholic reformers who remained loyal to the papacy thought they were refashioning not only Catholicism in the sense of a Roman hierarchy but Christianity.

For the entire late-medieval and Reformation period, therefore, a book title that reflects our thesis would be "The Refashioning of Christianity." This book would treat all the movements—Protestant, Radical, and Catholic—as reworkings of late-medieval religion that attempted to renovate Christianity in Europe. With hindsight we can see that the Roman hierarchy did guarantee structural continuity between Western medieval Christianity and the Roman Catholicism that emerged after Trent. Despite this continuity, however, and the competition that developed with Protestants, Catholic reform shared the general Reformation vision of a renewed Christianity in Europe.

Catholic Christianization

The association of Catholic reform with Christianization recalls the work of Jean Delumeau, briefly discussed in chapter 1. Since he believed that rural people in sixteenth- and seventeenth-century France were mostly ignorant of Christianity and possessed of a "persistent pagan mentality,"[16] it followed for Delumeau that Catholic missionaries to the countryside were engaged in a process of Christianization. Like the reformers, who charged that people were no better than pagans owing to blatant superstition, Delumeau made it sound as if the religion of early modern Catholics was thoroughly unchristian. Catholics were, however, no more likely to be unchristian than the inhabitants of Protestant areas. Before Eamon Duffy suggested the term "lay Christianity" in place of superstition,[17] John Bossy proposed that the term "Christianity of the illiterate" would be fitting for a rural populace in which Christianity was not neutralized by the presence of folkloric elements.[18] Even for the literate citizens of European towns, Christianity existed not only in the idealized form preached by reformers but in hybrids that combined orthodox teaching by the reformers' standards with the unorthodox convictions of ordinary people.

Despite Delumeau's definition, Catholic reform can be described as Christianization because, like medieval and Protestant reformers, sixteenth-century Catholics were in their own way trying to make people more Christian than they had been. When missionaries and other preachers urged regular participation in worship, taught catechism, and corrected the way people prayed and confessed, they were trying to increase the level of devotion and to instill orthodox attitudes. They were not converting people to Christianity for the first time, but cleansing their faith and practice from superstition. In cooperation with the Milan and Roman Inquisitions, Charles Borromeo pressed the eradication of magic and lesser superstitions beyond what Trent and colleagues were seeking.[19] Catholic theologians distinguished between nominal and devout believers and wanted to see the former changed into the latter. Defending Catholic truth early in the process of reform, the Dominican theologian Ambrosius Catharinus (Lancellotto de' Politi, d. 1553) noted the difference between believers who were only marked with the sign of baptism and those who lived in a Christian manner and were prepared to die for the sake of Christ.[20] Like Protestants and Radicals, Catholic reformers wanted to see more such people committed to the faith.

Catholic Christianization was not the spiritualization of Christianity as suggested by Delumeau: "The two Reformations, Luther's and Rome's, were two processes, which apparently competed but which in fact converged, by which the masses were christianized and religion spiritualized."[21] For Delumeau, the spiritualization of religion meant overcoming the animist mentality and eliminating the folkloric and magical elements that dominated late-medieval religion. For example, he pointed to the way in which the Nativity of St. John the Baptist (June 24), near the summer solstice, was celebrated by the lighting of fires to ward off evil spirits. A manual for proper conduct of the ritual placed restrictions on the celebrations and gave them a Christian meaning as fires of joy over the birth of the forerunner of Christ. It also listed the superstitions that should be avoided: "Dancing around the fire, playing, holding feasts, singing vulgar songs, throwing grasses over the fire, gathering grasses before midnight or before breakfast, wearing grasses, keeping them for the whole year, keeping brands or cinders from the fire, and the like." A prominent ecclesiastic was to stay by the fire to prevent such activity and the fire was to be quickly doused and the ashes removed as soon as the ritual was complete.[22]

Since the fires were not eliminated, however, but regulated and endowed with Christian meaning, the rite was not spiritualized in the sense of being dematerialized. Some material objects, like the charcoal remains of these fires, may have been stripped of their magical powers, but other material objects, like the sacramental elements, were conduits of the divine presence. For Catholics, therefore, Christianizing religious practice was not a process of spiritualization but of reasserting the proper sacramental relationship between material things and their spiritual significance. This reassertion was no less needed than it had been in the Middle Ages. When Catholic missionaries tried to focus the faithful on the cross of Christ by planting large crosses in the countryside, they had to ward off superstitions attached to those crosses and ensure that adoration of the cross did not become idolatry.[23]

Protestants wrestled with the relationship between the spiritual and the material, and it caused serious disagreements among them over, for example, the presence of Christ in the Lord's Supper. The Lutheran assertion of a real presence of the body and blood of Christ in the bread and wine was too materialistic for other Protestants and too likely to rekindle superstitious notions about the elements. The Reformed churches and many Radicals reinterpreted sacraments in a more spiritual way than did Catholics and Lutherans, and that divide has been an obstacle to Protestant ecumenical efforts and caused some Lutherans to identify more with Catholics than with Protestants. Sixteenth-century Christianization was, therefore, by no means the spiritualization of Christianity but a complex process of defining the proper relationship of the material to the spiritual that resulted in a spectrum of views which did not fall neatly into Catholic, Protestant, and Radical categories. The Catholic reassertion of medieval sacramental doctrine, like the limited Lutheran retention of some medieval principles, was part of this broader process and belongs to the Reformation project of Christianization.

Catholic Christianization also involved a complex interaction between the clergy and the people that produced mixed results, especially when reforms mandated by the Council of Trent (1545–1563) were imposed on the populace. In the province of Galicia in northwestern Spain, the residents of the diocese of Ourense refused to abandon their local religion for the reform program of Trent. Some changes were made: more priests resided in their parishes and the use of secular names declined. By and large, however, the traditional Christianity of the Gallegans was able to resist attempts by the authorities to make it conform to the Tridentine standards of Christian practice.[24] In the bishopric of Speyer in Germany, a strong Catholic populace disregarded most attempts to reform it and revived their traditional Christianity by reaching a compromise with the clergy. The people accepted some mandates from Trent, like the requirement that priests reside in their parishes, but they resisted others like the restrictions on popular festivals and the reorganization of parish structures. A crucial role was played by the local clergy, both the less educated peasant-priests of the seventeenth century and new seminary-educated and reform-minded priests of the eighteenth. The latter did not simply impose Tridentine reforms on the people but supported the traditional forms of Christianity that enjoyed a resurgence in the early 1700s.[25]

Catholic reform in another part of Spain, however, did bring significant religious change to the diocese of Cuenca, partly because it combined clerical initiative and compulsion with the people's religious fervor. The clergy taught catechism and rebuked sexual misconduct, magic, and heterodox beliefs. The Inquisition forced people to confess such sins and to denounce the sins of others. At the same time, the bourgeois and other laity disavowed superstition, learned from their clerical teachers, and donated more money to charity and to religious foundations. Funeral practices and a decline in the incidence of illegitimate pregnancies also pointed to a deeper personal faith and to improved moral conduct.[26]

Many things made Catholic Christianization distinctive: the theological rejection of Protestantism, the reassertion of papal authority, the pressure of the Inquisitions, the lucid formulations of Catholic belief by the Council of Trent and its calls for clerical and episcopal reform, the reorganization of the Roman curia, and Catholic missions to Asia, Africa, and the Americas. For the people of Catholic Europe, however, Christianization meant the reform of traditional Christianity. Instead of discrediting monastic attempts at perfection, as Protestants did, Catholics created new orders for active ministry. In place of disallowing the veneration of the saints, Catholics tried to control and purify it. Instead of abolishing the priesthood, Catholicism tried to discipline and upgrade it. Instead of reducing the number of sacraments, Catholics clarified their theological basis, refined their administration, and encouraged the faithful to use them more frequently. The sacrament of penance, for example, already popular in the late Middle Ages, was transformed by the confessional and pushed into the strategic center of Catholic reform. The role of confessor offered to priests greater access to the lives and thoughts of their parishioners and more frequent opportunity to correct their beliefs and affect their behavior. Instead of abolishing traditional structures and replanting new ones, as Protestants and dissenters often did, Catholics tried to reinvigorate the old forms.[27] This reinvigoration was more than a quickening of the religious urge, as Evennett proposed. Rather, it was a sustained effort to deepen the adherence of laypeople and clergy to the explicit teachings of the Christian faith and to conform their devotion to those teachings.

Protestants and dissenters did not see Catholic reform as a competing form of Christianization. They accused Catholics of teaching doctrines and abiding by rituals that were heretical at best and pagan at worst. Catholics returned the favor. In addition to the decrees of Trent, an impressive array of theologians rebutted Protestant positions with arguments from Scripture, from the writings of patristic and medieval theologians, and from papal and conciliar decrees contained in canon law. They also wrote commentaries on biblical books, scholastic tracts, and manuals for pastors and teachers. Thomas Cajetan (d. 1534), the Italian Dominican cardinal and papal legate who met with Luther at Augsburg in 1518, produced a commentary on the *Summa Theologica* of Thomas Aquinas, studies of the sacrament of penance, and a handbook for confessors. The German theologian Jerome Emser (d. 1527) published in 1527 his own German translation of the New Testament after criticizing Luther's. John Fabri (d. 1541), a German priest who served as bishop of Vienna, debated Zwingli in Zurich in 1523 and wrote against Luther, Zwingli, and the radical reformers Balthasar Hubmaier and Caspar Schwenckfeld (d. 1561). Ambrosius Catharinus (d. 1553), papal theologian at the first session of the Council of Trent, had defended the "true Catholic and apostolic faith" against Luther and published a work against the Italian general of the Capuchins, Bernardino Ochino (d. 1564), who fled Italy in 1542 and adopted Calvinism. John Eck, the German professor at Ingolstadt, debated Luther skillfully at Leipzig and represented Catholics at the important Diets of Augsburg (1530) and Regensburg (1541). He published an extensive defense of the sacrifice of the mass, and his *Handbook of Commonplaces* used passages from Scripture and other authorities to disprove Protestant teachings on authority, sacraments, the clergy, veneration of the saints, and other forms of piety and ritual.

At the end of the sixteenth century, a Jesuit cardinal and professor in Rome, Robert Bellarmine (d. 1621), presented comprehensive counterarguments against Protestant positions in his *Disputations concerning the Controversies of the Christian Faith against the Heretics of This Age* (1586–1593). For example, on the formal cause of justification, Bellarmine summarized the positions of six theologians—Luther, Melanchthon, Andrew Osiander, Matthias Flacius Illyricus, Calvin, and Bucer—and found five errors among them. After quoting the position of the Council of Trent and succinctly defining the issue, he proceeded to challenge the Protestant errors with the words: "Now let us come to arguments for the truth."[28] For Bellarmine and other theologians, the backbone of Catholic Christianization was the establishment of Catholic doctrine as the true Christian faith against Protestants who were making the same claim for their teaching.

Teaching Christianity

All but one of the male religious orders that sprang up during the Reformation were dedicated as never before to an active ministry in the world.

That ministry was diverse and extensive. It included local pastoral work such as preaching, teaching, hearing confession, and administering sacraments. Members of these orders also went as missionaries to Asia, Africa, and the Americas, served as chaplains in armies, hospitals, and confraternities, and published books for the study of theology and the practice of devotion.[29] In all these roles, their mission was to plant and to replant Christianity wherever they served. This active ministry was embodied in remarkable ways by the Capuchins, founded by the observant Franciscan Matteo da Basci, who wanted to emulate St. Francis and his earliest followers. Espousing both the contemplative and the active life, the order grew rapidly and by 1600 Capuchins had spread across Europe, where they numbered around 17,000 members in some 1,200 houses. They preached to all classes in order to strengthen the faith of Catholics and to convert Protestants and unbelievers; after 1600 they also joined the mission overseas.

Despite traditional restrictions and expectations, new orders of women also pursued an active ministry. The Order of St. Ursula, founded at Brescia in 1535 by Angela Merici, concentrated its efforts on teaching doctrine to girls, but the members also made regular visits to the sick and dying. At first these religious women stayed with their families, but in 1563 the Council of Trent required that "the enclosure of nuns be restored where it has been violated and that it be preserved where it has not been violated."[30] At Milan the Tridentine reforming bishop, Charles Borromeo (d. 1584), established three convents of Ursulines and required them to wear a distinctive habit, but the Ursulines continued to teach catechism to women of all ages, especially to girls who came to the convents.[31] At Annecy in Savoy, Jane Frances de Chantal co-founded the order of Visitation Nuns with Francis de Sales, the bishop of Geneva, who lived in Annecy. The nuns led a simple common life while caring for the sick and needy and offering their convent as a place of retreat.

The order that attracted the most members, however, was the Daughters of Charity, founded around 1630 in France by Vincent de Paul and Louise de Marillac. They started as a small group of aristocratic women, the Ladies of Charity, working to help the poor. In 1633 they were transformed into a confraternity of young rural women working under the direction of the Ladies. Gradually they assumed features of a religious order like the creation of a motherhouse and the taking of simple vows. They were able to avoid enclosure, however, because they created "a unique identity that was neither that of a nun nor a worldly single woman."[32] They were neither a true confraternity nor a traditional order, but a unique organization in which lay women with strong religious convictions could pursue an active ministry of charity without interference. They called themselves a confraternity until they received the support of the French government; papal approval followed in 1668. By that time, the Daughters of Charity had expanded their active ministry to include hospital work, orphanages, and teaching catechism.[33]

The same active ministry was the focus of the Jesuits, the Society of Jesus. Founded by Ignatius of Loyola and six companions at Paris in 1534, the society was conceived as a modest missionary enterprise. After completing their studies, the members vowed to travel to Palestine to convert souls to Christianity. When war prevented their departure from Venice in 1537, they placed themselves at the disposal of Pope Paul III. On his way to Rome, Ignatius had a definitive vision at La Storta. According to his autobiography, Ignatius "was at prayer in a church and experienced such a change in his soul and saw so clearly that God the Father placed him with Christ his Son that he would not dare doubt it. . . ."[34] Other reports of the incident pictured Christ carrying the cross with God the Father nearby telling Christ that he should take Ignatius for his servant. Ignatius had always longed to be "with Christ," and he took this vision as confirmation of his devotion to Jesus and of an earlier decision by the company to identify themselves by his name.[35] That name, the Society of *Jesus*, was symbolic of their mission and of the agenda that they pursued.

According to O'Malley, their mission can be summarized in two concepts: *reformatio* and *christianitas*. For the most part, "reformation" meant conversion, "the change of heart effected in individuals through the *Spiritual Exercises* and the other ministries in which the Jesuits were engaged."[36] "Christianity" was the goal of Jesuit instruction designated by the bull that approved the order on September 27, 1540. Members were held to work for the "progress of souls in Christian life and doctrine, the propagation of the faith through public preaching . . . , spiritual exercises, and works of charity, expressly through the instruction of children and the uneducated in Christianity (*in christianismo*), and by hearing confessions for the spiritual consolation of the faithful of Christ."[37] True to its name, the Society of Jesus was to be engaged in making Christians. This mission entailed more than teaching doctrine, however. It meant the formation of a Christian identity that was expressed "in life and doctrine" and that was generated and sustained by all the means listed in the bull: spiritual exercises, preaching, teaching, works of charity, and confession. In Asia and the Americas, Jesuits would be making people Christian for the first time, but in Europe their goal was to remake those already baptized into more devoted Christians.

The elements of the Jesuit mission named in the bull derived from two early works of Ignatius. The list of ministries was taken almost verbatim from the *Formula of the Institute,* a statement of purpose created for the process of papal approval in 1539. The *Formula* mentioned additional ministries and the persons to whom they should be directed: "the Turks or any other infidels, even those who live in the region called the Indies, or . . . any heretics whatever, or schismatics, or any of the faithful."[38] Although some activities were identical to those of parish priests and members of orders, the *Formula* gave the Jesuits a sense that their ministries were different, perhaps because they were independent missionaries. They were bound to no particular diocese or cloister; in fact, they were to take a special vow to minister anywhere in the world at the behest of the pope.[39] They were neither parish priests nor monks. They said the divine office in private, not as a community, and they did not chant the hours. They wore no distinctive habit, only the black cassock of diocesan priests, but they were not subject to bishops, only to their superior general who resided in Rome. Most of them were priests who engaged in the active ministry of "making Christians" wherever they were assigned.

The reformation desired by these ministries was described by Ignatius in his most famous work, the *Spiritual Exercises.* It was not a literary treatise but a teacher's guide for directing spiritual retreats that led to personal conversion. Divided into four "Weeks," the *Exercises* were followed by people who were already baptized, Jesuit novices included, in order to deepen their commitment to a Christian way of life. This purpose was stated at the outset:

> For, just as taking a walk, traveling on foot, and running are physical exercises, so is the name of spiritual exercises given to any means of preparing and disposing our soul to rid itself of all its disordered affections and then, after their removal, of seeking and finding God's will in the ordering of our life for the salvation of our soul.[40]

Although this reordering of the soul was described in the most general terms, the *Exercises* envisioned a life that was conformed to Christ. The most perfect way of being humble, outlined in the Second Week, entailed choosing poverty rather than wealth, contempt with Christ rather than honors, and the desire to be regarded as a "useless fool for Christ" rather than "a wise or prudent person in this world."[41] This humility could be adopted as a general orientation or as preparation for a specific decision, or "election," about one's vocation for which the *Exercises* were especially suited. Either way, their purpose was to inspire an intentional commitment to live in conformity with Christ, whose life was the organizing principle of the last three Weeks. This conformity was also encouraged by sections devoted to the "Kingdom of Christ" and the "Two Standards." In both cases, the faithful were enjoined to serve under the standard of Christ by means of spiritual poverty and, if they were called to it, by suffering actual poverty and reproach.[42]

The conformity with Christ envisioned by the *Exercises* derived from the late-medieval piety on which Ignatius drew during his early years: the *Life of Christ* by Ludolph of Saxony (d. 1378) and the *Imitation of Christ* by Thomas à Kempis (d. 1471). Part of the contemplation proposed for the second week was to "ask for an interior knowledge of our Lord, who became human for me, that I may love him more intensely and follow him more closely."[43] This request could have been made not only by Thomas à Kempis but also by any Protestant or dissenter, and it recalls the important influence of the gospels on all forms of Reformation piety. Ignatius, it is true, meant for the *Exercises* to prepare some retreatants for the election of a religious vocation, a state that he called "evangelical perfection." For Ignatius, however, perfection did not mean a state of sinlessness but the fulfillment of God's intention for lives that were not restricted to religious orders. Those making a vocational election should think, he said, about how they should dispose themselves "in order to come to perfection in whatsoever state of life God our Lord may grant us to elect."[44]

The piety proposed by Ignatius, so similar to that of Protestants and dissenters in its christocentric emphasis, differed from theirs by its acceptance of traditional forms of devotion. The *Exercises* upheld, among other things, prayer to the saints and the veneration of their relics, pilgrimages, indulgences for jubilees and crusades, and precepts of fasting and abstinence. This affirmation was included in the best-known section of the *Exercises*, the "Rules for Thinking with the Church."[45] By praising these traditional forms of devotion, the rules balanced the rest of the *Exercises* where external practices were "taken so little into account."[46] For Ignatius and the Society of Jesus, to Christianize their society meant to teach *christianitas* as advocated in the *Exercises* within the bounds of loyalty to the Roman Church and to the traditional piety still endorsed by it. The ninth rule clearly enjoined retreatants to "praise all the precepts of the Church, while keeping our mind ready to look for reasons for defending them and not for attacking them in any way."[47]

Jesuits adhered to the traditional forms in their own way. The *Exercises*, for example, advocated reading the *Imitation of Christ* and the lives of saints, but they mentioned no specific saints other than Mary and a few biblical figures.[48] People were free to venerate their favorite saints, and the Litany of the Saints was recited in Jesuit schools. Daily recitation of the Litany was imposed on Jesuit communities in Germany by their superior, Peter Canisius, who also authored the most popular Catholic catechisms of the Reformation.[49] The trusted agent of Ignatius, Jerónimo Nadal, believed in the authenticity of relics like Veronica's veil and appreciated the popular appeal that saints held for Catholics and Protestants. He preached at a ceremony welcoming two of the heads that had belonged to the eleven thousand virgin martyrs of St. Ursula in Cologne and were being transferred by the Jesuits to Messina. Nadal was careful, however, to subordinate veneration of the saints to worship of God: "Take care lest devotion to the saints and their invocation weaken devotion to God and invocation of him, which ought always to be on the increase. The latter differs totally from the former and altogether excels it."[50]

In the same spirit Jesuits encouraged traditional practices like the veneration of Mary when they were attacked by Protestants. Beginning in 1563, they founded popular sodalities dedicated to Mary; the Company of the Holy Sacrament, organized in Paris in 1629, eventually enrolled more than 4,000 members.[51] They also endorsed pilgrimages and the indulgences sponsored by the sodalities. Ignatius had referred to himself as "the pilgrim," and this image was used in early Jesuit writings to describe their mission. They rejected, however, practices they considered superstitious and attempted to correlate acts of piety with the Christian teaching that was the core of their mission.[52] After they were admitted to Münster in 1588, the Jesuits stressed classical learning in their schools and made Mary the center of their students' piety. This attention to mind and heart was highly successful, and more than anything else their pedagogy was instrumental in reshaping the religious culture of the city.[53]

In the diocese of Cuenca, which was rife with popular religious notions prior to the Council of Trent, the Jesuits opened five schools between 1554 and 1620.[54] After starting the first school, they found themselves also teaching doctrine in town and a year later two fathers spent the Lenten season teaching and preaching in the countryside. Typically, one Jesuit would walk through a village ringing a bell to attract the children and then he would teach them the catechism, prayers, and the rudiments of self-examination and confession. They also held competitions for the children and awarded prizes to the best performers. One Jesuit reported enthusiastically on the success of these methods:

It melted my heart to see the eagerness with which the children came to doctrine, and they went singing it in the streets and fields, so that almost nothing else was heard. Some women were crying with devotion, and when we asked them why they didn't know the Ten Commandments, they said, "Because they didn't teach it to us like now in the streets."[55]

The determination of the Jesuits to rehabilitate Christian doctrine and piety epitomized the Catholic attempt to Christianize Europe. Their schools were not just one ministry among others but a community platform from which all their ministries could be launched. They adapted the teaching and ritual of medieval Christianity to a style of being Christian that emphasized basic doctrine and encouraged personal practice of the faith. That style applied both to the Jesuits and to the people they served:

In everything they should try and desire to give the advantage to others, esteeming them all in their hearts as better than themselves [Phil 2:3] and showing exteriorly, in an unassuming and simple religious manner, the respect and reverence befitting each one's state, in such a way that by observing one another they grow in devotion and praise God our Lord, whom each one should endeavor to recognize in his neighbor as in His image.[56]

Jesuit ministries attempted to reach people of all ages and levels of education. Their versatility was exhibited, for example, by the German father, Graf Friedrich Spee von Langenfeld, whose missionary vision had to be redirected toward the academic circles of seventeenth-century Europe. When he entered the Society at age nineteen, he wanted to serve in the India mission but this wish was denied. Instead, Spee became a teacher of theology after studying in Mainz and receiving ordination in 1622. As professor of philosophy in Paderborn and of moral theology in Trier, Spee was best known for criticizing witch trials, but he also worked hard at presenting an attractive form of Catholic religiosity to his own culture. His "Golden Virtue-Book," published posthumously in 1649, aimed at the inculcation of divine virtues in the faithful, and he composed religious poetry and hymns to facilitate this effort. By emphasizing the importance of religious experience within the framework of Catholic worship and church life,[57] Spee made an important and representative Jesuit contribution to the devotional literature of Catholic reform.

The New Devotion

The Reformation vision of a Christian Europe included the overhaul of piety as well as the recovery of true faith. Since Catholic reform retained many traditional doctrines and practices, however, can its agenda truly be compared with Protestant reform? The active ministries pursued by new orders and the Tridentine decrees suggest a positive answer; an even stronger argument is provided by the increase of religious fervor. Traditional piety was refined and intensified to such an extent that one can call it, as historians have done, a new Catholic devotion. This language is used mainly of the *dévots* and *dévotes*, men and women of the seventeenth and eighteenth centuries whose diligent practice of Christianity contributed to the rise of a devout society in Catholic territories.[58] The new style of devotion, however, was already being formed in the sixteenth century.

Catholic reform did not consider the practice of traditional piety business as usual but tried to coordinate it with sound doctrine. The Council of Trent vigorously denied, for example, that veneration of the saints amounted to idolatry or that it was inconsistent with the honor of Christ as sole mediator. Clergy were charged to

> instruct the faithful diligently in matters relating to intercession and invocation of the saints, the veneration of relics, and the legitimate use of images, teaching them that the saints who reign together with Christ offer up their prayers to God for [us], that it is good and beneficial suppliantly to invoke them and to have recourse to their prayers, assistance and support in order to obtain favors from God through his Son, Jesus Christ our Lord, who alone is our redeemer and savior; and that they think impiously who deny that the saints who enjoy eternal happiness in heaven are to be invoked, or who assert that they do not pray for [us], or that our invocation of them to pray for each of us individually is idolatry, or that it is opposed to the word of God and inconsistent with the honor of the "one mediator of God and men, Jesus Christ" (1 Tim 2:5), or that it is foolish to pray vocally or mentally to those who reign in heaven.[59]

This decree was directed not only against Protestant teaching but also against the Catholic faithful who were enthusiastically seeking miraculous cures at the shrines of the saints. In Bavaria, where Protestant attacks had caused a decline in the number of miracles reported at shrines, Martin

Eisengrein (d. 1578) revived the cult of Our Lady at Altötting by publishing a book that wove an elaborate myth of the shrine's origins and made claims for extensive miracles performed by the Virgin.[60] Although laypeople were encouraged by such apologetic pilgrimage books to seek thaumaturgic results from their prayers to saints, the process of canonizing saints was already downplaying their miracles in favor of their exemplary lives to be followed by others. This trend became stronger in the seventeenth century as the road to sainthood was crowded by recent Catholic reformers who excelled in one or more of the following roles: founder of a religious order, missionary, provider of charity, good pastor, and mystic or spiritual leader.[61] Famous examples in three of these roles, Ignatius, Francis Xavier, and Teresa of Avila, were all canonized in 1622. Protestants were also willing to emulate models of piety without canonizing them, and martyrs played an important role for Protestants, dissenters, and Catholics. The honoring of Christian conviction to the point of death became a common feature of the Reformation even when its traditions disagreed about who died for the truth and who did not:

> Protestant, Anabaptist, and Catholic martyrs were all keenly aware of standing in this [biblical] tradition. Their respective accents varied within a framework of a common language. The ongoing story of the unjustly persecuted included both an ancient foundation and a modern reenactment.[62]

Because Protestants had rejected many traditional forms of piety, Trent also defended their necessity:

> And since [human] nature is such that it cannot without external means be raised easily to meditation on divine things, holy mother Church has instituted certain rites, namely, that some things in the mass be pronounced in a low tone and others in a louder tone. She has likewise, in accordance with the apostolic tradition, made use of ceremonies, such as mystical blessings, lights, incense, vestments, and many other things of this kind, whereby both the majesty of so great a sacrifice might be emphasized and the minds of the faithful excited by those visible signs of religion and piety to the contemplation of those most sublime things which are hidden in this sacrifice.[63]

Concern for the honor of Christ and for the necessity of external means expressed in these passages was not unlike arguments made by many Protestants. Disagreement involved not these concerns as such but the way they were expressed, or failed to be, in doctrines and concrete practices. Did the veneration of saints or the celebration of the mass as a sacrifice promote the affirmation of Christ as sole mediator or not? Disagreement on this question was sharp and could not be overcome. Nevertheless, Catholic reform was sensitive to the basic concerns raised by Protestants and included those concerns in its agenda for reform.

Religious women played a major role in the new devotion. By the seventeenth century the number of female religious in France outnumbered male.[64] Two of the three prominent orders that pursued an active ministry, the Visitation nuns in Savoy and the Daughters of Charity, were founded in France, and in the seventeenth century Ursuline convents became widespread in the same country. Like the Ursulines, the Visitation nuns had to accept enclosure, but their co-founders Jane Frances de Chantal and Francis de Sales wrote primarily for people who lived in the world. A popular guide by Francis, *Introduction to a Devout Life* (1609), was based on spiritual instructions written for a pious woman, Louise de Chastel. In that work he urged Christians to adapt their devotion to their station in life and to "the strength, activities, and duties of each particular person." In addition to the stations that men would occupy, Francis specifically addressed the roles of widow, young girl, and married woman.[65] Jane recommended the *Devout Life* and a proper attitude toward worldly possessions to her daughter Françoise before she married a wealthy member of French society:

> Don't waste time fussing about jewelry and fashion. You will be living in plenty, but, my darling, remember always that we are meant to use the good things God gives us without being attached to them. Such is the attitude we should always have toward the world. From now on, try to live honorably, modestly, sensibly in the new way of life that is before you.[66]

Royal women often combined the new devotion with their lives at court. In 1599, Margarita of Austria took her German Jesuit confessor, Richard Haller, with her to Spain when she married Philip III. The relationship between Margarita and Haller has been described as a typical case of mutual dependence that existed between early modern women and their confessors.[67] Every morning Haller said mass in the queen's chamber and listened to Margarita's confession. They also discussed political matters, and both of them represented Austrian Hapsburg interests at the

Spanish court. A mutual dependence it may have been, but their relationship also gave evidence of mutual respect and a complementary zeal for promoting piety. They nurtured contacts with other Jesuits, with priests, and with religious women for whom Margarita intervened. She also contributed indirectly to a more thorough Christianizing of Spain by supporting Philip's expulsion of the Moriscos in 1609. Margarita made Haller one of the executors of her will and left a sizable portion of her wealth to the Jesuit school at Salamanca.

At the request of her confessors and directors, Teresa of Avila (d. 1582) composed the *Book of Her Life*, one of the most compelling documents of the new devotion. The Spanish town in which she was born and spent most of her life was a center of Catholic reform and supplied her with inspiration and important contacts.[68] Reformist priests, holy women, a new Jesuit college, a nascent seminary, and a school for teaching doctrine to children—all of these were elements of a Christianizing process underway in Avila while Teresa was finding her way in the convent of the Incarnation and founding a new Carmelite house dedicated to St. Joseph.

Teresa's journey was hard. She compared it to a voyage on a tempestuous sea and called it one of the most painful lives she could imagine, "for neither did I enjoy God nor did I find happiness in the world."[69] In addition to sickness and temptation, Teresa was caught "between friendship with God and friendship with the world,"[70] but at last friendship with God won out. The practice of mental prayer, that is, silent personal prayer, finally brought her will into conformity with the will of God:

> For mental prayer in my opinion is nothing else than an intimate sharing between friends; it means taking time frequently to be alone with him who we know loves us. In order that love be true and the friendship endure, the wills of the friends must be in accord. The will of the Lord, it is already known, cannot be at fault; our will is vicious, sensual, and ungrateful. And if you do not yet love him as he loves you because you have not reached the degree of conformity with his will, you will endure this pain of spending a long while with one who is so different from you when you see how much it benefits you to possess his friendship and how much he loves you.[71]

This intensification of Teresa's relationship with God was a prominent example of the religious dedication that marked Catholic reform and that justifies its inclusion under the rubric of Christianization. The conformity with God's will and the raptures she experienced[72] were part of medieval contemplative traditions, but Teresa also took initiative that was typical of Catholic reform. She founded a new convent for Carmelite nuns (St. Joseph in Avila) that would keep more strictly the ancient rule of Carmel adopted by a group of hermits in the Holy Land in the early thirteenth century. It prescribed continual prayer, a daily Eucharist and recitation of the Psalter, and perpetual abstinence from meat. From Peter of Alcantara, a strict Franciscan whose asceticism she admired, Teresa also adopted the practice of wearing only sandals or no shoes at all. This practice gave the name "Discalced" to the Carmelite reform that gradually expanded to include new convents for women and houses for men.

Teresa's enthusiasm for monastic reform was not shared, however, by those women who pursued an active ministry while eschewing the cloister. They adopted a semireligious life that was closer to life in non-cloistered orders than it was to the convent. For example, in 1606 Ida Schnabels and nine companions in Cologne founded the Company of St. Ursula (not to be confused with the new Ursuline order). Formally approved in 1611, the women cooperated with the Jesuits in teaching catechism to children and providing pastoral care to women. Their goal was "to live a non-worldly life in the world"[73] by taking a vow of celibacy, wearing clergy-like garb, and observing their own liturgical celebrations. According to canon law, they were not clergy, but additional companies of these "female Jesuits" appeared outside Cologne and they remained instruments of pastoral care well into the eighteenth century.[74]

The new devotion also found expression in confraternities that emerged during the sixteenth and seventeenth centuries.[75] Impetus for these foundations—dedicated to the Sacrament, the Name of God, the Rosary, Christian Doctrine—came from clergy and laity whose primary objective was to increase religious knowledge and fervor. In the diocese of Milan, Bishop Charles Borromeo required membership in a eucharistic confraternity that was closely tied to the parish church. The purpose of these Corpus Christi confraternities, named after the festival that honored the Eucharist, was to strengthen religious life in the parish and to focus it on celebrations that would attract people and enhance both their piety and their loyalty. The consolidation and promotion of confraternities was an important component of Borromeo's campaign to Christianize Milan,[76] but they were also a crucial feature of Catholic revival in Italy, France, the Iberian peninsula, and parts of Germany.

By serving social and philanthropic purposes, lay confraternities supplemented the active ministries of religious companies like the Daughters of Charity and the Jesuits. Although the Jesuits are best known for their

Marian congregations, three confraternities founded in the 1540s specifically illustrate how their active campaign of Christianization blended both social and missionary goals.[77] The *Compagnia della grazia* was established in Rome to oversee a house for former prostitutes who wanted to alter their lives. To prevent the daughters of prostitutes and other vulnerable young girls from taking a similar road, Ignatius founded the *Compagnia delle vergini miserabili di Santa Caterina*. To effect a different kind of conversion, the Jesuits also opened Catechumen houses for the instruction of Jews and Muslims. These houses were connected to the confraternity of S. Giuseppe that supplied a suitable patron to support the neophytes during their transition to Christianity. During the early decades, Jesuits pursued their missionary activity and their ministry of charity through the foundation of many such confraternities.[78]

It is difficult to assess the depth and endurance of the new devotion in Catholic Europe. According to Châtellier, by 1700 the effects of the Tridentine mission appeared mixed.[79] That judgment is no more surprising for Catholic reform than it is for Protestants and dissenters. In 1603 Francis de Sales eloquently described the difference between the "grand and glorious preparations of the heart" a believer could make for God and their execution:

> [The heart] prepares for Him a body that is mortified and not rebellious, an attention to prayer that is not distracted, gentle conversation free of rancor, and a humility in which there are no bursts of vanity. All this is very good; these are fine preparations, but there is still more we must do to serve God as we should. When all this preparation is done, it remains to be seen who will carry it out, for when it comes to putting all this into practice, we fall short and realize that these perfections can be neither so grand nor so absolute in us. We can mortify the flesh, but not so perfectly that it doesn't rebel; in prayer, our attention will be often interrupted by distractions; and so with the other things I have mentioned.[80]

De Sales was generous about this inevitable imperfection; he told believers not to be discouraged and not to strive for perfection in one day. Popular preachers, however, did not hesitate to challenge people with a call for renewal and a threat of judgment. The Franciscan bishop of Bitonto, Cornelio Musso, proclaimed that the sum of Christianity lay in the virtues of faith, hope, and love, but he also kept people on the traditional tightrope between fear of hell and hope of heaven.[81] The customary piety proved to have a tenacious hold on the people as well. In the countryside around Speyer, calls for frequent confession and communion, private prayer, and strict self-discipline encountered little response. People were reluctant to give up the old forms of worship that emphasized the community over the individual; they attended mass sporadically as before and they retained traditional processions and local pilgrimages.[82]

Another reason for lay resistance may have been the quasi-monastic style of Christian existence that pervaded most forms of the new devotion. The broad-based attempt to Christianize the clergy and laity on Catholic terms was at the same time an attempt to Christianize them on monastic terms. Although Jesuits and most female communities directed their energy to active ministries in the world, their personal discipline and devotion may have been too austere for most Catholic laypeople who were presented with monastic and mystical models. In Milan, the rigorous enforcement of frequent confession and the use of public penance encountered resistance from local clergy and laity. It is doubtful that frequent confession was taken seriously outside small groups of the devout and confraternities that officially called for its practice.[83] When the monks at the charterhouse of St. Barbara in Cologne shed their tradition of silence and spoke up in favor of reform, they did so by publishing the works of their Carthusian forebear, Dionysius (Denys Ryckel), who had called for a monastic style of piety in the fifteenth century. The monks at St. Barbara urged reading Dionysius as a defense against Protestants and reading mystical writers as the path to inner reform.[84] Protestants and dissenters, however, were also calling for inner reform and for their own semimonastic style of being religious in the world. Although they rejected convents and confraternities, Protestants were bent on creating a devout Christian laity through preaching, praying, catechisms, and their own systems of discipline.

A horticultural image of the new devotion was supplied by the *Spiritual Exercises* of the Capuchins in 1683. Comparing the regular practice of piety to the tree of life, the Capuchins described in ideal terms how the soul could be restored in a well-tended garden:

> Our brothers describe this practice as a tree of life, whose leaf is the power of God, preserving as well as restoring everyone who believes unto salvation. Indeed, the aromatic flower revives and attracts anxious hearts; the fruit, which is desired at length, recreates the soul meditating on these things in such a way that it is always satisfied and will never feel distaste as long as it does not follow the example of

lying Adam and choose the tree of the knowledge of good and evil over the tree of life, but prefers faith to reason, simplicity to curiosity, and the sacred cross of Christ to wisdom of the flesh, through which cross the love of the Holy Spirit is poured out and nourished in our hearts.[85]

Expanding the Vineyard

The clearest evidence for the Christianizing agenda of Catholic reform was its missionary expansion into the world beyond Europe. For the most part, this expansion went hand in hand with the colonizing of the Americas, Africa, and Asia by Spain, Portugal, and France. Given the success of early efforts (perhaps as many as ten million converts in the Americas by 1550),[86] it was natural for Catholics to think that God was at work replacing the European lands lost to Protestants with the new territories gained for Roman Catholicism outside Europe. This success inspired the production of a universal image of the Pentecost in Rome. Newly commissioned frescoes showed the Holy Spirit descending not just upon Mary and the twelve apostles but tongues of fire hovering over all the foreigners gathered in Jerusalem for the festival.[87]

The conquest of Mexico (1519) by Cortés was witnessed by Franciscan friars who planted Christian enclaves in place of the Aztec temples that were destroyed.[88] The enclaves grew into a full-scale church that replicated European institutions like ecclesiastical councils and the Inquisition. To become Christian meant to accept many Spanish ways. On the Yucatan peninsula Franciscan missionaries converted the Mayans who had been conquered in 1544. At first they were enthusiastic about the new faith but, after suffering Spanish reprisals, the Mayans displayed resistance to colonial rule and to Christianity.

Christianization also encountered opposition in Peru. It took years to suppress traditional Andean religion, but after 1570, alongside new Spanish towns, a resettlement campaign created communities of Indians that were at least nominally Christianized. Nominal Christianity was not acceptable in Peru, however, just as it was not adequate in Europe, and both bishops and missionaries had to decide how to eradicate the remnants of Andean ritual and belief in order to enhance Christian identity.[89] In developing their strategy, the missionaries invoked early medieval models that used both the carrot and the stick against idolatry and superstition; coercion and destruction were employed alongside preaching and edification.[90] The destruction of Andean objects of worship was advocated by José de Acosta, the Jesuit provincial administrator in Peru between 1576 and 1581. On this point he differed from the famous Dominican missionary, Bartolomé de Las Casas, who had opposed the enslavement of Indians in the New World and argued that persuasion and example were the only legitimate means of conversion.[91] Many years and much frustration later, the campaign against idolatry in Peru took the form of investigations that were aggressively prosecuted throughout the archdiocese of Lima. People were broken, sometimes to the point of suicide, and entire villages were alienated from their indigenous religious leaders.[92]

The use of coercion was by no means the whole story. The pastoral strategy advocated by Las Casas and others was also wisely employed in the campaign of Christianization. Many missionaries to the Americas learned the native languages so well they were able to preach, hear confessions, and write catechisms in the vernacular. Acosta, for example, promoted the learning of Quechua and the publication of religious texts in Spanish, Quechua, and Aymara. He also appreciated the importance of exemplary living for the process of conversion. The miracle that would make missionaries in the Andes as successful as the missionaries of early Christianity was "the virtuous living of the missionaries themselves."[93] The Jesuits in general were instructed to respect the humanity of all people to whom they ministered, including the indigenous people of Brazil. Five months before the Jesuit missionary, Francis Xavier, and his companions arrived in Japan (1549), six Portuguese Jesuits landed in Brazil. They taught catechism to the Portuguese colonists and to natives along the coast before moving into the forests where they conducted a successful ministry among the Tupi Indians. A young Basque missionary, José de Anchieta, composed a grammar of the Tupi language and was able to set doctrines to music in order to facilitate the teaching of Christianity.[94] A successful campaign of Christianization occurred in the Guarani mission in Paraguay, where the Jesuits resettled nomadic Indians in Christian communities for which they provided direct spiritual leadership. This strategy had been recommended by Acosta in his treatise *On Securing the Salvation of the Indies* (1588), a remarkable analysis of the different non-Christians encountered by missionaries and of the most fitting way to convert them.[95]

In 1622 Pope Gregory XV created the Congregation for the Propagation of the Faith in order to coordinate and to oversee the missionary campaign. In Spanish and Portuguese America, it had little success in loosening the bonds between missionary churches and colonial governments; but in Asia it did support the indigenization of Christianity by encouraging the training of native clergy and accommodation to non-European ways.[96] The most famous practitioners of this accommodation were two Jesuits: Robert de Nobili, whose controversial methods of attracting Hindu brahmins were finally approved by the same Pope Gregory, and de Nobili's model, Matteo Ricci, whose openness to Confucian customs and scholarship enabled Christianity to secure a foothold in China.[97] Francis Xavier, who died in 1552 while waiting to enter China, had also demonstrated flexibility in Japan, but the Christian community founded by him suffered heavy persecution and was eventually forced underground in the early seventeenth century. Besides Jesuits, Franciscans, and Dominicans, the Congregation sent other orders into the mission field—Capuchins, Discalced Carmelites, and Lazarists, for example. They went not only to Asia and to the Americas, but also to the Middle East and to critical areas in Europe. The Congregation's agenda embraced both the conversion of non-Christian regions and the reconversion of those areas that had been lost to Protestants.

Reformers and missionaries were aware that their Christianizing work outside Europe corresponded to their ministry in Europe. Franciscans had a tradition of mission to the Holy Land that went back to Francis himself; in 1219 he went to Egypt on the fifth crusade and preached before Ayyubid sultan al-Kamil. Sixteenth-century Capuchins noted that the spirit of Francis "was none other than the conversion of sinners and the salvation of souls, so that his life was simply a continual mission."[98] That spirit could be invoked everywhere. The field of Jesuit activity was often delineated by the traditional missionary image of the "vineyard of the Lord." Part VII of the *Constitutions* described the "distribution of the incorporated members in Christ's vineyard and their relations there with their neighbor." This vineyard had no boundaries. The fourth vow taken by Jesuits to go anywhere the pope might send them "meant that the members were to go any place whatsoever where he judges it expedient to send them for the greater glory of God and the good of souls, *whether among the faithful or the infidels.*"[99] In his commentary on this paragraph, Nadal wrote that Jesuits undertook such journeys to help souls "in whatever way and in whatever situation they need spiritual help, whether we are sent to idolaters, to Muslims, to heretics, or to Christians who are perishing or in danger because of a lack of ministers or their neglect."[100] In 1602, when the Jesuit novice, Giuseppe Cocollo, told his provincial in southern Italy that he wanted to go to the Indies, the provincial advised him to apply himself to perfection in "these Indies down here" and that later he would be sent to "the other Indies."[101]

For Catholics, therefore, the vineyard of the Lord was ubiquitous, and it was an appropriate image for their Reformation agenda. Protestants used it and the parables on which it was based (Is 5:1–7; Mt 20:1–16) to advocate the replanting of Christianity in Europe where they thought the vineyard had become barren. Catholics, specifically Jesuits, used the metaphor for the planting of Christianity outside Europe and for the replanting of Christianity at home where they thought Protestants were engaged in its destruction.[102] This replanting in Europe was every bit a missionary enterprise, both corresponding to Catholic expansion overseas and competing with the missionary-like Protestant expansion at home.

In seventeenth-century Holland, for example, Dutch Calvinists were still warning the populace against Catholicism as a virulent form of idolatry and superstition.[103] Instead of rolling over and playing dead in a culture in which their public worship was prohibited, Dutch Catholics used the de facto toleration they enjoyed to regain lost ground and vitality. As it did for the overseas mission, the Congregation for the Propagation of the Faith supported the appointment of apostolic vicars, clergy who were direct representatives of the pope, to lead a clandestine Holland Mission. The Mission eventually consisted of several hundred priests who set up mission "stations" and traveled widely from station to station to minister to Catholic laity in towns and in rural areas. These priests were missionaries in an environment that was officially hostile and they could have been expelled, but the existence of the Mission was widely known, and most of the time Catholic believers were left alone by authorities, especially if a little "recognition money" changed hands.[104] The toleration of the Holland Mission resulted in a respectable number of conversions, especially by *klopjes*, unmarried Catholic laywomen who served the Mission by housing priests and providing worship space in which they and their neighbors could attend Catholic worship.[105]

The survival of Catholicism in Protestant England was also the result of a concerted missionary effort. The first missionaries were Marian priests who had served publicly during the reign of the Catholic Queen (1553–1558). At the accession of Elizabeth they first left the country but some of them returned in the 1560s to serve clandestinely in Catholic homes. The last surviving Marian priest was still alive in 1616, providing support to a nephew who was leaving for seminary training at the English College in Rome.[106] One of these Marian Catholics, William Allen, founded the English College at Douai in northern France, which prepared English-speaking priests for service in England. It was the first seminary north of the Alps to embody the proposals of the Council of Trent for the preparation of clergy. The first priest to return to England was Louis Barlow in 1574; by the end of Elizabeth's reign (1603), Douai had sent around 400 clergy to England, transforming a beleaguered confession into a vital, if illegal and persecuted, competitor to the Church of England.

The Marian and Douai priests were aided by the Jesuits, who initiated a mission to England in the 1580s. Its leader was Robert Parsons (1546–1610), who returned to the continent after his companion, Edmund Campion (1540–1581), was arrested and executed. Other Jesuits followed, however, like the uncle of John Donne, the translator and poet Jasper Heywood (1535–1598), who returned to England in 1581 and served as a missionary until he was arrested, imprisoned in the Tower of London, and finally exiled to the continent. Donne's mother grew up in a prominent recusant family that refused to attend Anglican services and so, presumably, did Donne himself before he was converted to the Church of England. Donne's younger brother, Henry, was arrested when a Catholic priest was found in his rooms, and he later died in prison.[107] Most Catholic families, however, did not attain such notoriety and indeed sought to avoid it, although so-called Church Papists conformed to the Church of England and attended its services.[108] At risk to themselves, Catholic laity of all classes, especially women, sustained the faith by sheltering clergy, providing food, horses, clothes, mass vessels, and vestments, and even arranging itineraries. Sometimes one house sheltered Marian priests, seminary priests, and Jesuits on the same night.[109] The clergy were diligent in pastoral care, the laity devoted, and the English Catholic community survived persecution to gain limited toleration late in the seventeenth century.

The Poland-Lithuanian commonwealth, which had sealed the formation of European Christendom in the fourteenth century, was also subject to a Catholic missionary campaign during the late sixteenth and seventeenth centuries. Protestantism had reached its high-water mark in 1572, when it held a near majority in the diet and claimed one-sixth of the parishes in the country. Lutherans, Calvinists, and Bohemian Brethren had come to a mutual understanding at Sendomir in 1570 while trying to distance themselves from the antitrinitarian movement led by Faustus Socinus. Under the guidance of Cardinal Stanisław Hosius (d. 1579) after he returned from the last session of the Council of Trent, Catholicism made a gradual recovery. In 1564 the cardinal brought to Poland Jesuit missionaries who established five highly regarded schools that attracted both Catholics and Protestants.[110] The reconversion of Poland was not accomplished by Jesuits alone. They had assistance from other orders such as the Observant Franciscans, who in Poland were called Bernardines or *reformati*. By the mid-seventeenth century they were on the offensive against Protestants and keeping records of their conversions. These records indicate that Catholic piety and ritual, like pilgrimages to Marian shrines and the spectacle of the mass, had more influence on converts than theology and politics.[111] Since a divided Protestantism had never struck deep roots in the Polish peasantry,[112] the concerted missionary outreach to all classes resulted in a predominantly Catholic Poland.

Near the end of the Anabaptist kingdom at Münster in 1535, the superior of St. Barbara's Carthusian cloister in nearby Cologne, Theodore Loher, ventured a prediction that was reminiscent of the warning that had been issued in 1524 by Martin Luther. The Wittenberg reformer had admonished Germans to seize the gospel that had already come and gone "like a passing shower of rain" from the lands of the Jews, the Greeks, and the Romans.[113] Loher decided it was probably too late for Christianity in Germany and France to thrive because they seemed to be falling away from the true faith, but he believed the church would prosper in other parts of the world to which God would send the gospel. History was his guide. When the church had declined in the East, God turned toward the West where Christianity then flourished. Now, with the Western church in decline, said Loher, God was calling people from America, Asia, and Africa to membership in the kingdom. God had once transferred the gospel from the ungrateful Jews to the Gentiles. Now that Protestants had defiled this gift through heresy and dissension, God would grant it to new nations where the church would survive.[114]

Loher's prognosis about early modern Europe was wrong. Catholicism not only survived, it made a strong comeback, especially in France and Germany, where it was never lost. He was right, however, about the rest of the world. When he made this prediction in 1535, Loher enjoyed only a glimpse of the expansion of Christianity abroad. Nevertheless, he was anticipating, however unawares, the Catholic agenda to Christianize both non-European peoples and believers at home. Although his prophecy, like Luther's, was couched in a theology of history, it turns out he was right in believing that the vineyard was expanding beyond the borders of Europe. Although Christianity had long been present in parts of Asia and Africa, it would now be carried by Europeans, in its Reformation forms, to other continents on an unprecedented scale.

Chapter 6

Confessionalizing the Agendas

The Outcome of Christianization

Ideals and Impact

The Reformation had two primary goals, one of which is easier to measure than the other. The first and more measurable goal was to reform the rituals of late-medieval piety in conformity with sound doctrine. Even though reformers did not agree on which practices needed to be abolished and which could simply be purified, the changes made to devotional practices were documented in parish inventories, church constitutions, orders of worship, and visitation reports.[1] Some of the most dramatic evidence comes from England, where centralized legislation and its swift execution led to a relentless makeover of people's religious lives. Although many parishioners objected to the radical alteration of their piety and found private ways to resist it, the reforms stuck in many places, and in those places Protestantism was established. The alteration of doctrine and ritual was most evident in Protestant and Radical reform, but Catholic reformers were also concerned that devotion be sincere and less tainted with superstition.

The second goal was to create more sincere and intentional believers by transforming people's minds and hearts. This goal applied to people's internal life and was accordingly harder to measure. Since actions are easier to evaluate than attitudes, how could reformers tell if faith had become deeper and love more ardent? Protestants insisted that a good tree produced good fruit and that faith and love could be measured by the actions to which they led. If obeying the first commandment entailed obedience to the rest, as Luther claimed, then one would notice whether people had kept the Sabbath by attending church and whether they had refrained from murder, adultery, and theft. The new Catholic devotion could be tested by

the orders founded and the number of people who joined them, the popularity of confraternities, and the change in clerical education and behavior. But the "preparations of the heart," as de Sales called them, remained
elusive unless they issued in conduct that approached perfection.

On this score, the Reformation's success is debatable. In 1978 Gerald
Strauss unleashed a prolonged controversy with his statement: "If it was
the central purpose [of the Protestant Reformation] to make people—all
people—think, feel, and act as Christians, to imbue them with a Christian mind-set, motivational drive, and way of life, it failed."[2] Strauss's
conclusion has been so provocative because his description of this Reformation objective is so accurate. Strauss based his evaluation on German
visitation records, that is, reports from the civil and ecclesiastical inspectors who visited Lutheran parishes during the second half of the sixteenth
century. The inspectors registered lax church attendance, ignorance of the
catechism, public misconduct, and the people's eager consultation with
soothsayers and wise women. The visitors also uncovered ignorance and
negligence among the clergy, although the long-winded preaching about
which some laypeople complained may have resulted from a misguided
zeal to excel at this vital Protestant function.

There have been three general responses to Strauss's thesis. First, some
historians focused on his methodology, pointing out that inspectors were
more likely to note cases of misconduct and ignorance than to give credit
to people who attended church and behaved themselves. The inspection
reports, they observed, were not court records or consistory registers in
which offenders made a formal appearance, but cases of deviance were still
more likely to attract attention than cases of compliance.

Second, other historians contended that Strauss did not pay enough
attention to positive judgments that do appear in Protestant records. In
rural parishes around Strasbourg, for example, catechetical instruction was
a success even if memorization does not prove that people became the kind
of Christians envisioned by reformers.[3] In the Palatinate by the end of the
sixteenth century, a Protestant folk piety that consisted of regular church
attendance existed alongside smaller pockets of religious zeal and hostile
indifference.[4] An examination of visitation records in Württemberg produced "no evidence of widespread disaffection from the state church nor
of the existence of an alternative folk religion."[5] In Joachimsthal, the ample
use of Lutheran hymnody in public and private settings by the laity pointed
to successful cultivation of a Protestant mind-set.[6] In Geneva, a few people
held onto old beliefs and practices, but most Genevans converted to
Protestantism, and, even though the conversion took time, by the late

1550s they were schooled in the basics of Reformed teaching and had given up old religious habits.[7] In the French Calvinist communities that were illegal and subject to persecution, allegiance to Protestantism ran deep. Parisian Protestants roundly rejected Catholic practices and gave evidence that justification by faith had shaped their belief.[8]

Judgments about the impact of Catholic reform have varied as well, but Bireley believes that it was relatively successful: "Features of late medieval Christianity—such as processions, pilgrimages, and confraternities, which Protestants had criticized vigorously—revived after a brief lull, gradually shedding many if not all of their more profane or raucous elements. A new emphasis on charitable good works and the needs of the poor and unfortunate was evident. . . ."[9] In chapter 5 we noted evidence of mixed results for Catholic laity, but on the whole Bireley's judgment seems well supported. As far as the clergy were concerned, for example, in the northwestern German Duchy of Jülich by 1560 the reform of the priesthood seemed to be well underway. One analysis of visitation records concluded that a much higher share (35 percent versus 9 percent) of the clergy had received formal education and that the proportion of underpaid curates had declined since 1530 from 31 percent to 25 percent.[10] The number of priests living with concubines had increased by 14 percent, but that number contradicts other studies; in most western and southern German dioceses after 1600 concubinage was no longer a problem.[11] In Cuenca, the younger secular clergy were not only better educated than their older colleagues, but they were also less frequently accused of concubinage and solicitation in the confessional.[12] The Council of Trent strictly forbade concubinage and threatened priests who ignored the admonitions of their superiors with the ultimate loss of their livelihoods.[13] The strong stand taken by Trent on clerical reform had a noticeable impact even though that impact was felt more quickly in some areas than in others.

It is no surprise that Protestant reform produced mixed results. Instilling the full Protestant message had been a challenge from the start. Reformers had to admonish their hearers that justification by faith and not by works did not mean they could stay away from church or ignore the Ten Commandments. By 1535 the German superintendent Urbanus Rhegius was already blaming young Protestant clergy for leading people astray:

> In striving to present Paul's teaching about the law and its office, some preachers brazenly teach the following: "The ten commandments were not given for us to obey." Here they abruptly stop the

sermon and move on to another topic, although they should explain in detail why the law was given at all since it cannot justify the sinner. Unless they already understand Paul perfectly, people who hear such things cannot avoid taking offense. Right away they think that meditating upon the law, keeping it, and doing good works are unnecessary and that it is permitted to steal and to commit adultery and murder. For one hears these things said publicly by people who have listened to such foolish sermons.[14]

A third response to Strauss's conclusions argued that he misread the agenda of Lutheran reformers. Oberman, for example, vigorously denied that the transformation of hearts and minds had ever been Luther's goal. In Luther, Oberman detected very little desire for the improvement and renovation that dominated the thought of city reformers like Bucer, Zwingli, and Calvin. For Luther, argued Oberman, moral reformation as transformation did not fail; it was never part of his agenda.[15] Human reform was preparation for the divine reformation that would come in fullness at the Last Day. In 1543 Calvin wrote that success depended on God's works and not on human hopes and opinions.[16] Taking the Reformation out of human hands, however, and placing it in divine arms does little to explain the discrepancy between the high expectations of the reformers and the mixed results that sometimes disappointed them.

It is tempting to play down interior transformation in favor of observable changes made by Protestants: new orders of worship that emphasized preaching, reading the Bible, teaching catechism, praying directly to God through Christ, organizing charity for the poor and the sick, expanding public education, and upholding secular callings. These changes were more measurable than attitudes and, besides, reformers acknowledged that sin and idolatry persisted in human hearts.[17] More was at stake for Protestants, however, than the replacement of one set of rituals by another; the survival of Christianity was in doubt. As Cranach illustrated, Protestant reformers thought that Christendom had been ruined by medieval religion; the vineyard had to be recultivated so that faith would take root and produce new fruit. Protestants replaced rituals and practices that they considered idolatrous with a Christianity centered on preaching, teaching, and learning the faith. These public changes were essential, but they should also lead to interior transformation and a corresponding improvement of conduct. Radical reformers made even deeper cuts in the old faith and demanded greater evidence of improvement. Catholic reformers vigorously denied that Christianity was nearly lost, but instead of abolishing the old faith, they reasserted its teachings, purged worship of its superstitions, and refocused it on the weekly mass and the sacrament of penance. They also intended for these changes to inspire in the Catholic faithful a new level of devotion. Alongside ritual and institutional change, therefore, the Reformation also envisioned the transformation of minds, hearts, and conduct.

On this point, reformers remained idealists even though they did not achieve the results for which they hoped. Occasionally they recognized that hearts and minds would not automatically change when new teaching and worship were introduced. For example, in his Large Catechism Luther argued that the "false worship" of medieval religion led people into idolatry because they relied on such things as endowments, fasts, and masses instead of trusting in God alone for every good thing. He conceded, however, that "this reasoning is a little too subtle and is not suitable for young pupils."[18] Despite containing a dash of realism, however, Luther's words probably overestimated the capacity and willingness of adults to see what children could not. Most of the time Luther wrote as if teaching people to trust in God alone would cause them to do so. In that sense, he was an idealist, and so were other Protestant reformers. In the Hamburg Church Order of 1529, John Bugenhagen made the same assumption when he transformed St. Cecilia's Day into a Protestant day of thanksgiving:

[T]his good city once made a vow to celebrate St. Cecilia's Day [November 22] because [in the year 1412] there arose such a terrible wind and such an unusually high tide that everyone feared the city might be destroyed. Now, so that superstitious people may not attribute the honor of God to the holy virgin Cecilia and to be sure that God receives both honor and the annual tribute that our vow requires, we have decided it is best for us to make our common thanksgiving on this day. And as we should always do, let us give thanks for eternal blessings in Christ as well as for the deliverance of our bodies from all our worldly distress. And let us pray that we might remain with Christ and never be forsaken by God, our merciful Father, in times of bodily need, through Jesus Christ our Lord, Amen.[19]

Late-medieval believers who became Protestants eventually learned this theology after their traditional piety was banned. They stopped praying to saints, simplified their worship, withdrew their relatives from convents, and sent their children to catechism and to Protestant schools.

Nothing guaranteed, however, that deep in their hearts these Protestants trusted in God alone as their help and salvation. In fact, there is considerable evidence, not just from the sixteenth century, that pure convictions of this kind were seldom generated. Skeptics remained, and even devout Protestants hedged their bets with soothsayers, prayer vigils, veneration of the Bible, and new forms of endowment giving. Seldom did the daily life of Protestants embody the Sermon on the Mount or the Ten Commandments as reformers had wished. On this point visitation reports and consistory records only confirm what historians know from other sources. The results were mixed. There was no uniform sanctity in the religious lives of early modern men and women, Protestant or Catholic. Religion did change "but, on the whole, very slowly,"[20] not only in Geneva and Cuenca, as we have seen, but also in Wittenberg and Cologne.

Change that was too slow for preachers and reformers may have been too rapid for laity, and the impact of the Reformation has to be evaluated from their vantage point as well. Not all people shared the grand vision of the reformers for a more Christian society. Their reasons for supporting the Reformation were more concrete and related to their own social and political goals. From the peasantry to the nobility, the Reformation held out the possibility of change that would better the conditions under which people lived. Late-medieval burghers in Germany and Switzerland supported Protestant preachers in part because it gave them political leverage over the patricians who had long held power in the towns. German princes who adopted the Reformation realized that it gave them leverage over against the Catholic emperor. In addition, anticlerical feeling was present in all social groups and resentment against clerical privilege ran deep. Protestant laity were glad to reduce the control that Catholic clergy had over their lives, but they condemned the Protestant clergy as new papists when they tried to enforce new patterns of worship and conduct beyond what the laity found tolerable. Visitation reports and consistory records indicate that Protestant and Catholic laity alike, especially in rural areas, held on to aspects of the old faith that they considered useful when reformers tried to take it away.[21]

At the same time, many laypeople did heed the admonitions to change their beliefs and the ways they worshiped. Around 5,000 people in Western Europe suffered martyrdom for the faith they believed to be true.[22] Remarkable conviction was demonstrated by Anabaptists, whose testimonies at trial indicate their resolve to live and worship differently no matter the cost. These people and others who did not die for the faith were obviously convinced by Protestant, Radical, and Catholic leaders that their faith and worship were worthy of defending to the end. Even if most believers did not live up to the ideal of the reformers, their reform of doctrine and piety slowly produced a new shape of Christianity that partially embodied their vision in a diversity they had not anticipated. The impact of the Reformation, therefore, lay not in the creation of ideal Christians, but in the rise of new churches in which the different agendas for attaining that ideal could be pursued.

How does this evaluation of its impact affect charges that the Reformation failed to halt the encroachment of secularization upon Europe[23] or to rid the continent of magic and superstition? The charges are quite different, but they are both connected to the work of Max Weber (d. 1920) and to his view of the Reformation.[24] The general argument for secularization claims that the Reformation showered Europe with a new kind of Christianity, namely Protestantism, which spiritualized religion and made it congruous with secular forces like the rise of capitalism and the autonomy of the state. For Weber, the Reformation, especially in its Calvinist expressions, helped Europe become modern by "disenchanting the world,"[25] that is, by transforming its otherworldliness into a this-worldly asceticism that drove believers to be productive and to see their productivity as a sign of God's blessing.[26] Robert Scribner strongly disagreed with Weber. He argued that the Reformation by no means led to a "disenchantment of the world" but that Protestants continued to share with Catholics a sacred view of the universe.[27]

Elements of secularization were present in the Reformation. To the extent that Protestants affirmed life in the world over monasticism—the dignity of daily work, domestic roles, and civic responsibility—they enhanced the value of worldly vocations, and without rejecting monasticism Catholics affirmed lay vocations as a Christian way of life.[28] This secularization was not secularism, however, in the sense of discarding a sacred view of the universe. Reformers certainly wanted to eliminate magic and superstition, but instead of disenchanting or desacralizing the world, they attempted to Christianize it by removing what they deemed to be remnants of folk religion that did not belong to historically orthodox teaching, worship, and piety. Protestants, and Catholics to a lesser extent, also moved the location of the sacred from consecrated physical objects to the faithful themselves who were baptized and empowered to live a holy life. The theology of radical Christians embodied this relocation of the holy most distinctly. It was less sweeping for Lutherans, who insisted on Christ's physical presence in the Lord's Supper and on the Holy Spirit in baptism, than it was for the Reformed tradition, which had always protested that nothing material could contain the divine.[29] The sacred universe of Catholics remained largely untouched, but the faithful were called to personal holiness with an urgency that seemed greater than before. The displacement of the holy from the physical to the personal was not a removal of the sacred from the world but a different way of giving the faithful access to the sacred.

According to Patrick Collinson, the Reformation can be seen as an "episode of re-christianization or even primary Christianization," which decelerated or arrested "a process of secularization with much deeper roots."[30] Whether or not this was true, reformers did not think of themselves as slowing down a process of secularization but of combating, to different degrees, the improper sacralization of Christendom, namely, those practices that reformers considered remnants of paganism or superstitious accretions. Historians can debate, of course, what reformers could not yet see, that is, the effects of the Reformation on European culture that may have led to a readier acceptance of the Enlightenment and to a process of de-christianization. By dividing Christianity into different confessions and fighting both academic and military battles over which confession possessed the truth, the Reformation did make Christianity less credible for those Europeans who were disturbed by the conflicts and sought a more rational religion. It is also true that in the eighteenth century explicit Christian content began to lose public stature and be relegated to the private sphere.[31] In the sixteenth century, however, far from creating a secular Europe, the non-radical Reformation reaffirmed Christendom as a civil society that privileged Christianity in its new confessional diversity. This diversity was not part of its original vision, but it was the legal and institutional result of that vision, which was destined to have a long history despite the secularization that eventually came.

Confessionalization and Christianization

Confessional Christianity was the most tangible outcome of the Reformation. Reformed or Calvinist churches were prominent in Switzerland, Scotland, Holland, southern France, and in parts of western Germany, England, and eastern Europe. They adhered to various Reformed confessions produced locally: in Switzerland, the *First and Second Helvetic Confessions* (1536, 1566); in Germany, the *Heidelberg Catechism* (1563); in France and Scotland, the *Gallican and Scottish Confessions* (1559); in the Low Countries, the *Belgic Confession* (1561) and the *Articles of the Synod of Dort* (1619); and in England, the *Westminster Confession* (1647) and *Catechisms*

(1648). Lutherans dominated Scandinavia, the Baltic countries, small pockets of eastern Europe, and half of Germany, where their confessions were produced and gathered into the *Book of Concord* (1580).[32]

The outcome of the Reformation in England was settled under Elizabeth I in 1559, but the new Church of England took longer to establish its identity according to the *Thirty-nine Articles of Religion* (1563, 1571) and the *Book of Common Prayer* (1549, 1552, 1662). In the beginning its theology was largely Calvinist, and controversy persisted between those believers who were loyal to the settlement with its episcopal and liturgical structure (the first "Anglicans") and those who desired a more Calvinist style of worship and piety ("Puritans"). The new Roman Catholic confession was defined by a process of codification that produced the canons and decrees of the Council of Trent (1564), the *Tridentine Profession of Faith* (1564), the *Index of Forbidden Books* (1564), the *Roman Catechism* (1566), and a new *Roman Missal* (1570).[33] In the realm of radical dissent, two traditions established an ongoing confessional identity after the early Anabaptists agreed to a set of articles at Schleitheim in 1527. Mennonites adopted the *Dordrecht Confession* (1632), and Hutterites recognized the *Account of Our Faith* (*Rechenschaft*, 1542, 1565) written by Peter Riedemann (d. 1556).[34]

The term confessionalization refers not to the documents, however, but to the process through which reforms were installed in early modern Europe. Confessional churches were by and large territorial churches, that is, they became the officially approved churches in a single town, territory, or country.[35] In Germany the distribution of confessional churches stabilized over a long period that extended from the first legal settlement of the Reformation, the Peace of Augsburg (1555), to the Treaty of Westphalia that ended the Thirty Years' War (1648). Some parts of Germany became Lutheran, some Roman Catholic, some Calvinist; and some areas were biconfessional. The confessional character of this era was emphasized by Ernst Walter Zeeden;[36] but confessionalization as the process by which these churches were established has been studied intensively by Wolfgang Reinhard,[37] Heinz Schilling,[38] and other scholars, such as Heinrich Richard Schmidt,[39] in conversation with them. Their work has focused on three aspects of the new confessional cultures: (1) the churches themselves; (2) the state and society; (3) the rise of other forces that led to the end of confessional Europe.[40] A prime subject of interest has been the process of social discipline by which church and state cooperated in overseeing belief and behavior for the purpose of creating obedient subjects.[41] Since that process could turn obliging clergy into virtual agents of government, confessionalization helped to consolidate the power of the early modern state and to make Christianity a servant of the political process. As clergy tried to make their parishioners conform to the teaching and practices of the reigning confession, they contributed to the stability of the social and political order. Seen in the light of social discipline, one impact of the Reformation was to shape up people as believers and as subjects.

Although regulation was a fundamental dynamic of confessionalization, it does not have to be seen only as social discipline.[42] Confessionalization was the continuation of efforts to Christianize European cities and territories. The adoption of a specific confession with its theological statements and church orders regulated the structure of parishes and the rituals that governed the lives of believers. The primary purpose of regulating belief and behavior was to instill the new Protestant or renewed Catholic version of Christianity and thus to curb whatever improper notions and practices still existed. Before creating obedient subjects, the process of confessionalization strove to create wholehearted supporters of the new creed in each branch of Christendom. In seventeenth-century Rostock, for example, the Lutheran clergy used all means of church discipline at their disposal to reinvigorate religious life even if it meant criticizing the city's magistrates. Their reform movement was not "state-imposed social control through a bureaucratized church apparatus," but a religious campaign that can be called "a re-sacralization of confessional Lutheranism."[43]

The religious motive for discipline operated without apology among English Puritans, for example. In St. Mary's parish at Kidderminster, Richard Baxter implemented a parish-based system of church discipline based on the model of Martin Bucer. Baxter had served as a chaplain in the new model army of Oliver Cromwell, and his system was introduced during the interregnum in England (the 1650s) when political influence on the churches was spotty. By the application of discipline, Baxter, like most sixteenth-century reformers, wanted to raise the level of Christian devotion in the parish at large, not to foment schism by taking the most committed laity out of the parish. According to Baxter, it was the fault of ministers that parishes "were not in a better case," and he suggested that believers who advocated separation from the parish system ("Independents" and "Baptists," for example) might change their mind when they saw "what was done at Kidderminster" and began to realize that "it is a better Work thus to reform the Parishes than gather Churches out of them."[44]

In order that more informed pastors and parishioners might be created, education became an essential feature of confessionalization. Reformers such as Luther had long since made education of the young a priority for restoring Christendom.[45] The new church orders not only regulated parish life and expectations of the clergy, but they set up schools as well. The first eight chapters of the church order written by Bugenhagen for Hamburg designated the kinds of schools to be supported by the city and described their structure and curricula. In his preface Bugenhagen wrote: "The purpose of this order is to provide a good school for the youth and good preachers of the word of God for us all, and, as is right and Christian, remuneration for those who work and a dedicated system of caring for the poor."[46] Bugenhagen also proposed a school system for the city of Braunschweig that established Latin and vernacular schools for boys and girls.[47] Although the clergy were to play a limited role, the purpose of these urban institutions was to educate future citizens for public life in a Christian community. Morality and discipline were taught, to be sure, but as part of a broader curriculum that sought to ensure the long-term impact of the Reformation.

In Germany, confessional churches disagreed over the success of this long-term goal. Calvinists believed Lutherans were doing an inadequate job of educating the minds and molding the conduct of Protestant believers. Although Lutherans had succeeded with the reformation of doctrine, Calvinists believed they had failed to follow through with a reformation of life. Calvinist clergy campaigned, therefore, for the conversion of Lutheran territories to their confession. The first territory to turn Calvinist was the Palatinate, and in 1613 the Elector John Sigismund of Brandenburg also renounced Lutheranism for Calvinism.[48] This conversion from one Protestant confession to another is called by some historians a second reformation, a term introduced by Jürgen Moltmann in his study of Christoph Pezel, the student of Philipp Melanchthon who facilitated the transfer of Nassau-Dillenberg and Bremen to Calvinism.[49] The term was also applied to theologians in Electoral Saxony who had been students of Melanchthon and felt that his views, especially on the presence of Christ in the sacrament, were closer to Calvin than to Luther.[50]

Did the process of confessionalization in Germany include a second Protestant reformation? According to Wilhelm Neuser, Pezel spoke not of two reformations but rather of a single reformation whose second stage had begun with the transition to Calvinism.[51] The term "second reformation" is problematic because it distorts the impact of the Reformation and draws a false distinction between Lutherans and Calvinists. In the sense of improved behavior and increased devotion, Lutherans desired the reformation of life as much as Calvinists did, and not only during the early years of reform. In the mid-seventeenth century (1641–1645), Duke

Ernest of Saxe-Gotha authorized a general visitation of the church and schools in the heartland of Lutheranism that expressly aimed at the "reformation of life." This term and similar expressions were used by Lutheran theologians of the seventeenth century, like Johan Valentin Andreae (d. 1654), to describe their vision of a Christian society that could be achieved through lifelong education and the consistent application of church discipline.[52] As a young man, Duke Ernest had been one of the founders of the "fruit-bearing society," an association dedicated to the Christian and political renewal of the Holy Roman Empire through educational reform and the inculcation of virtue.[53]

When it came to proper ritual, however, Lutherans and Calvinists disagreed as they had always done over which features of medieval religion needed to be abolished. These features included exorcism (renunciation of the devil in baptism), altars, crucifixes, pictures, the wearing of chasubles and other vestments, candles, and any features of the Lord's Supper, like elevating the host, that could lead to an inappropriate adoration of the elements. Calvinists believed that Lutherans had not purified medieval worship of these superfluous and allegedly magical features, and they were determined, as one preacher put it, to "sweep the leftover papal dung completely out of Christ's stable."[54] In the late sixteenth and early seventeenth centuries the competition between Calvinists and Lutherans drew clergy away from the general vision of Christianization that had prevailed in the late Middle Ages and the early Reformation. That transition can be observed in handbooks that were produced for parish priests. Late medieval manuals for parish priests advised them how to celebrate the liturgy and the sacraments correctly in the Christian community. A Lutheran manual written in 1582 emphasized the correct teaching of doctrine as the primary way in which a pastor preserved people from error and confounded the devil.[55]

The formation of confessions was the outcome of the conflicting agendas of Christianization. The disagreement over how to realize the Reformation vision in teaching and practice began with individual reformers and coalesced around their followers and political advocates in the confessional cultures of early modern Europe. The year 1555, when Lutheran areas received legal sanction alongside Catholic territories, was an important date for the political development of the Reformation, but it did not divide the Reformation from a subsequent age of confessionalization or confessional Europe. Confessionalization was not a separate age, but the last stage of installing new forms of Christendom into distinct cultures. This stage began with disagreements that became visible prior to 1555, and it continued well after that date as Catholic, Lutheran, and Calvinist clergy, in cooperation with magistrates, pursued local campaigns of Christianizing their flocks. Their agendas led to diverse patterns of theology and piety and formed different sociopolitical contexts that historians call the confessional groupings of early modern Europe.

The diversification of Christianity was actually under way prior to the Reformation. In the fourteenth and fifteenth centuries Christianity became more and more regionalized, and political leaders challenged the universal claims of the papacy with regularity. Unlike in early medieval Europe, a single universal church hierarchy was no longer needed to unify and Christianize a new civilization.[56] Although reformers envisioned the renewal of Christendom entire, Protestants and dissenters among them pursued their agendas to the point of exclusion from the Roman Church because they, like the rulers who protected them, believed their replantings of Christianity no longer required a single church hierarchy. Western Christendom was certainly divided by the Reformation of the sixteenth century, its wars of religion, and the devastating Thirty Years' War (1618–1648) that arose in part from that division. Even without the Reformation, however, it is not certain that Western Christendom would have remained unified, since Europe was becoming more conscious of its diversity and religion was being used as a weapon in political and social conflicts. The rise of different confessions was not part of the original vision of the Reformation but its unintended structural outcome.[57] Nevertheless, those confessions became the molds through which Christianity made its imprint on modern Europe for generations to come.

The Reformation Abroad

The impact of the Reformation vision was felt strongly outside Europe. Because colonial expansion took place for the most part after 1500, the religion carried to the rest of the world by European colonists was Christianity in the confessional forms generated by the Reformation. Prior to the Reformation, Christianity was not a global religion, but it did extend far beyond Western Europe. After its birth at the eastern end of the Mediterranean, it had moved deeper into Asia and southwestward into Africa while it was also being carried into Europe along the pathways and sea lanes of the Roman Empire.[58] By the fourth century Syriac Christianity had reached southern India, and Nestorian Christianity arrived in China by the seventh century. Nordic Christianity probably touched the northeastern coast of North America with the earliest Viking settlements.

By that time Christianity had been overwhelmed by Islam in North Africa and in the land of its origin. In Europe, however, Christianization was proceeding apace and Christianity was becoming the dominant religion of the Middle Ages.

The global expansion of Christianity accelerated during the Reformation. Owing to the far-flung empires of Spain and Portugal and to the French exploration of North America, Roman Catholicism permeated the Americas. It also benefited from the missionary commitment of its religious orders; Antonio Possevino, a prominent Jesuit diplomat and writer, developed his own plan for world evangelization.[59] When the Congregation for the Propagation of the Faith was founded in 1622, Roman Catholicism was the predominant form of Christianity outside Europe, extending its reach into Asia and covering South and Central America and the southwestern part of North America. It had reached the interior of North America with the French, but it was challenged by British Protestantism in Canada and in the colonies that became the United States. Not until the late seventeenth century did European Protestantism pursue its missionary enterprise in earnest and plant Reformation confessions in Africa, Asia and, with greater diversity, in North America. In Tranquebar (South India), for example, when the king of Tanjore granted Denmark the right to conduct trade in 1621, the treaty in the Tamil language guaranteed the right of the Danes to practice their Lutheranism as "the religion of Augsburg."[60] Almost a century went by, however, before Lutherans from the Danish-Halle mission, Bartholomäus Ziegenbalg and Heinrich Plütschau, established in 1706 the first intentional Protestant mission in Asia. Other Protestant missionary societies that arose in the eighteenth and nineteenth centuries, like the Society for the Propagation of the Gospel (1701) and the Basel Mission (1815), were also offspring of the Reformation.

Where European colonial cultures were planted, Christianity in one or more of its Reformation forms was planted as well. That transplantation was not foreign to the Reformation vision, but it caused a certain ambivalence. On the one hand, reformers in Europe had understood themselves to be Christianizing a syncretistic culture and defending a pure religion. Hence their heirs were hesitant to support cultural exchange between Christianity and non-Christian religions in other parts of the world. That hesitation sometimes led to aloofness from the host culture and the transplantation of Christianity remained shallow. During the Dutch colonial era in Ceylon, the Reformed church baptized Buddhists and Hindus by the thousands, but after the British took over in 1796 very few Christians

were left to greet the new British and American missionaries. Conversion
had provided access to the public life and educational benefits of colonial
society more than it had changed religious conviction and identity.[61] In
India, both Catholics and Protestants eventually became uncomfortable
with the successful enculturation of Christianity that they encountered.
The St. Thomas Christians, who traced their ancestry to early Syriac
churches, had already flourished for centuries in a Hindu environment.
Although they had maintained contact with the bishops of Antioch, they
emerged as an important class within Hindu society and participated in
extensive cultural exchange.[62] Eventually, Portuguese colonial authorities
tried to impose the authority of Rome on the Syrian Christians. In the
Coonen Cross Event of 1653, a substantial minority of the St. Thomas
Christians refused to submit and persisted in their allegiance to the Syrian Church. They came under pressure again after 1816, when the British
Resident, Colonel John Munro, used personnel from the British Church
Missionary Society to support his campaign of cleansing Syrian Christians
of "popery."[63] Although this campaign by colonial forms of Reformation
Christianity challenged the long-standing affiliation of St. Thomas Christians with Indian culture, they remained quite caste conscious and maintained their Indian rites.

On the other hand, the Reformation vision lent itself to missionary
agendas and could itself be understood as a process of enculturation. The
Reformation churches and the missionary societies linked to them did
engage other cultures and found themselves changed in the process. In
1606 the Jesuit Robert de Nobili arrived in Madurai in South India and
set about learning the languages and religious traditions of the Brahmins.
His acculturation of Christianity to the Hindu upper caste conflicted with
the lower-caste Paravas, a Christian community that traced its history
to the earlier mission of Francis Xavier, but both missions were genuine
cultural engagements. The later Hindu reaction to the arrival of missionaries from different Reformation churches facilitated that engagement.
Since there were no words in Hindi or regional languages for confessional designations, missionaries were received simply as propagators of
another religion and tended to emphasize that they were Christians and
not Roman Catholics or Presbyterians. When Ziegenbalg was asked in
1708 who he was and what he was doing, he did not respond that he was
Lutheran but that he was a servant of the living God, the creator of heaven
and earth, who was sent to "warn you to leave the idols of your own
making and to turn to the worship of the true God."[64] The results of

confessionalization gave way to the Christianizing goal of the Reformation vision.

The recent growth of indigenous Christianity in southern Africa is being facilitated by a way of appropriating the faith that is not completely unlike the Reformation. In medieval Europe, Christianity was imposed on traditional cultures from the outside by constructing a unified ecclesiastical culture in the Latin language. The Christianization of Europe during the Reformation presented people with more adaptable, vernacular forms of the faith that resulted in new Christian confessions. These European confessions were then taken to Africa by their colonial hosts and introduced to the traditional cultures. They were often imposed from the outside, to be sure, but Christianity in Africa has also been assimilated from the inside out, that is, by a process through which Africans spontaneously recognized an affinity between their traditional religions and Christianity.[65] This recognition was facilitated by the translation of Christianity into the vernacular languages of Africa, in contrast to Islam, which has generally insisted upon the sacred nature of Arabic and its indispensability.[66]

Similar to the Reformation or not, Christianity in Africa had gained over 300 million adherents by the close of the twentieth century,[67] and largely because of that, it is becoming increasingly a non-Western religion.[68] Some of that non-Westernness is still closely connected to its roots in Reformation confessionalization, especially within Roman Catholicism and the worldwide communions of Lutheran, Reformed, and Anglican churches. But the global impact of the Reformation may recede if Christianity loses more and more of its conscious European heritage. Modern studies of Christian missions indicate that the notion of true Christianity changes with time, because the way in which converts adapt the faith to their culture expands what the elites (theologians, clergy, and missionaries) find tolerable.[69] That change happened in sixteenth-century Europe and, for the same reason, many indigenous forms of Christianity can no longer be tied to the Reformation traditions of colonialism. Outside Europe, Reformation Christianity in its different forms has undergone a transformation that is similar to the change that it brought to late-medieval religion within Europe. In the sixteenth century, Reformation confessions were the new indigenous churches of Europe, but now they are being altered as Christianity is replanted and redefined in other cultures around the world.

The Reformation's own sources state plainly how reformers saw their enterprise as a missionary campaign to renew and replant Christianity in

European culture. In the global perspective of five hundred years, the impact of this vision can now be better assessed. In the first place, the Reformation was only one stage in a process by which Christianity, a historical religion with no sacred homeland, was trying to embed itself in European culture. No pure Christianity is available apart from its cultural expressions, and the history of Christianity demonstrates how new cultural forms of the Christian religion, like the sixteenth-century confessions in Europe, have to formulate definitions of the faith in their own languages and cultural symbols. As a process in the history of Christianity, therefore, the Reformation was not unique, but its moment and the extent of its vision were exceptional. In the second place, because of colonial expansion, the influence of the Reformation extended far beyond Europe and should be evaluated in broader terms. Its long-term impact on Europe is only part of its legacy; the global impact of its vision should be given equal weight. The Reformation gave rise to the confessional forms in which Christianity was transmitted to much of the modern non-European world. That history is a complex story of aloofness, triumphalism, and engagement, but the Reformation has remained an important historical factor for half a millennium.

Islam and Judaism

In Europe the Reformation failed to advance the relationship between Christianity and non-Christian religions. Given the vision of a more Christian society, a different result was hardly to be expected. Although Protestants hoped the evangelical movement would lead to the conversion of both Jews and Muslims, they were disappointed. At times, in fact, reformers were afraid that European Christendom would lose ground to Islam and to Judaism. This fear was for the most part irrational, but it helps to explain the hostility that finally dominated their stance toward these religions. An intensive campaign of Christianization was not likely to improve relations with religions that had already suffered at the hands of medieval believers.

During the sixteenth century, Islam was more of a threat to European Christendom than was Judaism. The Ottoman Turks made several forays into central Europe during the reign of Suleiman the Magnificent (1520–1566).[70] In 1526 he marched against the Hungarians and shattered their army at Mohács. He then pushed on to Buda and Pest, before retreating down the Danube toward Belgrade and returning to Turkey, where there was pressure on the eastern frontier. In 1529 Suleiman's army returned to the Danube in support of John Zápolyai, a Turkish vassal who ruled the kingdom of Hungary, against Archduke Ferdinand of Austria, who coveted the same crown for the Hapsburgs. Suleiman headed straight for Vienna, but he was unable to take the city and had to retreat again down the Danube. Suleiman returned to Austria in 1532 and to Hungary in 1541 and 1543 in order to quash Ferdinand's claims once and for all. The dispute lasted until 1562, resulting in three Hungaries, two under Ottoman control and one Austrian buffer zone.[71] There was conflict in the Mediterranean as well until the Christian fleet won the Battle of Lepanto in 1571. With the conquest of Tunis in 1574, the Ottomans saved North Africa for Islamic rule, but in Europe the Turks were not able to penetrate completely the shield erected by Ferdinand.

Islam was never on the verge of overwhelming central and western Europe, but sixteenth-century people did not know that. In Germany Hapsburg propaganda exaggerated the Turkish threat in order to justify the claims of Archduke Ferdinand to the Hungarian throne. Protestant princes and cities benefited from publicizing the threat. They gained leverage for the Reformation because Emperor Charles V needed their money and troops for his defense against Suleiman. People in England were also urged to give money to the crown to replace the 40,000 ducats that King Henry VIII had sent to Charles for war against the Turks. The collection was disappointing, however, and suggested "that few English parishioners regarded the Turk as a tangible threat to their own corner of Christendom."[72] The Turkish advance was frightening to central Europeans nonetheless, because the conflict between the Hapsburg and Ottoman empires was cast as a war between Christendom and Islam and between Christ and Antichrist.[73]

This interpretation of the conflict was the work of theologians and pamphleteers who popularized the threat of Islam.[74] In his exposition of Daniel 7, the Wittenberger Justus Jonas argued that the Turkish empire was entirely opposed to God and that it was the duty of a Christian ruler to resist it.[75] Despite the shrill language, however, the attitude of reformers toward war with the Turk was cautious. Huldrych Zwingli received regular reports about the Turkish threat and how the pope and the emperor were planning to meet it.[76] Zwingli was suspicious of the pope's sincerity, however, and in 1530, as he was sketching his own plan for resistance to the emperor, Zwingli imagined the Turks and John Zápolyai as Protestant allies.[77] His successor in Zurich, Heinrich Bullinger, stayed well informed about later developments in Hungary and the conflict between Ferdinand and Suleiman. Erasmus's opposition to war in general led him to recommend that the Turks be conquered with piety rather than with weapons.[78] This stance strongly influenced the Zurich biblical scholar Theodor Bibliander, who published a book on the Turks and how "Christian people" should understand and respond to their advance (1542). Bibliander believed the Turks were an agent of God's wrath against the sins of Christendom and that the only proper response was repentance and rededication to a godly life.[79]

Much of what reformers knew about Islam was influenced by a normative tradition that they inherited from the Middle Ages.[80] Among sixteenth-century commentators, however, Bibliander was probably the best informed. In 1542 he revised and prepared for publication a Latin version of the Qur'an that originally dated from the twelfth century. Martin Luther urged the city council of Basel to allow it to be printed,[81] and both he and Philipp Melanchthon provided prefaces for the work.[82] Luther himself published several works on the Turks that appeared in two clusters corresponding to the high-water marks of the Ottoman advance: 1529–1530 and 1541–1543. In three of them he discussed the Christian response to the Turkish threat, and in the others, all prefaces, he compared Islam with Christianity.[83] These writings reflect the way in which the Reformation vision shaped the attitude of reformers toward Islam. This attitude had three components: (1) Islam was a form of idolatry that was incompatible with Christianity; (2) Muslim discipline and conduct sometimes excelled that of Christians and could teach them a lesson; (3) Christians should try to convert Muslims where they could. None of these attitudes originated in the Reformation, but they were all given new life by the campaigns to Christianize Europe.

1. Luther's analysis of Islam concluded that it was idolatry because it patched together Jewish, Christian, and pagan beliefs. The Turk allowed no article of faith to stand, he claimed, except the resurrection. Consequently, Islam had "no redeemer, savior or king; there is no forgiveness of sins, no grace, no Holy Ghost." Who would not rather be dead, he asked, than to live under a government where speech about Christ was forbidden and blasphemy and abomination were so plain?[84] There was obviously no place for Islam in Luther's Christianized Europe, but he did not advocate a crusade against the Turks. If the emperor, claimed Luther wryly, set about to destroy unbelievers and non-Christians, then "he would have to begin with the pope, bishop, and clergy, and perhaps not spare us or himself; for there is enough horrible idolatry in his own empire to make it unnecessary to fight the Turks for this reason. There are entirely too many Turks, Jews, heathen, and non-

Christians among us with open false doctrine and with offensive, shameful lives."[85] According to Luther, there was enough idolatry to occupy all the reformers without attacking Islam.

2. Although Luther regarded Islam as a religion of works righteousness, he expressed grudging admiration for the piety of the Turks and conjectured that their discipline would put any monk to shame.[86] The admiration was grudging because Luther also found much to criticize about the Muslim way of life: it had destroyed not only true faith but also true government and true marriage.[87] Despite this criticism, Luther found polemical use for the impressive ceremonies and self-discipline of the Turks: it should teach the papists "that the Christian religion [was] by far something other than good customs or good works. For this book shows that the Turks are far superior to our Christians in these things as well."[88] Luther hoped it would warn "our people" not to be so impressed with a religion of ceremonies that they would "deny Christ and follow Muhammad." It is doubtful that Luther saw Christian defections to Islam as a serious threat, but the Muslim respect for ritual served his agenda well in two ways. It provided a foil for criticizing medieval religion, and it reminded evangelical believers that, as important as they were, the essence of Christianity was deeper than proper rituals.

Other Protestants used Islam as a pedagogical tool. Sebastian Franck, an independent scholar, dissenter, and critic of Luther, published a late-medieval description of Turkish life and religion. Franck praised the morals of the Turks and believed they could teach Christians a lesson. He used Islam to needle Lutherans in particular. Although the Turks had works without faith, he said, Lutherans had faith without works and needed the example of the Turks as motivation to improve their conduct. Franck wished that leadership, discipline, and conduct in Germany were more like that of the Turks.[89] Thomas Müntzer took a radical theological approach. Although he did not accept them as Christian, he believed that Muslims had been granted the gift of the Holy Spirit and that they were spiritually equal to Christians in a universal church of the elect. Muslims and Christians had the same access to God through the order of nature, in which the Spirit of God was revealed; hence, they could exchange with one another their experiences of the Spirit and of divine revelation. In Müntzer's opinion, that exchange would convince Muslims that biblical prophecies of a purified and restored Christendom were true.[90] Contact with Islam thus served the agendas of both Müntzer and Franck. Although they paid some attention to Islam itself, they were more interested in the way it could benefit the new Christendom of the Reformation.

3. The effort to convert Muslims had strong precedents in the Middle Ages, when Islam was often regarded as a Christian heresy. The experience of missionaries like Ricoldo da Monte Croce indicated that conversion was almost impossible, but a sixteenth-century mission to the Turks was nonetheless supported by Erasmus, Luther, Bullinger, and Bibliander.[91] Luther's strategy was mainly restricted to the situation in which Christians were Turkish captives. In that case, he speculated that Christians might so impress their captors with their faithfulness, diligence, and patience that many Muslims might convert.[92] In his 1541 appeal for prayer against the Turk, Luther urged that children be taught the catechism so that, in case they were taken captive during an invasion, they might "at least take something of the Christian faith with them. Who knows what God might be able to accomplish through them?"[93] Erasmus asserted that the greatest victory for Christ over the Turks would be their conversion instead of their annihilation. The only pious and acceptable homicide would be to cut a Turk's throat in such a way that a Christian might come to life and to cast down the ungodly that the godly might arise.[94] Bibliander emphasized that God willed all peoples, including Muslims, to be saved but that time was growing short before the final judgment. He believed, nevertheless, that the gospel would soon appear in Arabic, and he was prepared to undertake his own missionary journey to the lands of Islam.[95]

The missionary consequence of the Reformation vision was easily applied, therefore, to Muslims as well as to Christians. It also embraced Jews.[96] In 1523, when Luther wrote *That Jesus Christ Was Born a Jew*, he hoped that many Jews would convert to Christianity or, as he put it, come "back to their own true faith."[97] This hope was part of Luther's perception that the Reformation was blanketing Germany with the unadulterated and attractive message of early Christianity. Although no coordinated drive to convert Jews ever developed in German lands, some clergy actively proselytized Jews well into the seventeenth century.[98] As late as the 1650s, Jews were being readmitted to England in part because Cromwell still shared the Protestant hope of converting them to Christianity.[99]

When significant conversions did not take place among Jews, however, reformers turned against them. Luther reproached the Jews harshly for their refusal to acknowledge Jesus as the Messiah, tried to refute their scriptural interpretation, and supported restrictions against contemporary Jewish communities.[100] He associated their resistance with the opposition of Turks and papists to the Reformation, and cast all three as agents of the Antichrist in the final assault against the renewal of Christian life. The greatest Christian Hebrew scholar of the sixteenth century, the Basel professor Sebastian Münster, had a similar reaction. He published almost sixty works of Hebraica, including a Hebrew translation of the Gospel of Matthew; but when Jews failed to convert to Christianity, Münster began to fear that Hebrew studies might gain too much influence and lead to the Judaization of Christianity.[101]

Luther's harsh criticism of the Jews was shared by other reformers, including Martin Bucer and John Eck. This criticism, like the hope for conversion, was facilitated by the assertive Christianizing agendas of the Reformation. They were able to make use of anti-Jewish propaganda delivered by converts from Judaism like Antonius Margaritha, whose book, *The Entire Jewish Faith* (1530), falsely charged that Jewish ritual was full of anti-Christian content.[102] Reformers who knew that Jews were being expelled from their homes failed to realize that a campaign to Christianize the continent would not attract a people who had long suffered at the hands of a triumphalistic Christendom. That reformers could have high expectations of conversion is striking testimony to their idealism; and their harsh rejection of the Jews, a reaction reminiscent of jilted suitors, points not only to bad information but to the vulnerability of their vision.

That same vision also explains why several reformers, notably Luther and Urbanus Rhegius, defended at length the Christian interpretation of messianic passages in books from the Hebrew Scriptures. This proof-texting by Christians was not new; a canon of such texts was already in existence and known to sixteenth-century theologians.[103] In the midst of an overwhelmingly Christian society, however, why would scholars spend so much time on this project? In *The Jews and Their Lies* (1543), the book in which Luther made notorious recommendations about contemporary Jews, 85 percent of the treatise was devoted to a defense of key messianic passages which, Luther alleged, the Jews had contradicted with their "lies."[104] In one of his most popular and novel works,[105] composed as a dialogue with his wife, Anna, Rhegius explained how a multitude of passages from the Old Testament pointed to the messianic identity of Jesus. Rhegius claimed to make explicit what Jesus allegedly did on the first Easter when, "beginning with Moses and all the prophets," he explained to the disciples on the road to Emmaus "the things about himself in all the scriptures" (Lk 24:27). Rhegius's interest in these texts was stimulated by his participation in several dialogues with rabbis.[106] Still, to invest so much energy in proving that Jesus was the Messiah indicates how intently and broadly reformers were pursuing the Christianizing of Europe; and it suggests how much their vision was threatened by the refusal of this ancient non-Christian community to help them succeed.

The Reformation arose in a culture that was already restricting and expelling Jews and that was feeling threatened by Islam. Although Catholic and Protestant reformers had hoped for their conversion, the Reformation eventually assumed a hostile stance toward both religions. This hostility was exacerbated by the Reformation campaign to Christianize Europe and by the disappointed expectations of reformers. Although attempts were made to renew the ancient conversation between Christians and Jews, neither this conversation nor the encounter with Islam benefited from the Reformation.

History and Theology

Although the Reformation failed to advance interreligious understanding, it did promote intense deliberation over the fundamental nature of Christianity. The theological disagreements to which the major confessions owed their origins still shape the identity of the churches and continue to be debated in ecumenical conversations. In some cases, however, the doctrines that are analyzed and debated have become separated from the pressing sixteenth-century issues which formed their historical context. To be sure, reformers debated questions like the operation of the sacraments, or the effect of religious performance on one's status before God, as academic issues in the terms bequeathed to them by medieval theology. Those academic debates arose, however, because of the contradictions between doctrine and practice, perceived first by Protestants, and the challenge presented by these contradictions to the core of Christianity as they identified it. Once Protestant and radical reformers decided that medieval religion needed to be Christianized, they were forced to develop coherent theological reasons for the changes they proposed.

Reformation theologies were born in this interaction between reform and reflection; that is, they were driven by the agendas of the reformers. Although the reformers' thought was shaped by the diversity of medieval theology, it is doubtful whether the differences between Luther and Eck or between Calvin and Menno can be traced mainly to the influence of conflicting scholastic traditions. Protestants set out to make changes to Christianity because they regarded both practice and the theology behind it as wrong. When Protestants insisted on changes that brought them into conflict with one another, they justified their positions with theological arguments based on conflicting interpretations of Scripture and backed up by appeals to early church theologians. Catholics defended traditional practices by invoking Scripture, early church theologians, canon law, and medieval theological authorities. Radicals generally abided by passages of Scripture that they considered prescriptive for the Christian life. Those theological arguments were gradually amplified and fashioned into coherent statements by the reformers in their writings, by confessions and conciliar decrees named above, and by the theologians of the late sixteenth and seventeenth centuries whom history has assigned to a period of orthodoxy because they produced systematic summaries and analyses of normative confessional statements. Throughout this process, theologians from all traditions insisted that they had identified the essence of Christianity and were attempting to preserve it.

Since Reformation theologies were based on scrutinizing the state of Christendom and shaped by the process of reform, they were intertwined with history from beginning to end. Reformers started with historical judgments that were reached by comparing Christianity as it was taught and practiced in late-medieval Europe with Christianity as they derived it from sources that they considered authoritative. The reformers of each tradition then decided what changes needed to be made, changes that were far less sweeping for Catholics than for Protestants and Radicals. Finally, they pressed for the urgent implementation of these changes because they believed the end of history was at hand. This historical perspective gave to Reformation theology as a whole distinctive features: its center was Christological; its shape was catechetical; and its horizon was eschatological.

To say that its center was Christological is not to make traditional doctrinal assertions about the two natures of Christ or a trinitarian conception of God. Reformers generally accepted these doctrines, although they were occasionally challenged by critics like Michael Servetus. To say theology was Christological means that reformers placed fresh emphasis on Jesus as the center and criterion of Christian faith. That emphasis on Christ was understood and applied differently by reformers, but Christology was important to most of them—outright humanists like Erasmus, mainline Protestants, Ignatius Loyola, and dissenters like Menno Simons and even Servetus. Ignatius was influenced by Ludolph of Saxony and Thomas à Kempis, medieval authors who paid direct attention to the life of Christ; but Protestant and Radical reformers considered medieval religion subchristian because the penitential system and the cult of the saints seemed to minimize the saving work of Christ. Protestants countered with the doctrine of justification by faith which meant that salvation came by the work of Christ alone. The way in which the saving work of Christ was mediated to believers became the hub of Reformation controversies, and reformers were forced to rethink the work of the Spirit, the sacraments, and the nature of the church. Encounters with Judaism and Islam exacerbated the need for that deliberation.

Deliberation was not enough, however. Reformers also wanted change. The significance of Jesus had to be taught in a way that moved people to conform their lives to his teaching more than medieval religion seemed to require. Reformation theologies, although known for their doctrines, were equally concerned about the impact of those doctrines, and they cast the faith in forms that made the transformation of lives inseparable from believing. The essence of Christianity was located in how one lived as well as in how one thought—even by Protestant theologians like Luther who are least known for stressing faith *and* love. Reformers differed over how Jesus caused this transformation—as example, as teacher, as mediator, or as the Spirit—but they were convinced that recapturing a Christological center was the way for their religion to change lives.

Reformers saw themselves in a missionary situation in which the faith had to be taught to a populace they judged to be inadequately informed. The shape of their theology became, therefore, catechetical. The basic doctrines and practices of Christianity had to be taught as a whole. For that reason Protestants and Catholics wrote hundreds of catechisms and preached sermons on their contents to children and adults alike.[107] Catechisms and catechetical sermons were well established prior to the Reformation, but reformers produced them in such numbers that their teachings and admonitions often reached the people in catechetical form. Protestant and Catholic catechisms used the Ten Commandments not only to teach reverence and morals but also to inculcate civil obedience in the subjects of German rulers.[108] Providing a catechism for the weekly noonday services in Geneva was a priority for John Calvin after he returned to Geneva in 1541.[109] Later he claimed he would not have accepted that call unless the Genevans had sworn to uphold both the catechism and the discipline. As he wrote the catechism, the completed pages were snatched out of his hand and taken immediately to the printer.[110] Calvin's *Institutes of the Christian Religion*, conceived as the foundation or basics of the Christian religion, fell into the same category. The subtitle of the original 1536 edition described their content as *Embracing Almost the Whole Sum of Piety, and Whatever Is Necessary to Know [of] the Doctrine of Salvation.* The purpose of the *Institutes* was catechetical: to provide a summary of the evangelical faith for the new Protestants in France.[111]

The translation of the Bible into languages of the people was also not unprecedented, but the missionary awareness of the Reformation and the appeals to scriptural authority made the translations crucial instruments for the agendas of Christianization. It was not coincidental that Martin Luther was translating the New Testament into German at the same time (1522) he was urging his colleagues in Wittenberg to preach the evangelical message in other cities.[112] After vehemently criticizing Luther's translation, the Catholic humanist scholar Jerome Emser prepared his own German New Testament, which was published in the year of his death (1527). The great English Bibles produced during the Reformation were intentional tools of evangelical reform, as were the Book of Common Prayer and the new liturgies produced on the continent. Protestants and dissenters were given access to the source of the doctrines and admonitions that had reshaped their religious lives, but this access also provided the basis of sharp disagreement among them because it was impossible for reformers to agree on what the Bible taught about controversial doctrines and how to follow its models of ministry, conduct, and worship. Vernacular translations were not the sole cause of the conflicts. Reformers also disagreed over how to interpret the Hebrew, Greek, and Latin versions that were also published. Disagreement did not impede production, however, but accelerated it. Many reformers published expositions of biblical books alongside collections of prayers and their own catechisms. Every preacher and pastor, it seemed, was equipped to become a teacher and a missionary.

Finally, the horizon of Reformation theology was eschatological. Signs of the end were everywhere: the bitter battles between Protestants and Catholics, the Peasants' War, the rise of false prophets like the Melchiorites who took over Münster, the martyrdom of believers on every side, the spread of the faith to distant lands, the resistance of Judaism and the advances of the Turks, confessional turncoats who seemed to be the devil at work. The true church had to be defended against all its enemies; true believers had to be consoled and given hope in their tribulation. Urbanus Rhegius justified almost every treatise he wrote with the need for comfort and endurance "during these last dangerous times." Explaining Psalm 15 in 1537 as a portrayal of the true church, Rhegius wrote: "It is necessary to know these things, especially now in these last times when people play such clever tricks with the sacred names Christian, Christendom, and Christian Church. Everyone wants to be the Christian Church even though they live in a way that is worse than Turks and pagans."[113]

Warnings that the end of the world was near made the improvement of life before the end and the stability of the churches more urgent. By the end of the Council of Trent (1563) and the death of Calvin (1564),

Catholic and Reformed Christians were well on the way to confessional consolidation despite the plight of believers in exile, wars of religion, martyrdom, and religious rivalry that continued to stoke eschatological fervor. Anabaptists had survived intense persecution and schisms in Mennonite and Hutterite communities. In England the Elizabethan settlement was fragile, and in Germany Lutherans were in conflict over the legacies of Luther and Melanchthon. In the midst of these uncertainties, reformers took refuge in the book of Revelation. In 1530, for example, Luther had already recommended Revelation for people who thought that no true Christians could be found. Revelation would teach them, he said, to see Christendom differently. It not only portrayed a time when the church seemed to be in greater danger, but it would also remind people that the statement "I believe in one holy Christian church" was an article of faith and that human reason would never be able to recognize the church even if it put on all the spectacles in the world.[114] Heinrich Bullinger preached a similar message in one hundred sermons on the book of Revelation delivered in the presence of Marian exiles in Zurich between 1554 and 1556. The faithful were to find comfort in the imminent victory of the crucified Christ that would justify their suffering and prove them right before all the world.[115] In these admonitions, the idealism of the early reformers was sustained and conveyed to their successors despite the setbacks they continued to face.

The Reformation was a missionary campaign that envisioned a renewed Christian society in Europe. That vision and the different agendas that sought to realize it resulted in the formation of confessional churches that changed the shape of Christianity and decisively influenced its expansion into other parts of the world. That result was not what early reformers expected. When they set out to recultivate the vineyard, they did not anticipate that it would be divided into so many competitive fields or that the harvest would be so uneven. Nevertheless, lingering disappointments were tempered by the expectation of a great harvest to come that they would not see but that would finally fulfill their vision. Christendom was the object of faith as well as a historical reality. By hoping for the transformation of hearts and minds, the reformers of early modern Europe were also hoping for a transformation of history, and if that transformation could not be accomplished in the present, then it would be completed, they believed, in an age yet to come.

Abbreviations

AHR	*American Historical Review*
ARG	*Archiv für Reformationsgeschichte*
CChr-SL	*Corpus Christianorum*, Series Latina
CH	*Church History: Studies in Christianity and Culture*
CHR	*Catholic Historical Review*
CR	*Corpus Reformatorum*
CWE	*Collected Works of Erasmus* (Toronto: University of Toronto Press, 1974–)
D-S	*Enchiridion symbolorum definitionum et declarationum de rebus fidei et morum*, ed. Henricus Denzinger and Adolfus Schönmetzer, 34th ed. (Freiburg: Herder, 1967)
EAS	*Erasmus of Rotterdam: Ausgewählte Schriften*, ed. Werner Welzig. 8 vols. (Darmstadt: Wissenschaftliche Buchgesellschaft, 1967–)
FC	*Fathers of the Church* (Washington, D.C.: Catholic University of America, 1947–)
JEH	*Journal of Ecclesiastical History*
LCC	Library of Christian Classics (London: SCM Press; Philadelphia: Westminster John Knox, 1953–1969)
LQ	*Lutheran Quarterly*
LuJ	*Lutherjahrbuch*
LW	*Luther's Works: American Edition*, ed. Helmut Lehmann and Jaroslav Pelikan, 55 vols. (Philadelphia: Fortress; St. Louis: Concordia, 1955–1986)
Mansi	Mansi, G. D. *Sacrorum conciliorum nova et amplissima collectio* (Florence: Expensis Antonii Zatta, 1761–1762; reprinted Graz, 1960–1961)
MPG	Migne, *Patrologiae cursus completus*, Series Graeca, ed. J.-P. Migne (Paris, 1857–1866)
MPL	Migne, *Patrologiae cursus completus*, Series Latina, ed. J.-P. Migne (Paris, 1844–1864)
MQR	*Mennonite Quarterly Review*
NRSV	*The HarperCollins Study Bible*, New Revised Standard Version, ed. W. A. Meeks et al. (New York: HarperCollins, 1993)

OER	*The Oxford Encyclopedia of the Reformation*, ed. Hans J. Hillerbrand, 4 vols. (New York and Oxford: Oxford University Press, 1996)
OS	*Joannis Calvini Opera Selecta*, ed. Peter Barth and Wilhelm Niesel, 5 vols. (Munich: Chr. Kaiser, 1926–1970)
SC	*Supplementa Calviniana* (Neukirchen: Neukirchener Verlag, 1961–)
SCJ	*The Sixteenth Century Journal*
StA	*Martin Luther Studienausgabe*, ed. Hans-Ulrich Delius, 6 vols. (Berlin: Evangelische Verlagsanstalt, 1979–1999)
TRE	*Theologische Realenzyclopädie*, ed. Gerhard Krause, Gerhard Müller, et al. (Berlin and New York: W. de Gruyter, 1977–)
Vulg.	*Biblia sacra iuxta vulgatam versionem*, ed. R. Weber et al., 2 vols. (Stuttgart: Württembergische Bibelanstalt, 1969)
WA	*D. Martin Luthers Werke: Kritische Gesamtausgabe*; Schriften, 69 vols. (Weimar: Böhlau, 1883–)
WABr	*D. Martin Luthers Werke: Kritische Gesamtausgabe*; Briefwechsel, 18 vols. (Weimar: Böhlau, 1930–1985)
WADB	*D. Martin Luthers Werke: Kritische Gesamtausgabe*; Deutsche Bibel, 12 vols. (Weimar: Böhlau, 1906–1961)
WATr	*D. Martin Luthers Werke: Kritische Gesamtausgabe*; Tischreden, 6 vols. (Weimar: Böhlau, 1912–1921)
ZKG	*Zeitschrift für Kirchengeschichte*

Notes

Introduction

1. See, e.g., Lindberg, *The European Reformations*.
2. Interesting local studies of medieval religion include Brentano, *A New World in a Small Place: Church and Religion in the Diocese of Rieti, 1188–1378*; French, *The People of the Parish: Community Life in a Late Medieval English Diocese*; Duffy, *The Voices of Morebath: Reformation and Rebellion in an English Village*.
3. For the importance of visual art to the Reformation, see Christensen, *Art and the Reformation in Germany*, and *Princes and Propaganda*; Scribner, *For the Sake of Simple Folk*; Matheson, *The Imaginative World of the Reformation*.
4. See the frontispiece to this volume. See also Lilienfein, *Lukas Cranach und seine Zeit*, illus. 25. The epitaph is portrayed in Junghans, *Martin Luther und Wittenberg*, 129, and in Junghans, *Spätmittelalter, Luthers Reformation, Kirche in Sachsen*, 260.
5. Lau, *Luther*, 81. See Junghans, "Plädoyer für 'Wildwuchs der Reformation' als Metapher (1998)," in Junghans, *Spätmittelalter, Luthers Reformation, Kirche in Sachsen*, 261–67.
6. For images of planting, watering, and growth in the humanist program of the Renaissance, see Horowitz, *Seeds of Virtue and Knowledge*.
7. Hamm, "Einheit und Vielfalt der Reformation—oder: was die Reformation zur Reformation machte," in Hamm, Moeller, and Wendebourg, *Reformationstheorien*, 127.
8. Chrisman, *Conflicting Visions of Reform*, 15.
9. Fasolt, "Europäische Geschichte, zweiter Akt: Die Reformation," 245–48.
10. Ibid., 247.
11. Gregory, *Salvation at Stake*, 10.
12. De Boer, "Calvin and Borromeo: A Comparative Approach to Social Discipline," 85: "Calvinism and Catholicism pursued like-minded efforts to impose social order and loyalty, but followed diverging paths to do so."
13. Historians also note the common sources that fed Catholic and Protestant piety in the late Reformation; see Brecht, "Der mittelalterliche (Pseudo-)Augustinismus als gemeinsame Wurzel katholischer und evangelischer Frömmigkeit."
14. Gregory, *Salvation at Stake*, 29.

Chapter 1: The Medieval Vision

1. Brown, *The Rise of Western Christendom: Triumph and Diversity, A.D. 200–1000*; Fletcher, *The Barbarian Conversion: From Paganism to Christianity*; MacMullen, *Christianity and Paganism in the Fourth to Eighth Centuries*.

2. Gregory of Tours, *History of the Franks*, 41. In sixteenth-century France, the baptism of Clovis and his religious leadership were important precedents for the Gallican tradition of asserting royal over papal authority; see Salmon, "Clovis and Constantine: The Uses of History in Sixteenth-Century Gallicanism."

3. For the conversion of Clovis, see Daly, "Clovis: How Barbaric, How Pagan?"; Spencer, "Dating the Baptism of Clovis 1886–1993"; Moorhead, "Clovis' Motives for Becoming a Catholic Christian."

4. Fletcher, *The Barbarian Conversion*, 507; Bartlett, *The Making of Europe*, 255.

5. Van Engen, "The Christian Middle Ages as an Historiographical Problem," 537.

6. Ibid., 552.

7. Dowden, *European Paganism*; Milis, ed., *The Pagan Middle Ages*; Jones and Pennick, *A History of Pagan Europe*.

8. *Christianity and Paganism, 350–750*, ed. Hillgarth, 170, 173.

9. *The Anglo-Saxon Missionaries in Germany*, ed. Talbot, 45.

10. Harmening, *Superstitio*, 49–75. Harmening identifies the sermons of Caesarius of Arles (d. 542) as a source of many pagan practices alleged in documents of the Middle Ages. For a broader discussion of sources, see Flint, *The Rise of Magic in Early Medieval Europe*, 36–58. Catalogues of "pagan" practices were sometimes based on literary sources and not on observation.

11. *The Anglo-Saxon Missionaries in Germany*, ed. Talbot, 46.

12. Ibid., 46–47.

13. Old, *The Reading and Preaching of the Scriptures*, 3:211–12.

14. Mary Alberi recommends the term magic in place of pagan ritual "so as not to disqualify as unchristian every modification or adaptation of these rituals and thus not to deny the legitimacy of medieval Christianity"; review of Milis, ed., *The Pagan Middle Ages*, in *CH* 68 (1999): 981. Cf. Flint, *The Rise of Magic in Early Medieval Europe*, 4, 7–9. For Wiesner-Hanks, all beliefs and practices through which cultures deal with supernatural forces are religious traditions and not "cults" or "magic"; *Gender in History*, 114.

15. Augustine, *In Iohannis evangelium* 61.2, in *CChr-SL* 36:481. For the early Luther, see WA 4:240.6–25, and for the later Luther, WA 43:428.30–429.7.

16. Peter Lombard, 3 *Sent.* d 23 c 4–5; Van Engen, "Faith as a Concept of Order in Medieval Christendom," 19–67.

17. Thomas Aquinas, *Summa theologiae* II-II, q. 2 a. 10: ". . . puta cum quis aut non haberet voluntatem, aut non habere promptam voluntatem ad credendum, nisi ratio humana induceretur. Et sic ratio humana inducta diminuit meritum fidei."

18. Oberman, *The Harvest of Medieval Theology*, 83–84.

19. Trompf, "The Concept of the Carolingian Renaissance." See Rosamond McKitterick, ed., *Carolingian Culture: Emulation and Innovation*; McKitterick, *Books, Scribes, and Learning in the Frankish Kingdoms, 6th–9th Centuries*.

20. Haskins, *The Renaissance of the Twelfth Century*; Constable, *The Reformation of the Twelfth Century*; Swanson, *The Twelfth-Century Renaissance*.

21. Moeller, "Piety in Germany around 1500"; Monter, "Popular Piety in Late Medieval Europe"; Van Engen, "The Church in the Fifteenth Century." For a comprehensive synthesis, see Swanson, *Religion and Devotion in Europe, c.1215–c.1515,* 311–42. For England, see Duffy, *The Stripping of the Altars.*
22. Huizinga's *Herfsttij der middeleeuwen* (1919) was first published in English as *The Waning of the Middle Ages* (London: E. Arnold, 1924). The title of a recent English translation is *The Autumn of the Middle Ages.* For earlier treatments of the fifteenth century in Germany and a plea that it be studied on its own terms apart from the Reformation, see Boockmann, "Das 15. Jahrhundert und die Reformation."
23. Huizinga, *The Autumn of the Middle Ages,* 203, 204.
24. Elm, "Antiklerikalismus im Deutschen Mittelalter."
25. Martin, *Mentalités médiévales, XIe–XVe siècle,* 217–58.
26. Ibid., 234.
27. Riley-Smith, *The First Crusaders, 1095–1131,* 149–53.
28. Donnelly and Maher, eds., *Confraternities and Catholic Reform in Italy, France, and Spain;* Terpstra, ed., *The Politics of Ritual Kinship: Confraternities and Social Order in Early Modern Italy.*
29. Martin, *Mentalités médiévales, XIe–XVe siècle,* 247.
30. Kamen, *Inquisition and Society in Spain in the Sixteenth and Seventeenth Centuries,* 199.
31. Boockmann, *Einführung in die Geschichte des Mittelalters,* 118.
32. E.g., Delumeau, *Sin and Fear.*
33. Le Roy Ladurie, *Montaillou,* viii.
34. Pegg, *The Corruption of* Angels, 92–103.
35. Ibid., 130.
36. Delumeau, *Sin and Fear,* 9–114.
37. Waldburg Wolfegg, *Venus and Mars: The World of the Medieval Housebook,* 34–35 (fol. 14r of the Housebook).
38. It was thus, e.g., in the diocese of Bath and Wells in England studied by French, *The People of the Parish.* Compare the lively portrait drawn for Morebath by Duffy, *The Voices of Morebath.*
39. It is possible to detect this evolution despite the fact that terms like superstition and paganism are notoriously vague. See MacMullen, *Christianizing the Roman Empire (A.D. 100–400),* 1–9, 78–79; Brown, *The Cult of the Saints,* 17–22.
40. Harmening, *Superstitio,* 43–44.
41. Thomas Aquinas, *Summa theologiae* II-II, q. 92 a. 2.
42. Augustine, *De doctrina christiana* 2.20.30, in *CChr-SL* 32:54. Thomas Aquinas, *Summa theologiae* II-II, q. 94 a. 4; q. 95 a. 4; q. 96 a. 1.
43. Thomas Aquinas, *Summa theologiae* II-II, q. 93 a. 2. Cf. the summary of his answer in q. 93 a. 2: "Ergo etiam in cultu divino potest esse superstitio ex aliqua superfluitate."
44. Brown, *The Rise of Western Christendom,* 297.
45. John of Damascus, *On the Divine Images,* 63–64.
46. Brown, *The Rise of Western Christendom,* 297.
47. Cameron, *The Reformation of the Heretics.*
48. This point is illustrated for the domains of daily life by Sautman (*La religion du quotidien,* 1): "Grossière erreur que d'envisager la culture populaire révolue comme un amas informe de 'superstitions' ou même comme un assemblage fortuit de 'pratiques.' Les gestes, les mythes qui les sous-tendent, appartiennent à une vision du monde selon

laquelle l'être humain bute constamment contre les exigences et les sollicitations du sacré."

49. *Adversus superstitionem in audiendo missam*, in *Jean Gerson: Oeuvres complètes*, 10:141–43 (no. 509).

50. *Jean Gerson: Oeuvres complètes*, 10:141.

51. Ibid., 10:142.

52. Ibid., 10:143.

53. *Contra superstitiosam dierum observantiam*, in *Jean Gerson: Oeuvres complètes*, 10:116–21 (no. 503).

54. *Jean Gerson: Oeuvres complètes*, 10:117.

55. Ibid., 10:119: "Vel secundo ex gentilium et paganorum et aliorum infidelium derelictione sicut in principio conversionis ad fidem frequenter inveniebatur."

56. Ibid., 10:120.

57. Burger, "Volksfrömmigkeit in Deutschland um 1500," 311–13.

58. Ibid., 322.

59. Ibid., 323–24.

60. Ibid., 321.

61. Hamm, "Wie Innovativ war die Reformation?" 10.

62. Seegets, *Passionstheologie und Passionsfrömmigkeit im ausgehenden Mittelalter*, 287–90.

63. Hamm, "Normative Centering in the Fifteenth and Sixteenth Centuries"; Hamm, *Frömmigkeitstheologie am Anfang des 16. Jahrhunderts*, 5, 132–216; Hamm, "Frömmigkeit als Gegenstand theologiegeschichtlicher Forschung"; Hamm, "Between Severity and Mercy."

64. Saak, *High Way to Heaven*, 351–68.

65. Hamm, "Wie Innovativ war die Reformation?" 14.

66. Denis the Carthusian, *De doctrina et regulis vitae christianorum libri duo*, Proemium, in *Opera Omnia*, 7:499. According to Wassermann, *Dionysius der Kartäuser*, 198–201, Denis cited long passages from a work entitled *De vita christiana*, which was attributed to Augustine but was in fact written by Pelagius. When citing this work and a few similar texts, Denis emphasized acts of mercy and charity more than he was wont to do. Normally, his view of the ideal Christian was more ascetic and called for the restraint of passion.

67. Denis the Carthusian, *De doctrina et regulis vitae christianorum* 1.1, in *Opera Omnia*, 7:504: "Itaque, sicut lex Christi cunctis legibus consistit perfectior, sic Christiani universis mundi hominibus virtuosiores, perfectiores magisque exemplares esse tenentur, et magis ordinati in omnibus intus et foris, in verbis et factis, in vestimentis, in cibo, potu, somno atque incessu, omnique usu rei creatae ac possessionis terrenae. Propterea venerabiles patres Cassianus et Climacus contestantur, illum esse indignum Christianum vocari, cuius conversatio, apparatus, mores, habitus et incessus non cogunt omnem etiam infidelem rite considerantem fateri, legislatorem illum qui talem instituit legem ac vitam, vere esse divinum, sapientem ac iustum."

68. Delaruelle, *La piété populaire au moyen age*, 411: "Ainsi le christianisme est la religion des bonnes oeuvres" and "Ce chrétien est d'abord un conformiste." According to Erwin Iserloh, a certain "externalization of religious life" was an immediate cause of the Reformation: Jedin, ed., *Handbuch der Kirchengeschichte* 4:6.

69. Jansen, *The Making of the Magdalen*, 203–44.

70. Burger, "Volksfrömmigkeit in Deutschland um 1500," 308, 326–27.

71. Winston-Allen, *Stories of the Rose*, 133–47.
72. Bossy, *Christianity in the West, 1400–1700*, 58, 62; Black, "The Development of Confraternity Studies over the Past Thirty Years," 25–29.
73. Rubin, *Corpus Christi*, 239.
74. Almazan, "The Pilgrim-Shell in Denmark."
75. Erasmus, "A Journey for Religion's Sake," in *Scheming Papists and Lutheran Fools*, 90.
76. Galpern, "The Legacy of Late Medieval Religion in Sixteenth-Century Champagne," 149; Gordon and Marshall, eds., *The Place of the Dead*, 3, 13.
77. Duffy, *The Stripping of the Altars*, 178.
78. Ibid., 8, 278.
79. Rubin, *Corpus Christi*, 164–76.
80. On Erasmus, see Auer, *Die vollkommene Frömmigkeit des Christen nach dem Enchiridion militis Christiani des Erasmus von Rotterdam*, 93.
81. Luther, *De libertate christiana* (1520), StA 2:298.39–300.5; *LW* 31:368.
82. Luther, *Von der Wiedertaufe an zwei Pfarrherrn* (1528), WA 26:147.13–15: "Wir bekennen aber, das unter dem Bapstum viel christliches gutes, ia alles Christlich gut sey, Und auch daselbs herkomen sey an uns."
83. Luther, *De libertate christiana* (1520), StA 2:296.13–17: "Vitam christianorum ab Apostolo in hanc regulam esse positam, ut omnia opera nostra ad aliorum comoditatem ordinentur, cum per fidem quisque suam sic abundet, ut omnia alia opera totaque vita ei superfluant, quibus proximo spontanea benevolentia serviat et benefaciat." *LW* 31:365–66.
84. Kavka, "Bohemia," 150–51; Fudge, *The Magnificent Ride*, 1–3.
85. Erika Rummel suggests that "the Reformation of the sixteenth century blended the voices of 'forerunners' in a manner that ultimately precludes an analysis into separate intellectual genealogies.'" Rummel, "Voices of Reform from Hus to Erasmus," 2:61.
86. See, e.g., Hendrix, "'We are all Hussites': Hus and Luther Revisited," and the earlier literature cited there.
87. Hus, *The Letters of John Hus*, 178.
88. An English translation of Delumeau's book appeared in 1977: Delumeau, *Catholicism between Luther and Voltaire*. A sixth edition of the French version has been published: Delumeau and Cottret, *Le Catholicisme entre Luther et Voltaire*, 1996.
89. Delumeau, *Catholicism between Luther and Voltaire*, 176.
90. Ibid., 161.
91. This negative picture has been criticized because it contrasts popular religion unfairly with a literate and enlightened Christianity that Delumeau presumably preferred. See Despland, "How Close Are We to Having a Full History of Christianity? The Work of Jean Delumeau"; and see the appraisal by John Bossy in the introduction to Delumeau, *Catholicism between Luther and Voltaire*, xiii–xviii.
92. For humanism in Wittenberg and Luther's place in it, see Junghans, "Martin Luthers Einfluss auf die Wittenberger Universitätsreform." See also Luther to John Lang, 18 May 1517, WABr 1:99.8–14; *LW* 48:42. It is true, as Leif Grane emphasized, that Luther came forward as a reformer of theology, not as a reformer of the church, and that theology remained important for his agenda. Nevertheless, as a reformer of theology Luther was also a reformer of piety. Grane, *Reformationsstudien*, 83–98.
93. Van Engen, "The Sayings of the Fathers: An Inside Look at the New Devout in Deventer," 293–94.

182   *Notes*

94. Elm, "Reform- und Observanzbestrebungen im spätmittelalterlichen Ordenswesen"; Elm, "Verfall und Erneuerung des Ordenwesens im Spätmittelalter"; Becker, "Benediktinische Reformbewegungen und klösterliches Bildungsstreben"; Ziegler, "Reformation und Klosterauflösung."
95. F. X. Martin, "The Augustinian Observant Movement."
96. See Neidiger, "Die Observanzbewegungen der Bettelorden in Südwestdeutschland."
97. On Eberlin and his contribution to the Reformation, see Dipple, *Antifraternalism and Anticlericalism in the German Reformation.*
98. Moeller, "Ambrosius Blarer als Alpirsbacher Mönch," in Moeller, *Luther-Rezeption,* 156–66.
99. Ziegler, "Reformation und Klosterauflösung," 588. For a summary of Augustinian reform, see Zschoch, *Klosterreform und monastische Spiritualität im 15. Jahrhundert,* 13–33. See also F. X. Martin, "The Augustinian Observant Movement," and Kunzelmann, *Die sächsisch-thüringische Provinz und die sächsische Reformkongregation.*
100. Dohna, "Von der Ordensreform zur Reformation: Johann von Staupitz."
101. Staupitz, *Tübinger Predigten* (1498), in *Sämtliche Schriften,* 1:315.366–316.372.
102. Steinmetz, *Luther and Staupitz,* 3–9, 30–34.
103. Dohna, "Von der Ordensreform zur Reformation," 579; Oberman, "'Tuus sum, salvum me fac': Augustinréveil zwischen Renaissance und Reformation."
104. Bowd, *Reform before the Reformation,* 103–22, and 233: "On balance, the continuities in reform thought and action between bishops and monks, clerics and laypeople, Lateran V and Trent, are more striking than the discontinuities."
105. Oecolampadius, letter to Beatus Rhenanus (?), February 1522, in *Briefe und Akten,* ed. Staehelin, 1:168 (no. 119); see Kuhr, *"Die Macht des Bannes und der Busse,"* 42.
106. Köpf, "Martin Luthers Lebensgang als Mönch"; Moeller, "Die frühe Reformation in Deutschland als neues Mönchtum," 80–82.
107. Luther, *Vorrede zum 1. Band der Wittenberger Ausgabe* (1539), WA 50:657–61; *LW* 34:283–88.
108. Luther, *Genesis-Vorlesung* (1535–1545), WA 42:441.15–21; 453.13–455.22; *LW* 2:251–53. WA 42:548.27–29: "[Abraham] habet uxorem, servos, ancillas, sed omnia haec habet, tanquam non habens, et est verus Monachus, contemnit enim vere voluptates, glorias, divitias mundi, et toto animo occupatur expectatione promissionis de Christo." *LW* 2:398.
109. Luther, *Das fünfte, sechste und siebente Kapitel Matthaei gepredigt und ausgelegt* (1532), WA 32:309.33–41; *LW* 21:3–6. See Schwarz, "Luthers unveräusserte Erbschaft an der monastischen Theologie," 219–22.
110. D. D. Martin, "The Via Moderna, Humanism, and the Hermeneutics of Late Medieval Monastic Life," 194.
111. Constable, *The Reformation of the Twelfth Century,* 3, 6, 7.
112. Cowdrey, *Popes and Church Reform in the 11th Century,* v, 33–54.
113. Howe, *Church Reform and Social Change,* xiv.
114. Ibid., 22 n. 57.
115. Constable, *The Reformation of the Twelfth Century,* 7.
116. See Van Engen, "The 'Crisis of Cenobitism' Reconsidered: Benedictine Monasticism in the Years 1050–1150."
117. Constable, *The Reformation of the Twelfth Century,* 138.
118. Saak, *High Way to Heaven,* 581–83, 722–35.

119. Ibid., 581.
120. Feld, "Konrad Summenhart: Theologe der kirchlichen Reform vor der Reformation," 102–3.
121. Bernard was appreciated by both Luther and Calvin. For Luther, see Lohse, "Luther und Bernhard von Clairvaux"; Bell, *Divus Bernhardus: Bernhard von Clairvaux in Martin Luthers Schriften*; Hendrix, "American Luther Research in the Twentieth Century," 9 n. 7. For Calvin, see Lane, *Calvin and Bernard of Clairvaux*.
122. D. D. Martin, "The Via Moderna, Humanism, and the Hermeneutics of Late Medieval Monastic Life," 190–96.
123. Zschoch, *Klosterreform und monastische Spiritualität im 15. Jahrhundert*, 243–44.
124. Moeller, "Die frühe Reformation in Deutschland als neues Mönchtum," 91. Cf. Johannes Schilling, *Gewesene Mönche*, 28: "So könnte man sagen, dass die Reformation sich selbst gleichsam als ein neues Mönchtum verstand oder doch so verstanden werden konnte."
125. Trinkaus, *"In Our Image and Likeness,"* 2:681.
126. Lauster, "Religion als Lebensform: Zur Erinnerung an Marsilio Ficinos Programm eines platonischen Christentums."
127. Trinkaus, *"In Our Image and Likeness,"* 1:12.
128. Ibid., 2:681.
129. Rummel, *The Confessionalization of Humanism*, 6–7.
130. After he died, Adelmann was described by Veit Bild as "Christianissimus Christianus" (cited by Thurnhofer, *Bernhard Adelmann von Adelmannsfelden*, 80 n. 2).
131. Erasmus, *The Education of a Christian Prince*, 83.
132. Adelmann to Pirckheimer, 7 August 1516, in Pirckheimer, *Willibald Pirckheimers Briefwechsel*, 3:22.5–11. See Thurnhofer, *Bernhard Adelmann von Adelmannsfelden*, 49.
133. Rublack, "Anticlericalism in German Reformation Pamphlets," 466.
134. Seidel Menchi, S., *Erasmus als Ketzer*, 143–44, 223–28, 235–40.
135. Erasmus, *The Education of a Christian Prince*, 21–22.
136. DeMolen, "Erasmus' Commitment to the Canons Regular of St. Augustine."
137. Erasmus to Servatius Rogerus, 8 July 1514, in *CWE* 2:297.88–93.
138. Erasmus to Paul Volz, 14 August 1518, in *CWE* 6:89.591–94. Cf. *Ausgewählte Werke*, ed. Holborn, 19.20–22. Witt, "The Humanist Movement," 2:118: "In an attack on the hierarchical conception of ways of life, Erasmus sought to bring the monastery into the world by insisting on the same level of Christian conduct for all believers."
139. Rummel, *"Monachatus non est pietas*: Interpretations and Misinterpretations of a Dictum." Cf. Auer, *Die vollkommene Frömmigkeit des Christen*, 81.
140. DeMolen, "The Interior Erasmus."
141. Erasmus, *The Handbook of the Christian Soldier* (1501), in *CWE* 66:127. Cf. *Ausgewählte Werke*, ed. Holborn, 135.8–13. Rummel, *"Monachatus non est pietas,"* 48–49: "Being a monk is not a guarantee of piety."
142. Rummel, *"Monachatus non est pietas,"* 51–52.
143. Erasmus, *The Handbook of the Christian Soldier* (1501), in *CWE* 66:62.
144. Walter, "Kirche und Kirchenreform nach Erasmus von Rotterdam," 142.
145. Erasmus, "A Journey for Religion's Sake" (1526), in Rummel, ed., *Scheming Papists and Lutheran Fools*, 93–94.
146. Erasmus to Albert of Brandenburg, 22 December 1517, in *CWE* 5:250.51–55. See Walter, "Kirche und Kirchenreform nach Erasmus von Rotterdam," 141.

Chapter 2: Martin Luther's Agenda

1. See below, note 8.
2. *Von beider Gestalt des Sakraments zu nehmen,* WA 10,2:11–41; *LW* 36:231–67.
3. *Acht Sermone D. M. Luthers* (1522), *StA* 2:534.12–24; *LW* 51:74.
4. Canon 21, in *D-S,* 264 (no. 812).
5. *Von beider Gestalt,* WA 10,2:24.16–21; *LW* 36:249.
6. Ibid., WA 10,2:22.16–19; *LW* 36:247.
7. Ibid., WA 10,2:24.14–16; *LW* 36:249.
8. Ibid., WA 10,2:39.1–13; *LW* 36:264.
9. Ibid., WA 10,2:39.14–17; *LW* 36:264.
10. Ibid., WA 10,2:39.17–21; *LW* 36:265.
11. *De libertate christiana* (1520), *StA* 2:302.23–27; *LW* 31:370.
12. *Von beider Gestalt,* WA 10,2:37.8–16; *LW* 36:262.
13. Ibid., WA 10,2:26.15–28.19; *LW* 36:251–53.
14. Ibid., WA 10,2:32.11–17; *LW* 36:257–58.
15. Ibid., WA 10,2:29.22–24; *LW* 36:254.
16. Ibid., WA 10,2:30.15–16; *LW* 36:255.
17. Ibid., WA 10,2:30.22–24; *LW* 36:256–57.
18. Ibid., WA 10,2:32.18–26; *LW* 36:258.
19. Ibid., WA 10,2:33.18–34.14; *LW* 36:259.
20. Ibid., WA 10,2:34.20–36.5; *LW* 36:260–61.
21. Ibid., WA 10,2:36.6–27; *LW* 36:261.
22. Ibid., WA 10,2:36.28–37.3; *LW* 36:262.
23. *De libertate christiana,* *StA* 2:264.17–18: "Christianus homo, omnium dominus est liberrimus, nulli subiectus. Christianus homo, omnium servus est officiosissimus omnibus subiectus." *LW* 31:344.
24. *An den christlichen Adel deutscher Nation von des christlichen Standes Besserung* (1520), *StA* 2:88–167; *LW* 44:115–217.
25. Ibid., *StA* 2:96.8–17; *LW* 44:123.
26. Ibid., *StA* 2:98.11: "der elenden Christenheit iamer vnd not." *LW* 44:126.
27. Ibid., *StA* 2:98.20–22; *LW* 44:126.
28. Ibid., *StA* 2:101.27–102.5: "Ists nit vnnaturlich / schweyg vnchristlich / das ein glid dem andern nit helffen / seinem vorterben nit weren sol? Ja yhe edler das glidmasz ist / yhe mehr die andern yhm helffen sollen. Drumb sag ich / die weil weltlich gewalt von got geordnet ist die boszen zu straffen / vnd die frumen zuschutzen / szo sol man yhr ampt lassen frey gehn vnuorhyndert durch den gantzen corper der Christenheit / niemants angesehen / sie treff Bapst / Bischoff / pfaffen / munch / Nonnen / odder was es ist." *LW* 44:130.
29. *An den christlichen Adel,* *StA* 2:99.19–31; *LW* 44:127.
30. If secularization specifically means declericalization, then this consolidation of clergy and laity into one Christian estate was secularization; but it was not secularization or secularism in the sense of de-christianizing public life or substituting nonreligious values for religious ones. See Headley, "Luther and the Problem of Secularization."
31. *An den christlichen Adel,* *StA* 2:125.18–21: "Ich wil nur angeregt vnd vrsach zugedencken geben haben / denen / die do mugen vnd geneygt sein / deutscher Nation zuhelffen /

widderumb Christen vnd frey werden / noch dem elenden / heydnischen vnd vnchristlichen regiment des Bapsts." *LW* 44:161.

32. *Von dem Papsttum zu Rom wider den hochberühmten Romanisten zu Leipzig* (1520), WA 6:285–324; *LW* 39:49–104. The terms "zu Rom" and "Romanisten" (the Leipzig Franciscan Augustine Alveld) were intentionally included in the title; they signaled that Luther would dispute the claim of the papacy that the church was bound to Rome.

33. *Von dem Papsttum zu Rom*, WA 6:293.1–5: "Diesz gemeyne odder samlung heysset aller der / die in rechtem glauben / hoffnung und lieb leben. Also das der Christenheyt wesen leben / und natur sey / nit leyplich vorsamlung / sondern ein vorsamlung der hertzen in einem glauben / wie Paulus sagt [Eph 4:4–6]. . . ." *LW* 39:65. Cf. *Crucigers Sommerpostille* (1544), [on Jn 10:12–16], WA 21:333.17–35. See Hendrix, "Luther and the Church."

34. *Von der Wiedertaufe an zwei Pfarrherrn*, WA 26:148.5–13; *LW* 40:232–33.

35. Grane, *Reformationsstudien: Beiträge zu Luther und zur dänischen Reformation*, 23–24; cf. Grane, *Modus loquendi theologicus*, 23–27.

36. Luther to John Lang, 18 May 1517, WABr 1:99.8–13; *LW* 48:42. Junghans, "Martin Luther's Einfluss auf die Wittenberger Universitätsreform." Specific changes to the faculty and to the curriculum were costly, however, and slow in coming; less than a year later Luther expressed concern that proposed reforms might not be carried out: Luther to Georg Spalatin, 11 March 1518, WABr 1:153.5–8.

37. Scheurl to Georg Spalatin, 17 December 1518, in *Christoph Scheurls Briefbuch*, 2:66 (no. 180).

38. For the way in which Luther's theology spoke to the crisis of late-medieval piety, see Lottes, "Luther und die Frömmigkeitskrise des Spätmittelalters."

39. *StA* 5:618–38; *LW* 34:325–38.

40. *StA* 5:635.17–637.14; *LW* 34:336–37.

41. *StA* 5:636.5–637.7; *LW* 34:337.

42. *Disputatio pro declaratione virtutis indulgentiarum* (1517): "Non christiana predicant: qui docent quod redempturis animas vel confessionalia non sit necessaria contritio" (no. 35), *StA* 1:180.1–2; *LW* 31:28.

43. "Quilibet christianus vere compunctus habet remissionem plenariam a pena et culpa etiam sine literis veniarum sibi debitam" (no. 36), *StA* 1:180.3–4; *LW* 31:28.

44. "Quilibet verus christianus sive vivus sive mortuus habet participationem omnium bonorum Christi et Ecclesie etiam sine literis veniarum a deo sibi datam" (no. 37), *StA* 1:180.5–8; *LW* 31:29.

45. "Docendi sunt christiani quod dans pauperi aut mutuans egenti melius facit quam si venias redimeret" (no. 43), *StA* 1:180.18–19; *LW* 31:29.

46. In theses 42–55, *StA* 1:180.16–181.19; *LW* 31:29–30.

47. From the Wartburg in 1522 Luther claimed that Psalm 10 showed "how the pope and his anti-Christian regime shall be destroyed"; *Eine treue Vermahnung M. Luthers zu allen Christen, sich zu hüten vor Aufruhr und Empörung*, *StA* 3:17.6–25; *LW* 45:60.

48. Adelmann to Pirckheimer, 19 December 1517, in *Willibald Pirckheimers Briefwechsel*, 3:247.28–31 (no. 501); 11 January 1518, 3:275.7–12 (no. 515).

49. *Die sieben Busspsalmen mit deutscher Auslegung* (1517), WA 1:158–220. In 1516 Luther had published an incomplete version of *A German Theology* with his own preface; WA 1:153.

50. *Ein Sermon vom Sakrament der Busse*, *StA* 1:247–57; *LW* 35:3–22. *Ein Sermon von dem heiligen hochwürdigen Sakrament der Taufe*, *StA* 1:259–69; *LW* 35:23–43. *Ein Sermon von*

dem hochwürdigen Sakrament des heiligen wahren Leichnams Christi und von den Bruder-schaften, StA 1:272–87; *LW* 35:45–73. *Ein Sermon von dem Neuen Testament, das ist von der heiligen Messe*, StA 1:291–311; *LW* 35:75–111.

51. Stolt, *Martin Luthers Rhetorik des Herzens*, 30.

52. *Eine kurze Form der zehn Gebote, des Glaubens, und des Vaterunsers*, WA 7:204–29. These sermons became the core of his popular *Betbüchlein*, first published in 1522: WA 10,2:375–501; *LW* 43:3–45.

53. Dannenbauer, *Luther als religiöser Volksschriftsteller 1517–1520*, 6, 30, 33; cf. Edwards, *Printing, Propaganda, and Martin Luther*.

54. *Decem praecepta Wittenbergensi praedicata populo* (1518), WA 1: 398–521. For the dating of the sermons and their relationship to the published text of *Decem Praecepta* (1518), see Rieske-Braun, *Glaube und Aberglaube*, 22–30.

55. *Decem Praecepta* (1518), WA 1:399.11–27.

56. Ibid., WA 1:401.1–411.10.

57. Ibid., WA 1:411.1–5. Haustein, *Martin Luthers Stellung zum Zauber- und Hexenwesen*, 32–67.

58. Haustein, *Martin Luthers Stellung zum Zauber- und Hexenwesen*, 174–75.

59. *Decem Praecepta* (1518), WA 1:411.11–20.

60. Ibid., WA 1:412.6–416.18.

61. Ibid., WA 1:416.37–39.

62. Ibid., WA 1:420.17–20.

63. Ibid., WA 1:420.28–30.

64. *Operationes in psalmos* (1519–1521), WA 5:455.37–456.3.

65. Ibid., WA 5:479.7–11.

66. Eire, *War against the Idols*.

67. *Das Magnificat verdeutscht und ausgelegt* (1521), StA 1:337.22–25: "Aber nw findt man wol etlich die bey yhr als bey einem got hulff vnd trost suchen / das ich besorg es sey abgot-terey itzt mehr in der welt / denn yhe geweszen ist." WA 7:570.5–7; *LW* 21:323–24.

68. *De votis monasticis iudicium* (1521), WA 8:583.20–22: "Ecce fundamentum monastico-rum votorum impietas, blasphemia, sacrilegium, atque haec contingunt, quod Chris-tum ducem et lucem spernentes, alia et meliora sequi praesumunt." *LW* 44:261.

69. *De votis monasticis iudicium* (1521), WA 8:599.33–36; 600.7–11; *LW* 44:287, 288.

70. *Vom Missbrauch der Messe*, WA 8:540.36–541.3; *LW* 36:202.

71. Ibid., WA 8:560.8–11; *LW* 36:225–26.

72. *Ein Sendbrief D. M. Luthers an . . . Barth. von Starhemberg*, 1 September 1524, WA 18:7.1–5: "Sonderlich aber byt ich E. G., wellet die vigilien und selmessen nachlassen, dann das ist zumal ain unchristlich ding, daz got hochlich erzürnt; zwar in den vigilien sycht man wol, das weder ernst noch glaub da ist sonder ain lautter unnutz gemürmel."

73. *Vorrede auf den Propheten Jesaja* (1528), StA 1:414.17–21; *LW* 35:275. For idolatry among Christians see the preface to *Die Propheten alle deutsch* (1532), WADB 11,1:2–15; *LW* 35:270–73.

74. *Vermahnung an die Geistlichen, versammelt auf dem Reichstag zu Augsburg* (1530), StA 4:332.10–12; *LW* 34:16.

75. Ibid., StA 4:334.15–18; *LW* 34:17.

76. Ibid., StA 4:377.5–385.18; *LW* 34:54–59.

77. *Genesis-Vorlesung* (1535–1545), WA 43:228.34–229.5; *LW* 4:130. When Benno was can-onized in 1524, Luther wrote against "the new idol and old devil" being raised up in

Meissen: *Wider den neuen Abgott und alten Teufel, der zu Meissen soll erhoben werden* (1524), WA 15:183–98.

78. *Genesis-Vorlesung* (1535–1545), WA 43:305.13–21; *LW* 4:236.
79. Melanchthon, "Gutachten für Valentin Vigelius" (1542), CR 7:876 (MBW no. 3119); see Wengert, "Luther and Melanchthon on Consecrated Communion Wine (Eisleben 1542–43)," 27.
80. Rhegius, *Formulae quaedam caute*, in *Preaching the Reformation*, 109.
81. Grane, *Reformationsstudien*, 169–70.
82. Brenz, "Election Day Sermon, 1543," in *Godly Magistrates and Church Order*, 138; Brecht, "Johannes Brenz und das Hexenwesen," 391–92; Bast, *Honor Your Fathers*, 210.
83. More, *Responsio ad Lutherum*, in *The Complete Works of Thomas More*, vol. 5, I:689–90.
84. *In epistolam S. Pauli ad Galatas commentarius, ex praelectione D. M. Lutheri collectus* (1531; 1535), WA 40,1:362–64; *LW* 26:229 (Gal 3:6).
85. *Von den guten Werken* (1520), StA 2:24.4–11; *LW* 44:30–31.
86. *Acta Augustana* (1518), WA 2:17.37–18.6. For the encounter with Cajetan, see Hendrix, *Luther and the Papacy*, 56–65.
87. See Laemmer, *Die vortridentinisch-katholische Theologie des Reformations-Zeitalters aus den Quellen dargestellt*, 88–95.
88. Eck, *Enchiridion of Commonplaces against Luther and Other Enemies of the Church*, 13.
89. Osiander, *Bericht über das Marburger Religionsgespräch* (1529), in *Gesamtausgabe*, 3:437.9–16; *LW* 38:70–71.
90. Martin Luther to Hans Luther, 21 November 1521, WA 8:575.28–29: "Itaque iam sum monachus et non monachus, nova creatura, non Papae, sed Christi"; 8:576.15–18: ". . . et tanta libertate me donarit, ut, cum omnium servum fecerit, nulli tamen subditus sim nisi sibi soli. Ipse enim est meus immediatus (quod vocant) Episcopus, Abbas, Prior, dominus, pater et magister. Alium non novi amplius." *LW* 48:335, 336.
91. Erikson, *Young Man Luther*; Hendrix, *Tradition and Authority in the Reformation*, XIII, 236–58; Hendrix, "Beyond Erikson: The Relational Luther."
92. Martin Luther to Hans Luther, 21 November 1521, WA 8:576.18–20; *LW* 48:336; Hendrix, *Tradition and Authority in the Reformation*, XIV, 48–63.
93. *Ein Brief an die Fürsten zu Sachsen von dem aufrührerischen Geist* (1524), WA 15:216.21–28; 215.25–28; *LW* 40:54, 55.
94. Luther to Philipp Melanchthon, 13 July 1521, WABr 2:359.112–15; *LW* 48:262.
95. Ibid., WABr 2:359.116–19; *LW* 48:262.
96. Moeller, "Was wurde in der Frühzeit der Reformation in den deutschen Städten gepredigt?" 185. For a challenge to Moeller's thesis, see Karant-Nunn, "What Was Preached in German Cities in the Early Years of the Reformation? *Wildwuchs* versus Lutheran Unity."
97. *An die Ratherren aller Städte deutschen Landes, dass sie christliche Schulen aufrichten und halten sollen* (1524), WA 15:32.1–14; *LW* 45:352–53.
98. Luther to Marguerite of Angoulême, 1540, WABr 9:301.32–36.
99. *Ein Sermon D. M. Luthers von dem guten Hirten* (1523), WA 12:540.8–15: "Also ist nun alles eyn kirch oder gemeyn, ein glaub, ein hoffnung, eyn liebe, eyn tauff etc. Das weret noch heut zu tage ymmer dar, bis auff den Juengsten tag. Darumb muest yhrs nicht also verstehen, das die gantz welt und alle menschen an Christum werden glewben, denn wyr mussen ymmer das heylig Creutz haben, das yhr das mehr teyl sind, die die Christen verfolgen. So musz man auch ymmer das Euangelion predigen, das man ymmer

ettlich hertzu bringe, das sie Christen werden, denn das reych Christi stehet ym werden, nicht ynn geschehen."

100. Kohler, *Martin Luther und der Festbrauch*, 8.
101. Muir, *Ritual in Early Modern Europe*, 185; cf. Karant-Nunn, *The Reformation of Ritual*, 4: "Few other events [like the Reformation] have permitted the invention of ritual anew."
102. Luther was likely acquainted with the *Celifodina* and the *Supplementum Celifodine* by Paltz, but he never mentioned them; see Fischer, "Paltz und Luther," 12–17. Luther did cite various works by Gerson and seems to have known several of them well; see Pannen, "Luther über Johannes Gerson," 121–22.
103. *LW* 53:147–309.
104. *Formula missae et communionis pro ecclesia* (1523), *StA* 1:369.6–28; *LW* 53:19–20.
105. Ibid., *StA* 1:379.21–23; *LW* 53:31.
106. *De libertate christiana* (1520), *StA* 2:304.39–307.34; *LW* 31:372–73.
107. *Deutsche Messe und Ordnung Gottesdiensts* (1526), WA 19:75.3–23; *LW* 53:63–64.
108. Junghans, "Luthers Gottesdienstreform—Konzept oder Verlegenheit?" 88–89.
109. Later Protestant piety was centered on feeling instead of action and ritual; see Molitor, "Frömmigkeit in Spätmittelalter und früher Neuzeit als historisch-methodisches Problem."
110. Holsten, "Reformation und Mission," 9–10.
111. Sparn, "Wahrlich, dieser ist ein frommer Mensch gewesen!" 458.
112. *Grund und Ursach aller Artikel* (1521), *StA* 2:333.10–15: "Das alszo ditz leben nit ist / ein frumkeit / szondern ein frumb werden / nit ein gesuntheit szondernn eyn gesunt werdenn / nit eyn weszen sunderen ein werden / nit ein ruge szondernn eyn vbunge / wyr seyns noch nit / wyr werdens aber. Es ist noch nit gethan vnnd geschehenn / es ist aber ym gang vnnd schwanck. Es ist nit das end / es ist aber der weg / es gluwet vnd glintzt noch nit alles / es fegt sich aber allesz." *LW* 32:24.
113. Wunder, "iusticia, Teutonice fromkeyt."
114. Ibid., 328–29; Sparn, "Wahrlich, dieser ist ein frommer Mensch gewesen!" 461–62.
115. Wengert, "Philip Melanchthon and a Christian Politics," 41.
116. Luther to Philipp Melanchthon, 13 July 1521, WABr 2:357.32–359.107, esp. 358.88–92; *LW* 48:258–62.
117. *Von weltlicher Oberkeit wie weit man ihr Gehorsam schuldig sei* (1523), *StA* 3:40.16–21; *LW* 45:91.
118. Luther sharply criticized the restriction of Mt 5–7 to the monastic life: *Das fünfte, sechste und siebente Kapitel Matthaei gepredigt und ausgelegt* (1532), WA 32:301.17–27; *LW* 21:5.
119. *Von weltlicher Oberkeit* (1523), *StA* 3:48.32–49.4: "Vnd sey du gewiss / das disse lere Christi nicht eyn radt fur die volkomen sey / wie vnsser Sophisten lestern vnd liegen / sondern eyn gemeyn strengs gepott fur alle Christen. Das du wissest / wie die altzumal heyden sind vnter Christlichem namen / die sich rechen odder fur gericht vmb yhr guott vnd ehre rechten vnd zancken / Da wirt nicht anders auss / das sag ich dyr. Vnd kere dich nicht an die menge / vnd gemeynen brauch / Denn es sind wenig Christen auff erden / da zweyffel du nicht an / datzu sso ist Gottis wortt ettwas anders denn gemeyner brauch." *LW* 45:101–2.
120. See, e.g., Estes, "Erasmus, Melanchthon, and the Office of Christian Magistrate."
121. Cameron, "The Search for Luther's Place in the Reformation," 482.
122. *Vom ehelichen Leben* (1522), WA 10,2:283.8–16; *LW* 45:25.
123. Ibid., WA 10,2:288.10–22; *LW* 45:31.

124. *Bedenken über Bordelle* (1539), WABr 12:295.2–296.10: "Erstlich ist hie ein underscheid zu machen, ob eine herrschafft oder Volck auch wolle oder gedencke, sich für Christen oder Gottes Volck zu halten und zu halten lassen, oder ob sie Heiden sein und heissen wollen. Wollen sie Heiden sein und heissen, Christum und Gott sampt den Christlichen namen verleucken und abtretten, mügen sie wol nicht eines, sondern wie viel sie wollen Frawen heuser zulassen, auffrichten, auch drinnen leben und wonen, wo sie es ja so sehr gelüstet. Wollen sie aber Christen heissen und unter Gottes Namen sein, als die ihn angehören und selig zu werden gedencken, sind sie schüldig, bei ihrer Seelen seligkeit solche heuser nicht zu leiden . . ."

125. *Vom ehelichen Leben* (1522), WA 10,2:292.22–23; *LW* 45:36.

126. Ibid., WA 10,2:295.27–296.2; *LW* 45:39.

127. Harrington, *Reordering Marriage and Society in Reformation Germany*, 47, 271. Cf. Hendrix, "Luther on Marriage."

128. Rieth, "Luther on Greed," 338; Rieth, *"Habsucht" bei Martin Luther*, 156–58.

129. *Von Kaufhandlung und Wucher* (1524), WA 15:300.26–304.23; *LW* 45:255–61.

130. Ibid., WA 15:302.9–29; *LW* 45:257–58.

131. *Sermon von dem Wucher* (1520), WA 6:40.2–7; *LW* 45:278–79.

132. *An die Ratherren aller Städte deutschen Landes* (1524), WA 15:30.12–16; *LW* 45:350.

133. Ibid., WA 15:44.11–23; *LW* 45:367–68.

134. *Ordenung eyns gemeynen kastens: Radschlag wie die geystlichen gutter zu handeln sind* (1523), WA 12:13.20–30; 15.8–15; 24.25–25.29; *LW* 45:173, 175–76, 188.

135. Luther to Wenceslas Link, 20 June 1543, WABr 10:335.14–17; *LW* 50:242.

136. WATr 1:294.19–23 (no. 624); *LW* 54:110.

137. For example, Niebuhr, *Christ and Culture*, 217: "More than Luther, he [Calvin] looks for the present permeation of all life by the Gospel."

138. *Sermo de duplici iustitia* (1519), StA 1:225.15–33; *LW* 31:302–3.

139. Eck, *Enchiridion of Commonplaces against Luther and Other Enemies of the Church*, 50–56.

140. Erasmus, *De libero arbitrio Diatribe* (1524) Ia 8, in *EAS* 4:10–12; *LW* 33:30–32 n. 27.

141. *De servo arbitrio* (1525), StA 3:186.24–29: "Sed illud magis est intolerabile, quod caussam hanc liberi arbitrii inter ea numeras, quae sunt inutilia et non necessaria, Et loco eius nobis recenses, quae ad pietatem Christianam satis esse iudices, qualem formam certe describeret facile quilibet Iudaeus aut gentilis Christi prorsus ignarus, nam Christi ne uno quidem iota mentionem facis, ac si sentias, Christianam pietatem sine Christo esse posse . . ." *LW* 33:31.

142. Erasmus, *Hyperaspistes*, in *EAS* 4:294–96; *LW* 33:30–32 n. 27.

143. *De servo arbitrio* (1525), StA 3:189.15–18; *LW* 33:30, 35.

144. Ibid., StA 3:186.28–30: "Oportet igitur certissimam distinctionem habere, inter virtutem Dei et nostram, inter opus Dei et nostrum, si volumus pie vivere." *LW* 33:35.

145. Mehlhausen, *"Forma Christianismi*: Die theologische Bewertung eines kleinen katechetischen Lehrstücks durch Luther und Erasmus von Rotterdam," 72–73.

146. *De libero arbitrio Diatribe* (1524) Ia 10, in *EAS* 4:18.

147. Edwards, *Luther's Last Battles*, 113–14.

Chapter 3: The Urban Agenda

1. Moeller, *Imperial Cities and the Reformation*, 39–115. For the relationship of the urban reformation to the Reformed confessional churches, see Moeller, "Die Ursprünge der reformierten Kirche."

2. Moeller, *Reichsstadt und Reformation*, 69–97; cf. Hamm, "The Urban Reformation in the Holy Roman Empire." For the complexity of the Zwinglian Reformation, see Brecht, "Was war Zwinglianismus?"
3. Oberman, "*Europa afflicta*: The Reformation of the Refugees."
4. For a different view of Bullinger and the clergy in Zurich that emphasizes their independent voice, see Biel, *Doorkeepers at the House of Righteousness*.
5. Oberman, "*Europa afflicta*," 99.
6. Ibid., 102.
7. "Refugee events" were spawned by urban reform outside Calvin's sphere of influence, in Augsburg for example, throughout the sixteenth century; Tyler, "Refugees and Reform," 96.
8. Oberman, *Die Reformation: Von Wittenberg nach Genf*, 244–48. Zwingli's first biographer, Oswald Myconius (d. 1552), justified Zwingli's support of Protestant alliances by giving the largest possible scope to his religious agenda: "because in accordance with the course once begun he had resolved to eradicate vices and to establish the evangelical doctrines to the praise of God and the advantage of all Switzerland, [not] because he aimed at protecting the things of God in this way, but because he desired nothing more than that all nations might confess the Lord, and that the extent of the alliance might terrify the minds of the ungodly, and so more easily win them to Christ"; *Ulrich Zwingli, Early Writings*, 19–20. Cf. Myconius, *Vom Leben und Sterben Huldrych Zwinglis*, ed. Rusch, 66–67.
9. Mühling, *Heinrich Bullingers europäische Kirchenpolitik*, 276–77.
10. Bucer, *De Regno Christi* (1550), preface to book 1; *The Kingdom of Christ*, in *Melanchthon and Bucer*, 175–76; *Martini Buceri opera latina*, 15,1:2–3.
11. Gäbler, *Huldrych Zwingli*, 52.
12. Zwingli, *Von Erkiesen und Freiheit der Speisen*, CR 88:74–136; *Ulrich Zwingli, Early Writings*, 70–112.
13. Ibid., CR 88:101.28–29; *Ulrich Zwingli, Early Writings*, 82.
14. Rogge, *Anfänge der Reformation: Der junge Luther 1483–1521 / Der junge Zwingli 1484–1523*, 274; Gäbler, *Huldrych Zwingli*, 49–51. At the beginning of the *Sixty-seven Articles* (1523), Zwingli claims that he had preached their content "in the worthy city of Zurich as based upon the Scriptures"; *Ulrich Zwingli (1484–1531): Selected Works*, 111.
15. Schneider, "Zwinglis Marienpredigt und Luthers Magnifikat-Auslegung," 106–8.
16. Fast, "Reformation durch Provokation," 80–85. Most of the interruptions occurred later in 1522, or in 1523. On Grebel's involvement, see Goertz, *Konrad Grebel*, 45–46.
17. Fast, "Reformation durch Provokation," 85–86.
18. Stahl, *Die lutherische Kirche und die Union*, 11–45.
19. Ibid., 30–31.
20. Locher, *Huldrych Zwingli in neuer Sicht*, 11.
21. Ibid., 269; Gäbler, *Huldrych Zwingli*, 67.
22. *Ulrich Zwingli: Early Writings*, 9; Myconius, *Vom Leben und Sterben Huldrych Zwinglis*, ed. Rusch, 48, 49.
23. Locher, *Huldrych Zwingli in neuer Sicht*, 18.
24. Büsser, *Die Prophezei*, 15.
25. Junghans, *Der junge Luther und die Humanisten*, 9; Spitz, "Luther and Humanism," 88–89; Junghans, "Martin Luthers Einfluss auf die Wittenberger Universitätsreform." Mauer, *Der junge Melanchthon zwischen Humanismus und Reformation*, vol. 1, *Der Humanist*.

26. Hamm, *Zwinglis Reformation der Freiheit*, 134–35.

27. Ibid., 43–44.

28. Verkamp, "The Zwinglians and Adiaphorism," 495: "But to have called for such positive harmonization of church structures with Scripture did not necessarily mean that the Zwinglians were any less adiaphoristic in their thinking than other of the 'magisterial' reformers."

29. Hamm, *Zwinglis Reformation der Freiheit*, 53: "Gerade an dieser Stelle aber stehen Zwingli und Luther bemerkenswert nahe beieinander."

30. *De vera et falsa religione commentarius*, CR 90:705.7–11; *Commentary on True and False Religion*, 135.

31. *Ein göttlich vermanung* (1522), CR 88:170.22–23; *Ulrich Zwingli, Early Writings*, 135: "The people of our time, who do not recognize the fact that God has deserted us on account of our sins, are almost not to be counted, so numerous are they."

32. CR 88:59.201–24; *Ulrich Zwingli: Early Writings*, 54.

33. *De vera et falsa religione commentarius*, CR 90:630.33–35; *Commentary on True and False Religion*, 47.

34. *De vera et falsa religione commentarius*, CR 90:630.4–14; *Commentary on True and False Religion*, 46. On this text, see Sallmann, *Zwischen Gott und Mensch*, 8–10.

35. Hamm, *Zwinglis Reformation der Freiheit*, 72.

36. *Von Erkiesen et Freiheit der Speisen*, CR 88:97.28–33; *Ulrich Zwingli: Early Writings*, 79.

37. Ibid., CR 88:105.26–30; *Ulrich Zwingli: Early Writings*, 86.

38. Ibid., CR 88:97.3–4; *Ulrich Zwingli: Early Writings*, 78.

39. Ibid., CR 88:107.2–5; *Ulrich Zwingli: Early Writings*, 87.

40. *De vera et falsa religione commentarius*, CR 90:674.20–24; *Commentary on True and False Religion*, 97–98.

41. *Ein göttlich vermanung* (1522), CR 88:169.5–12; *Ulrich Zwingli: Early Writings*, 133.

42. Ibid., CR 88:169.20–23; *Ulrich Zwingli: Early Writings*, 134.

43. *Supplicatio . . . ad R. D. Hugonem episcopum Constantiensem* (1522), CR 90:203.13–19; *Ulrich Zwingli: Early Writings*, 159.

44. *Luther's and Zwingli's Propositions for Debate*, ed. Meyer, 36–41 (articles 1–16).

45. *Vorschlag wegen der Bilder und der Messe* (1524), CR 91:129.20–130.1. On idolatry in the thought of Zwingli and Bullinger, see Eire, *War against the Idols*, 76–88.

46. *Vorschlag wegen der Bilder und der Messe*, CR 91:130.11–13. For the larger implications of this statement, see Wandel, "The Reform of the Images"; cf. Wandel, *Always among Us: Images of the Poor in Zwingli's Zurich*.

47. *De vera et falsa religione commentarius*, CR 90:901.33–36: "Hac enim ratione distinguuntur unius ac veri dei cultores ab idololatris, quod nos deum colimus, qui invisibilis est, quique vetat, ne se ulla visibili figura exprimamus; isti autem deos suos qualibet specie induunt"; *Commentary on True and False Religion*, 332–33.

48. *Eine Antwort Valentin Compar gegeben* (1525), CR 91:89.12–14: "Daruss yetz volget, dass, welche by einer creatur, wer joch dieselb sye, suchend, das sy by dem einigen gott sol gesucht werden, nit ware glöubigen noch Christen sind."

49. Ibid., CR 91:108.23–113.19.

50. Ibid., CR 91:93.1: "Das ist eim yeden ein got, zu dem er in synem anligen loufft."

51. Luther, *The Large Catechism*, in *The Book of Concord*, 386, ¶2.

52. Ibid., 388, ¶21.

53. *Das Marburger Religionsgespräch 1529*, 69–70.

54. *De vera et falsa religione commentarius, CR* 90:774.32–775.1; *Commentary on True and False Religion,* 199. Stephens, "Zwingli and the Salvation of the Gentiles," 238: "Underlying this [sacramental] controversy is the fundamental opposition in Zwingli's theology to idolatry, that is, putting one's trust in the creature rather than the creator."

55. Zwingli, *Eine klare Unterrichtung vom Nachtmal Christi* (1526), *CR* 91:857.17–858.1; "On the Lord's Supper" (1526), in *Zwingli and Bullinger,* 234: "[Christ] himself instituted a remembrance of that deliverance by which he redeemed the whole world, that we might never forget that for our sakes he exposed his body to the ignominy of death, and not merely that we might not forget it in our hearts, but that we might publicly attest it with praise and thanksgiving, joining together for the greater magnifying and proclaiming of the matter in the eating and drinking of the sacrament of his sacred passion, which is a representation of Christ's giving of his body and shedding of his blood for our sakes."

56. Rott and Lienhard, "Die Anfänge der evangelischen Predigt in Strassburg."

57. For a vivid account of this preaching, see McKee, *Katharina Schütz Zell,* 1:31–40; cf. Stafford, *Domesticating the Clergy,* 12–46.

58. McKee, *Katharina Schütz Zell,* 1:40.

59. Stierle, *Capito als Humanist,* 33–54, 192–93.

60. Rott, "Die 'Gartner,' der Rat, und das Thomaskapitel."

61. McKee, *Katharina Schütz Zell,* 1:47–49.

62. Ibid., 1:64.

63. Bucer to Odile de Berckheim, 28 April 1524, in *Correspondance de Martin Bucer,* 1:237–45.

64. McKee, *Katharina Schütz Zell,* 1:54–55; Selderhuis, *Marriage and Divorce in the Thought of Martin Bucer,* 128–31.

65. Selderhuis, *Marriage and Divorce in the Thought of Martin Bucer,* 123–28.

66. *Das ym selbs niemant, sonder anderen leben soll, und wie der mensch dahyn kummen mög* (1523), in *Martin Bucers Deutsche Schriften,* 1:29–68.

67. Gäumann, *Reich Christi und Obrigkeit,* 53.

68. Bucer to Odile de Berckheim, 28 April 1524, in *Correspondance de Martin Bucer,* 1:239.48–57.

69. *Convents Confront the Reformation,* ed. and trans. Skocir and Wiesner-Hanks, 29. On Bernard Rem and the reform of convents in Augsburg, see Roper, *The Holy Household,* 232–33.

70. *Convents Confront the Reformation,* 33.

71. Wiesner-Hanks, "Ideology Meets the Empire," 51–52.

72. Brady, *Protestant Politics: Jacob Sturm (1489–1553) and the German Reformation,* 68–89.

73. Abray, *The People's Reformation,* 65.

74. Burnett, *The Yoke of Christ,* 1.

75. *Martin Bucers Deutsche Schriften,* 5:392.1–8 (article 14).

76. Ibid., 5:392.9–18 (article 15).

77. Lienhard, "Glaube und Skepsis im 16. Jahrhundert."

78. *Martin Bucers Deutsche Schriften,* 5:37.4–38.19.

79. Burnett, *The Yoke of Christ,* 105–6. Bucer also argued for penance because it had been required in early Christianity: *Von der wahren Seelsorge,* in *Martin Bucers Deutsche Schriften,* 7:162.20–21.

80. Burnett, *The Yoke of Christ,* 100. Cf. the petition of the Strasbourg clergy to the council: *Aufforderung der Strassburger Prediger an den Rat, endlich die Synodalbeschlüsse zu fassen*

[1534], in *Martin Bucers Deutsche Schriften*, 5:505.7–9: "Der päpstlichen oberenn hat man sich entzogen vnnd will auch kein christliche zucht gedulden. Darauss mag nichts guts kommen."

81. Burnett, *The Yoke of Christ*, 187.

82. Hammann, "Ecclesiological Motifs behind the Creation of the 'Christlichen Gemein-schaften.'"

83. Hammann, *Entre la secte et la cité*, 360–61.

84. *Ordenung der Christlichen Kirchenn zucht, für die Kirchen im Fürstenthumb Hessen* (1539), in *Die evangelischen Kirchenordnungen des XVI. Jahrhunderts*, 8,1:101–12.

85. Neuser, "Bucers Programm einer 'guten leidlichen Reformation' (1539–1541)."

86. Burnett, *The Yoke of Christ*, 143–62.

87. MacCulloch, *Thomas Cranmer: A Life*, 422.

88. Gäumann, *Reich Christi und Obrigkeit*, 131 n. 1.

89. Bucer, *De Regno Christi* (1550) 2.5, in *Melanchthon and Bucer*, 272, 273; *Martini Buceri opera latina*, 15,1:105–6.

90. Ibid., 2.7, in *Melanchthon and Bucer*, 277–78; *Martini Buceri opera latina*, 15,1:111.

91. Ibid., 2.4, in *Melanchthon and Bucer*, 269; *Martini Buceri opera latina*, 15,1:102–3.

92. Ibid., 2.5, in *Melanchthon and Bucer*, 273; *Martini Buceri opera latina*, 15,1:107.

93. Ibid., 2.7, in *Melanchthon and Bucer*, 278; *Martini Buceri opera latina*, 15,1:111–12.

94. Selderhuis, *Marriage and Divorce in the Thought of Martin Bucer*, 257–326.

95. Lienhard, "Glaube und Skepsis im 16. Jahrhundert," 161: "Ihm ging es nicht so sehr um das Heil des einzelnen und um die Frage des angefochtenen Gewissens als um die Errichtung eines christlichen Gemeinwesens unter Gottes Wort und zu Gottes Ehre."

96. Kohls, "Martin Bucer, 'Martinien,'" 197.

97. Holsten, "Reformation und Mission."

98. Ibid., 5.

99. Wendel, *Calvin*, 59.

100. Cottret, *Calvin: A Biography*, 120.

101. Preface to *Commentary on the Psalms* (1557), in *John Calvin: Selections from His Writings*, 28; CR 59:25–26.

102. Cottret, *Calvin: A Biography*, 138.

103. *Institutio Christianae religionis*, Prefatory Address, OS 3:9.6–11; LCC 20:9.

104. *Institutio*, John Calvin to the Reader (1559), OS 3:6.28–30; LCC 20:4. For the develop-ment of Calvin's prefaces to the *Institutes* and a rhetorical analysis of their context, see Jones, *Calvin and the Rhetoric of Piety*, 50–69.

105. Oberman, "*Initia Calvini*: The Matrix of Calvin's Reformation," 153.

106. Ibid., 154.

107. *Responsio ad Sadoletum* (1539), OS 1:475; *John Calvin: Selections from His Writings*, 102.

108. Kingdon, "The Genevan Revolution in Public Worship," 265.

109. Calvin, *Traité des reliques* (1543), in *La vraie piété*, 164; cf. "An Admonition Showing the Advantages Which Christendom Might Derive from an Inventory of Relics," in *Tracts Relating to the Reformation*, 1:291. For Calvin's attack on idolatry, see Eire, *War against the Idols*, 195–233.

110. *Registers of the Consistory of Geneva in the Time of Calvin*, 1:xxvii.

111. Ibid.

112. *Institutio* III.6.4, OS 4:149.13–15; LCC 20:687. Cf. Calvin, *Sermons sur le livre de Michée* (1550–1551), SC 5:163.13–15; *Documents on the Continental Reformation*, 53.

113. Calvin, *Sermon où il est montré quelle doit être la modestie des femmes en leurs habillements*, 19. On Calvin's campaign against luxury in Geneva and its classical sources, see Battles, "Against Luxury and License in Geneva: A Forgotten Fragment of Calvin."

114. Calvin, *Sermon où il est montré quelle doit être la modestie des femmes en leurs habillements*, 21–23 (italics mine).

115. *Institutio* III.6.4, *OS* 4:149.23–32; LCC 20:688.

116. Steinmetz, "Calvin and the Monastic Ideal."

117. *Institutio* III.7.2, *OS* 4:152.15–19; LCC 20:691.

118. *Institutio* IV.12.1, *OS* 5:212.24–26; LCC 21:1230. Cf. Calvin, *Responsio ad Sadoletum*, *OS* 1:479; *John Calvin: Selections from His Writings*, 107.

119. *Institutio* IV.12.5, *OS* 5:215.12–20; LCC 21:1232.

120. *Les ordonnances ecclesiastiques*, *OS* 2:358.19–20; *John Calvin: Selections from His Writings*, 241.

121. *Registres de la Compagnie des Pasteurs de Genève au temps de Calvin*, 1:29; *CR* 38,1:49–50.

122. *Registers of the Consistory of Geneva in the Time of Calvin*, 1: xx. See Lambert, "Preaching, Praying and Policing the Reform in Sixteenth-Century Geneva," 402–79.

123. For a more thorough treatment of this material, see Hendrix, "The Reform of Marriage in Calvin's Geneva."

124. *Ordonnances sur les mariages faictes par l'aucthorité de Messieurs*, in *Registres de la Compagnie des Pasteurs de Genève*, 1:33.

125. *Registres de la Compagnie des Pasteurs de Genève*, 1:137.

126. Kingdon, *Adultery and Divorce in Calvin's Geneva*, 176.

127. Ibid., 71–97, 143–65.

128. *Registres de la Compagnie des Pasteurs de Genève*, 1:138–40.

129. Calvin to Socinus, 7 December 1549, *CR* 41:485; "Four Letters from the Socinus-Calvin Correspondence (1549)," 228.

130. *Registers of the Consistory of Geneva in the Time of Calvin*, 1:46–47, and note 194.

131. Knox to Mrs. Locke, 9 December 1556, in *The Works of John Knox*, 4:240.

132. *Sermones in Acta Apostolorum*, *SC* 8:116.3–4.

133. *SC* 5:163; *Documents on the Continental Reformation*, 53–54.

134. *OS* 2:402.19–22; *John Calvin: Selections from His Writings*, 42.

135. Cottret, *Calvin: A Biography*, 220–21.

136. Reid, ed., *John Calvin: His Influence in the Western World*; Duke, Lewis, and Pettegree, ed., *Calvinism in Europe 1540–1610*; Graham, ed., *Later Calvinism: International Perspectives*.

137. Oberman, "*Europa afflicta*," 107–9.

138. Wilcox, "The Lectures of John Calvin and the Nature of His Audience, 1555–1564"; cf. Jones, *Calvin and the Rhetoric of Piety*, 62–69.

139. Berger, *Calvins Geschichtsauffassung*, 118–19, 184–85.

140. *De Necessitate Reformandae Ecclesiae*, in *Tracts Relating to the Reformation*, 1:200; *CR* 34:510–11.

141. Ibid., in *Tracts Relating to the Reformation*, 1:200–201; *CR* 34:511.

Chapter 4: The Radical Agendas

1. Estes, "*Officium principis christiani*: Erasmus and the Origins of the Protestant State Church." Cf. Estes, "Melanchthon's Confrontation with the 'Erasmian' *Via media* in Politics: The *De officio principum* of 1539."

2. Oehmig, "'Christliche Bürger'—'christliche Stadt'?" Bubenheimer, "Andreas Bodenstein von Karlstadt und seine fränkische Heimat," 47 (Letter of Karlstadt to Hektor
   Pömer, 27 March 1522).
3. Williams, *The Radical Reformation*, 1st ed., xxiv.
4. Ibid., xxv.
5. Ibid., xxv.
6. Vogler, "Gab es eine radikale Reformation?" 498.
7. Williams, "The Radical Reformation Revisited." Noting that the term "Reformation"
   was appropriate because "the Radicals regarded themselves as participants in the main
   movement and the expectancy of their age" (17–18), Williams also argued for "Radical
   Reformation" because "there is substantial data indicating that many participants in the
   Radical Reformation were in personal contact with each other through confrontations,
   colloquy, dialogue, and correspondence" (18).
8. Williams, *The Radical Reformation*, 3rd ed., 9: "Although the congeries of disparate ethical, societary, and theological radicals of various impulses and aspirations was surely no
   more homogeneous in their theology, sacramental usage, and conceptualization of the
   new currents, agitating them all alike, than the Magisterial Reformers, . . . still they may
   be grouped together as an entity, as *the* Radical Reformation, insofar as in the end, if not
   at once, they or their successors in their congregations, sects, conventicles, fellowships,
   communes, and synodal churches for a number of reasons became detached from the
   primary Magisterial Reformation motif of territorial reform of all the institutions in a
   given civil jurisdiction, whether city-state or national kingdom, and would come to
   appreciate and then defend their separation from the state and the state-supported
   ecclesiastical institutions—parish churches, cathedrals, schools, and the patronage of
   magistrates of various titles and authority, from landlord to Emperor. . . ."
9. For an older statement of early Reformation coherence, see Fast, "The Dependence of
   the First Anabaptists on Luther, Erasmus, and Zwingli."
10. Stayer, *Anabaptists and the Sword*, 337: "The mistake of those who would regard early
    Anabaptism as fundamentally violent is to miss the basic apoliticism of the movement.
    The mistake of those who say that all 'true' Anabaptists are non-resistant is that they
    miss the movement's inherent illegitimacy and radicalism, which is in some cases compatible with violence." See Stayer, *The German Peasants' War and Anabaptist Community
    of Goods*, 61–92.
11. Goertz, *Religiöse Bewegungen in der frühen Neuzeit*, 62–63.
12. Seebass, "Der 'linke Flügel der Reformation,'" 160: "Es scheint mir eines der
    wesentlichen Ergebnisse der neueren Forschung, dass die Vertreter des linken Flügels
    keineswegs von Anfang an auf die Bildung separierter Gemeinden drängten, sondern
    dass sie im Gegenteil, wenn auch in unterschiedlicher Weise, eine Christianisierung der
    Gesamtgesellschaft anstrebten."
13. Deppermann, "The Anabaptists and the State Churches," 105.
14. *Auslegung des anderen Unterschieds Danielis*, in *Schriften und Briefe*, 246.24–26: "Wan
    dieselbige [die forcht Gotis] allein in uns gantz und reyne vorsorget würde, dann so
    möchte die heylge christenheit leychtlich wider zum geist der weissheit und offenbarung götlichs willens kummen." Cf. Williams, *The Radical Reformation*, 16. Bernhard
    Rothmann entitled his treatise: *Eine Restitution oder eine Wiederherstellung der rechten und
    gesunden christlichen Lehre*, in *Flugschriften vom Bauernkrieg zum Täuferreich (1526–1535)*,
    2:1120–42.

15. *Auslegung des anderen Unterschieds Danielis*, in *Schriften und Briefe*, 255.20–22: "Dann so die christenheit nicht solt apostolisch werden, Act. 27 [Acts 2:17–21], do Johel [Joel 2:28–32] vorgetragen wirt, warumb solt man predigen? Wozu dienet dann die biblien von gesichten?"

16. "Thomas Müntzer's *Protestation* and *Imaginary Faith*," 125.

17. Ibid., 114–15, 125–26.

18. Friesen, *Thomas Müntzer*, 170; Bräuer, "Thomas Müntzers Kirchenverständnis vor seiner Allstedter Zeit," 115. For the text of the *Prague Manifesto*, see *The Radical Reformation*, 1–10.

19. Friesen, *Thomas Müntzer*, 194–98.

20. Schwarz, *Die apokalyptische Theologie Thomas Müntzers und der Taboriten*, 62–86.

21. Friesen, *Thomas Müntzer*, 252–59.

22. For a comparison of Müntzer's views with proposals for social renewal along the Upper Rhine in 1524 and 1525, see Fauth, "Verfassungs- und Rechtsvorstellungen im Bauernkrieg 1524/25."

23. "The Twelve Articles," in Blickle, *The Revolution of 1525*, 198, 200–201.

24. Blickle, *The Revolution of 1525*, 97–104.

25. Luther, *Ermahnung zum Frieden auf die zwölf Artikel der Bauernschaft in Schwaben* (1525), WA 18:292.24–30; *LW* 46:17–18.

26. Blickle, *Communal Reformation*, 50; cf. Seebass, *Artikelbrief, Bundesordnung und Verfassungsentwurf*, 44–46.

27. Luther, *Ermahnung zum Frieden*, WA 18:313.35–314.23; *LW* 46:31.

28. Ibid., WA 18:312.23–27; *LW* 46:30. WA 18:315.29–32; *LW* 46:32.

29. *The Schleitheim Articles*, in *The Radical Reformation*, 172, 173; cf. *Brüderliche Vereinigung* (also *Schleitheimer Artikel*, 24 February 1527), in *Quellen zur Geschichte der Täufer in der Schweiz*, 2:27–28.

30. *The Schleitheim Articles*, in *The Radical Reformation*, 175–76.

31. Zschoch, "Das Recht der Mächtigen und die Macht der Gerechten."

32. *Spiritual and Anabaptist Writers*, 44.

33. Goertz, *Konrad Grebel*, 111.

34. Packull, *Hutterite Beginnings*, 42–45.

35. Seebass, *Artikelbrief*, 177–79.

36. Hut, *Von dem geheimnus der tauf, baide des zaichens und des wesens*, in *Glaubenszeugnisse oberdeutscher Taufgesinnte* 1:15: "Dise ordnung muez gehalten werden, soll anderst ein rechte christenheit angericht werden, und solte die ganz welt darob zerbrechen." Cf. *Ein Sendbrief Hans Huts, eines einst vornehmen Vorstehers im Wiedertäuferorden, widerlegt durch Urbanus Rhegius*, in *Flugschriften vom Bauernkrieg zum Täuferreich (1526–1535)*, 1:858.6–10: "Dieweyl der allmechtig ewig Got unser getrewer vater, in diser letsten und aller gefärlichsten zeyt, die verwüsten und zerbrochnen kirchen, sein aynige gespons widerumb auffbawet, die so lang unfruchtbar gewesst, yetz aber an allen orten kinder gebirt zum erkantnus warhafftiger lieb und glaubens, durch krafft des heyligen geysts. . . ." See Seebass, "Das Zeichen der Erwählten."

37. Packull, *Hutterite Beginnings*, 58.

38. Ibid., 229.

39. Ibid., 106–19.

40. Boyd, *Pilgram Marpeck*, 111–12.

41. Ibid., 157.

42. Boyd, "Marpeck, Pilgram," in *OER* 3:15–17.
43. Deppermann, *Melchior Hoffman*, 178–86.
44. Hoffman, "The Ordinance of God," in *Spiritual and Anabaptist Writers*, 186.
45. Ibid., 188.
46. Deppermann, *Melchior Hoffman*, 275.
47. Ibid., 284–89. Believers' baptism was equated with the sealing of 144,000 in Rev 7:3.
48. Haude, *In the Shadow of "Savage Wolves,"* 16–26.
49. Packull, *Hutterite Beginnings*, 11.
50. Seebass, "Der 'linke Flügel der Reformation,'" 158; Weigelt, *Sebastian Franck und die lutherische Reformation*, 21–23.
51. Denck, *Vom Gesetz Gottes, wie das Gesetz aufgehoben sei und doch erfüllt werden muss* (1526), in *The Radical Reformation*, 131; *Flugschriften vom Bauernkrieg zum Täuferreich (1526–1535)*, 1:646.38–647.1. The ethical message of Ludwig Hätzer's Augsburg pamphlet, *Von den evangelischen Zechen / Von der Rede der Christen* (1525), is summarized by Goeters, *Ludwig Hätzer*, 57–61.
52. Rhegius, *Wider den newen Tauforden* (1527), in *Flugschriften vom Bauernkrieg zum Täuferreich (1526–1535)*, 2:1184.30–33.
53. Zschoch, "Gehorsamschristentum: Die 'göttliche und gründliche Offenbarung' des Augsburger Täuferführers Jakob Dachser." Cf. Dachser, *Eine göttliche und gründliche Offenbarung von den wahrhaftigen Wiedertäufern mit göttlicher Wahrheit angezeigt*, in *Flugschriften vom Bauernkrieg zum Täuferreich*, 1:772–97.
54. Rhegius, *Wider den newen Tauforden*, in *Flugschriften vom Bauernkrieg zum Täuferreich*, 2:1185.19–30.
55. Ibid., 2:1185.33–37. On the Anabaptist critique of Rhegius's ministry, see Grieser, "Anabaptism, Anticlericalism, and the Creation of a Protestant Clergy."
56. Rhegius, *Wider den newen Tauforden*, in *Flugschriften vom Bauernkrieg zum Täuferreich*, 2:1186.10–17: "Wa aber diser widertauffer vermainte, es sey keiner gebessert, oder ein christ, wenn er noch schwach ist, er müsse gantz volkommen sein, so beweysst er aber ein mal sein unwissenheyt inn götlicher schrifft, darynn wir lernen, das unser leben noch nicht ein ruw, sondern ein stetter fürzug ist auss Egypten, das wir in glauben, liebe, und hoffnung von tag zu tag müssen zunemen und bitten, das Gottes will geschech, seyn reych zukomme, sünd verzygen werd."
57. Ibid., 2:1188.37–1189.1: "Nun lieber widertauffer, kindestu ermessen was ein Christenmensch wer, unnd wie hin und wider Gottes kinder seind unnder dem grossen hauffen der unglaubigen vermischt geleych als rosen under den dörnen, die noch zu streyten haben mit blut und fleysch, so hetstu dein frevenlichs urtayl lassen anston."
58. Ibid., 2:1189.12–16.
59. Ibid., 2:1175.3–9.
60. Deppermann, *Melchior Hoffman*, 305–31. On Menno and Münster, see Voolstra, *Menno Simons*, 88–99; Stayer, *Anabaptists and the Sword*, 309–28.
61. "Foundation of Christian Doctrine" in *The Complete Writings of Menno Simons*, 121; *Dat Fundament des christelycken Leers*, 40. Reformers would have agreed with Menno's indictment of medieval piety as "consisting only in an outward appearance and human righteousness, such as hypocritical fastings, pilgrimages, praying and reading lots of Pater Nosters and Ave Marias, hearing frequent masses, going to confessionals and like hypocrisies"; *Complete Writings*, 111; *Dat Fundament*, 17.

62. "Foundation of Christian Doctrine," in *Complete Writings*, 106; *Dat Fundament*, 5. Voolstra, *Menno Simons*, 95: "If Menno had succeeded in finding a local or regional authority which could have implemented a reformation in the Anabaptist style—and the chance of this was quite real in East Friesland for some time—then this would not have been in conflict with his theology." Cf. Stayer, *Anabaptists and the Sword*, 318: "Menno represents the original Melchiorite teaching on the Sword in a more radical development. He never worked out a political ethic which completely separated Christians from the maintenance of the natural order of society."

63. Voolstra, "Themes in the Early Theology of Menno Simons," 49–50.

64. Peters, "The Ban in the Writings of Menno Simons."

65. Blok, "Discipleship in Menno Simons' *Dat Fundament*: An Exercise in Anabaptist Theology," 115–16.

66. Goertz, "Der fremde Menno Simons: Antiklerikale Argumentation im Werk eines melchioritischen Täufers," 36–37.

67. Bugenhagen, *Der Ehrbaren Stadt Hamburg Christliche Ordnung 1529*, 105.

68. Ibid.

69. Ibid., 107.

70. Simons, "On the Ban: Questions and Answers by Menno Simons," in *Spiritual and Anabaptist Writers*, 269.

71. Rhegius, *Wider den newen Tauforden*, in *Flugschriften vom Bauernkrieg zum Täuferreich*, 2:1190.18–21: "Was hilffts denn, das sich die widertauffer vast reyssen, von aussen ein zichtiges geystlichs leben anzurichten und inwendig noch keyn ernst vorhanden ist? Nichts hülfft es, ein newe müncherey würt darauss, die vil einfeltiger leüt mit falschem schein verfürt."

72. Luther, *Genesis-Vorlesung* (1535–1545), WA 42:494.35–38. Cf. *Apology of the Augsburg Confession*, XXVII.47–50, in *The Book of Concord*, 285.

73. Zwingli, *Refutation of the Tricks of the Catabaptists*, 1527, in *Ulrich Zwingli (1484–1531): Selected Works*, 197.

74. Friedman, *The Most Ancient Testimony*, 68.

75. Servetus, *Dialogues on the Trinity*, in *The Two Treatises of Servetus on the Trinity*, 189.

76. Ibid., 210.

77. Ibid., 216.

78. Ibid., xi.

79. Estes, "Melanchthon's Confrontation with the 'Erasmian' *Via media* in Politics," 90.

80. Guggisberg, *Sebastian Castellio*, 27–29, 38–41.

81. Ibid., *Sebastian Castellio*, 87.

82. Castellio, *De haereticis an sint persequendi* . . . (Basel: Oporinus, 1554).

83. Guggisberg, *Sebastian Castellio*, 89–91.

84. Hirsch, "Luther, Calvin, and the Doctrine of Tolerance of Sebastian Castellio," 637.

85. Guggisberg, *Sebastian Castellio*, 93–97.

86. Guggisberg, *Sebastian Castellio*, 169.

87. Blickle, *Communal Reformation*, 193: "The critical mass was reached around 1525, and thereafter the communal reformation turned into the reformation of the princes."

88. Stayer, "The Passing of the Radical Moment in the Radical Reformation," 148–49; Williams, *Radical Reformation*, 3rd ed., 1063–78, 1190–91.

89. See Blickle, *Die Reformation im Reich*, 36–37, 157–60; Blickle, *Communal Reformation*, 120–45; Blickle, "Politische Weiterungen der reformatorischen Theologie: Die Antwort des Gemeinen Mannes."

90. *Dass eine Christliche Versammlung oder Gemeine Recht und Macht habe, alle Lehre zu urteilen und Lehrer zu berufen, ein- und abzusetzen. Grund und Ursach aus der Schrift* (1523), WA 11:408–16; *LW* 39:301–14.
91. Hendrix, "Luther and the Church." Similar arguments can be made for the ecclesiology of the "city reformers," whose vision extended beyond their local communities.
92. Stayer, "Passing of the Radical Moment," 148.

Chapter 5: The Catholic Agenda

1. Bowd, *Reform before the Reformation*, 136–38.
2. O'Malley, *Trent and All That*, 18.
3. They followed the lead of Veit Ludwig von Seckendorff (d. 1692); see O'Malley, *Trent and All That*, 18–19.
4. O'Malley, *Trent and All That*, 20
5. Von Ranke, *Deutsche Geschichte im Zeitalter der Reformation.*
6. Ritter, *Deutsche Geschichte im Zeitalter der Gegenreformation und des Dreissigjährigen Krieges, 1555–1648.*
7. Jedin, "Katholische Reformation oder Gegenreformation" (1946).
8. Evennett, *The Spirit of the Counter-Reformation*, 24. For sources that sustain Evennett's judgment, see *The Catholic Reformation: Savonarola to Ignatius Loyola.*
9. Evennett, *The Spirit of the Counter-Reformation*, 124.
10. Hoffman, *Church and Community in the Diocese of Lyon, 1500–1789.*
11. Hsia, *The World of Catholic Renewal 1540–1770.*
12. Bireley, *The Refashioning of Catholicism, 1450–1700.*
13. Reinhard, "Reformation, Counter-Reformation, and the Early Modern State: A Reassessment," 105–28; cf. Reinhard, "Was ist katholische Konfessionalisierung?"
14. O'Malley, *Trent and All That*, 8, 140–43.
15. Bireley, *The Refashioning of Catholicism, 1450–1700*, 2.
16. Delumeau, *Catholicism between Luther and Voltaire*, 176.
17. Duffy, *The Stripping of the Altars*, 8, 278.
18. Delumeau, *Catholicism between Luther and Voltaire*, xvii.
19. De Boer, *The Conquest of the Soul*, 298–302.
20. Catharinus, *Apologia pro veritate catholicae et apostolicae fidei ac doctrinae*, in *Corpus Catholicorum* 27:159.17–20: "Sic et christianus vulgo aequivoce dicitur pro christiano simpliciter, qui baptismi sit caractere insignitus, et pro eo, qui christiane vivat et, ut ait Hieronymus, qui paratus sit mori pro Christo."
21. Delumeau, *Catholicism between Luther and Voltaire*, 161.
22. Ibid., 167, 177–78.
23. Châtellier, *The Religion of the Poor*, 108–17.
24. Poska, *Regulating the People*, 160–61.
25. Forster, *The Counter-Reformation in the Villages*, 8–9.
26. Nalle, *God in La Mancha*, 209–10.
27. Haliczer, *Sexuality in the Confessional*, 22–41.
28. Bellarmine, *Disputationes . . . de controversiis christianae fidei*, IV, 3:1027–30.
29. Donnelly, "The New Religious Orders, 1517–1648," 2:285.
30. *Canons and Decrees of the Council of Trent*, 220, 488. On the impact of this decree, see Dinan, "Confraternities as a Venue for Female Activism during the Catholic Reformation," 192–97.
31. Donnelly, "The New Religious Orders, 1517–1648," 2:301–2.

32. Dinan, "Confraternities as a Venue for Female Activism during the Catholic Reformation," 208.
33. Donnelly, "The New Religious Orders, 1517–1648," 2:303–4.
34. Ignatius of Loyola, *The "Spiritual Exercises" and Selected Works*, 109.
35. Ibid., 41–42; O'Malley, *The First Jesuits*, 34.
36. O'Malley, *Religious Culture in the Sixteenth Century: Preaching, Rhetoric, Spirituality, and Reform*, XII, 182.
37. Pope Paul III, *Regimini militantis* (27 September 1540), in *Quellen zur Geschichte des Papsttums und des Römischen Katholizismus*, 1:540.
38. O'Malley, *The First Jesuits*, 5–6.
39. O'Malley, *The First Jesuits*, 6.
40. Ignatius of Loyola, *The "Spiritual Exercises" and Selected Works*, 121.
41. Ibid., 160.
42. Ibid., 147, 155–56; O'Malley, *The First Jesuits*, 45.
43. Ignatius of Loyola, *The "Spiritual Exercises" and Selected Works*, 148.
44. Ibid., 154.
45. Ibid., 211–12.
46. O'Malley, *The First Jesuits*, 49.
47. Ignatius of Loyola, *The "Spiritual Exercises" and Selected Works*, 212.
48. O'Malley, *The First Jesuits*, 266.
49. Ibid., 268.
50. Ibid., 269.
51. Hsia, *The World of Catholic Renewal 1540–1770*, 195.
52. O'Malley, *The First Jesuits*, 271–72.
53. Hsia, *Society and Religion in Münster, 1535–1618*, 69.
54. Nalle, *God in La Mancha*, 29–30, 87–89.
55. Ibid., 112.
56. "Constitutions of the Society of Jesus and Their Declarations" [250], in Ignatius of Loyola, *The "Spiritual Exercises" and Selected Works*, 291.
57. Zschoch, "Graf Friedrich Spee von Langenfeld (1591–1635)," in *TRE* 31:635–41.
58. Châtellier, *The Europe of the Devout*; Rapley, *The Dévotes: Women and Church in Seventeenth-Century France*.
59. Session 25, "On the Invocation, Veneration, and Relics of Saints, and on Sacred Images," in *Canons and Decrees of the Council of Trent*, 215, 483.
60. Soergel, *Wondrous in His Saints*, 99–130.
61. Burke, "How to Become a Counter-Reformation Saint," 130–42.
62. Gregory, *Salvation at Stake*, 119.
63. *Canons and Decrees of the Council of Trent*, 147, 420.
64. Bireley, *The Refashioning of Catholicism, 1450–1700*, 37.
65. Ibid., 178–81.
66. Francis de Sales and Jane de Chantal, *Letters of Spiritual Direction*, 210.
67. Sánchez, "Confession and Complicity," 137.
68. Bilinkoff, *The Avila of Saint Teresa*, 78–107.
69. *The Collected Works of St. Teresa of Avila*, 1:94.
70. Ibid., 1:95.
71. Ibid., 1:96–97.
72. Ibid., 1:211–12.

73. Conrad, "Die Kölner Ursulagesellschaft und ihr 'weltgeistlicher Stand,'" 280.

74. Ibid., 286–93.

75. Black, "The Development of Confraternity Studies over the Past Thirty Years," 9–29.

76. Zardin, "Relaunching Confraternities in the Tridentine Era: Shaping Consciences and Christianizing Society in Milan and Lombardy." For comparison with Geneva, see De Boer, "Calvin and Borromeo: A Comparative Approach to Social Discipline."

77. Lazar, "The First Jesuit Confraternities and Marginalized Groups in Sixteenth-Century Rome."

78. Ibid., 146–47.

79. Châtellier, *The Religion of the Poor,* 58; de Boer, *The Conquest of the Soul,* 327–30.

80. Francis de Sales and Jane de Chantal, *Letters of Spiritual Direction,* 97.

81. Norman, *Humanist Taste and Franciscan Values,* 87.

82. Forster, *The Counter-Reformation in the Villages,* 9.

83. De Boer, *The Conquest of the Soul,* 212–37, 327–30.

84. Haude, "The Silent Monks Speak Up: The Changing Identity of the Carthusians in the Fifteenth and Sixteenth Centuries."

85. *Exercitia spiritualia pro tyronibus FF. Capucinorum Ordinis Minorum S. P. Francisci simplici calamo excepta,* 258.

86. Bireley, *The Refashioning of Catholicism, 1450–1700,* 147.

87. Valone, "The Pentecost: Image and Experience in Late Sixteenth-Century Rome."

88. A summary of Catholic expansion during the Iberian conquest is given by Hsia, *The World of Catholic Renewal,* 165–77.

89. MacCormack, "Ubi Ecclesia? Perceptions of Medieval Europe in Spanish America," 84.

90. The different approaches are classified as *Zwangsmission* and *Predigtmission* by Wriedt, "Kirche und Kolonien in der frühen Neuzeit: Der Aufbau des lateinamerikanischen Kirchenwesens im 16. Jahrhundert."

91. MacCormack, "Ubi ecclesia?" 86.

92. Ibid., 96; Hsia, *The World of Catholic Renewal,* 169.

93. MacCormack, "Ubi ecclesia?" 87.

94. O'Malley, *The First Jesuits,* 77.

95. Bireley, *The Refashioning of Catholicism, 1450–1700,* 148–49.

96. Ibid., 172–73.

97. Wiest, "Bringing Christ to the Nations: Shifting Models of Mission among Jesuits in China."

98. Châtellier, *The Religion of the Poor,* 7.

99. Ignatius of Loyola, *The "Spiritual Exercises" and Selected Works,* 306–7.

100. O'Malley, *The First Jesuits,* 301.

101. Selwyn, "Reverberations from the New World: The Jesuits' Civilizing Mission in the Early Modern Period," 122 (used by permission).

102. O'Malley, *The First Jesuits,* 298.

103. Kooi, "Converts and Apostates," 199.

104. Ibid., 202; Tracy, "Public Space: Restriction of Non-Calvinist Religious Behavior in the Province of Holland, 1572–1591," 104–7.

105. Kooi, "Converts and Apostates," 210.

106. Scarisbrick, *The Reformation and the English People,* 142.

107. *John Donne: Selections from Divine Poems, Sermons, Devotions, and Prayer,* 11–12.

108. Rosman, *From Catholic to Protestant*, 67–69; Walsham, *Church Papists: Catholicism, Conformity, and Confessional Polemic in Early Modern England*.
109. Scarisbrick, *The Reformation and the English People*, 149–59.
110. Kloczowski, "Catholic Reform in the Polish-Lithuanian Commonwealth (Poland, Lithuania, the Ukraine, and Belorussia)," 88–89.
111. Kowalski, "From the 'Land of Diverse Sects' to National Religion: Converts to Catholicism and Reformed Franciscans in Early Modern Poland."
112. Tazbir, "Poland," in *The Reformation in National Context*, 168–80.
113. Luther, *An die Ratherren aller Städte deutschen Landes, dass sie christliche Schulen aufrichten und halten sollen* (1524), WA 15:32.1–14; *LW* 45:352–53.
114. Haude, "The Silent Monks Speak Up," 135–37.

Chapter 6: Confessionalizing the Agendas

1. Even within Lutheranism, which retained more remnants of medieval piety than did Reformed and dissenting traditions, there was considerable variety and disagreement. See Zeeden, *Katholische Überlieferungen in den lutherischen Kirchenordnungen des 16. Jahrhunderts*.
2. Strauss, *Luther's House of Learning*, 307; cf. Strauss, "Success and Failure in the German Reformation."
3. Kittelson, "Successes and Failures in the German Reformation: The Report from Strasbourg."
4. Vogler, "Die Entstehung der protestantischen Volksfrömmigkeit in der rheinischen Pfalz zwischen 1555 und 1619."
5. Tolley, *Pastors and Parishioners in Württemberg during the Late Reformation, 1581–1621*, 113.
6. Brown, "Singing the Gospel."
7. Lambert, "Preaching, Praying and Policing the Reform in Sixteenth-Century Geneva," 525–26.
8. Diefendorf, *Beneath the Cross*, 112–13.
9. Bireley, *The Refashioning of Catholicism, 1450–1700*, 97.
10. Helmrath, "Visitationsberichte als Geschichtsquellen."
11. Bireley, *The Refashioning of Catholicism, 1450–1700*, 144–45.
12. Nalle, *God in La Mancha*, 98.
13. Session 25, "Decree concerning Reform," in *Canons and Decrees of the Council of Trent*, 246–48, 512–13.
14. Rhegius, *Formulae quaedam caute*, in *Preaching the Reformation*, 31.
15. Oberman, "Martin Luther: Vorläufer der Reformation."
16. Calvin, *De Necessitate Reformandae Ecclesiae*, in *Tracts Relating to the Reformation*, 1:200; CR 34:510–11.
17. Hendrix, *Tradition and Authority in the Reformation*, XVII, 3–14.
18. Luther, *The Large Catechism*, in *The Book of Concord*, 388–89, ¶22–23.
19. Bugenhagen, *Der Ehrbaren Stadt Hamburg Christliche Ordnung 1529*, 135.
20. Gordon, "Religion and Change in Early Modern Germany," 238.
21. Karant-Nunn, *The Reformation of Ritual*, 197–201.
22. Gregory, *Salvation at Stake*, 6; Kolb, *For All the Saints*.
23. Nichols, *History of Christianity 1650–1950: Secularization of the West*, 460: "The modern Christian churches inherited the great new enterprise of medieval and Reformation

Christianity, the endeavor to penetrate and 'Christianize' civilization. For three hundred years they continued this attempt, yet, on the whole, with ever less success."

24. Lehmann, *Max Webers "Protestantische Ethik,"* 42–49.

25. Weber, *The Protestant Ethic and the Spirit of Capitalism*, 105: "That great historic process in the development of religions, the elimination of magic from the world which had begun with the old Hebrew prophets and, in conjunction with Hellenistic scientific thought, had repudiated all magical means to salvation as superstition and sin, came here [in Puritanism] to its logical conclusion."

26. Van Dülmen, "Protestantismus und Kapitalismus."

27. Scribner, "The Reformation, Popular Magic, and the 'Disenchantment of the World.'" Cf. Scribner, Porter, and Teich, eds., *The Reformation in National Context*, 222: "In short, Protestantism in all its forms was no more successful in uprooting a magico-religious view of a sacramental universe than pre-Reformation Christianity had been in displacing paganism."

28. For Catholics, see Bireley, *The Refashioning of Catholicism, 1450–1700*, 176.

29. Karant-Nunn, *The Reformation of Ritual*, 190–92. I disagree, however, with Karant-Nunn's conclusion that the transferal of holiness rendered the faithful powerless.

30. Collinson, *The Religion of Protestants*, 199.

31. Rublack, "Reformation und Moderne," 32–33.

32. For a brief description of Reformation confessions, see Greengrass, *The Longman Companion to the European Reformation, c. 1500–1618*, 246–51.

33. Maron, "Die nachtridentinische Kodifikationsarbeit in ihrer Bedeutung für die katholische Konfessionalisierung."

34. Packull, "The Origins of Peter Riedemann's *Account of Our Faith.*"

35. For an overview of territories within the Holy Roman Empire, see Schindling and Ziegler, eds., *Die Territorien des Reichs im Zeitalter der Reformation und Konfessionalisierung*. See also Fata, *Ungarn, das Reich der Stephanskrone*.

36. Zeeden, *Das Zeitalter der Glaubenskämpfe, 1555–1648*, 13–18.

37. Reinhard, "Gegenreformation als Modernisierung?" Schilling, "Zwang zur Konfessionalisierung?"

38. Schilling, "Confessional Europe"; Schilling, "Die Konfessionalisierung im Reich"; Schilling, "Die Konfessionalisierung von Kirche, Staat und Gesellschaft"; Schilling, *Konfessionskonflikt und Staatsbildung*.

39. Schmidt, *Konfessionalisierung im 16. Jahrhundert*; Schmidt, "Sozialdisziplinierung? Ein Plädoyer für das Ende des Etatismus in der Konfessionalisierungsforschung." The bibliography of confessionalization in Germany now includes volumes on the three major traditions: Schilling, ed., *Die reformierte Konfessionalisierung in Deutschland*; Rublack, ed., *Die lutherische Konfessionalisierung in Deutschland*; Reinhard and Schilling, eds., *Die katholische Konfessionalisierung*.

40. Schilling, "Confessional Europe," 2:643–44.

41. Oestreich, *Geist und Gestalt des frühmodernen Staates*; Oestreich, *Strukturprobleme der frühen Neuzeit*.

42. H. R. Schmidt has shifted attention away from the state and toward the function that confessionalization served for the parish and for the religious life of parishioners; Schmidt, "Sozialdisziplinierung? Ein Plädoyer für das Ende des Etatismus in der Konfessionalisierungsforschung"; Schmidt, "Gemeinde und Sittenzucht im protestantischen Europa der Frühen Neuzeit."

43. Strom, *Orthodoxy and Reform*, 8.

44. Black, "From Martin Bucer to Richard Baxter," 670.

45. Luther, *Decem Praecepta Wittenbergensi predicata populo per P. Martinum Luther Augustinianum*, WA 1:494.10–11; see Witte, *Law and Protestantism*, 257–92.

46. Bugenhagen, *Der Ehrbaren Stadt Hamburg Christliche Ordnung 1529*, 37.

47. Witte, *Law and Protestantism*, 279–84.

48. Nischan, *Prince, People, and Confession*. Other territories which turned Calvinist were Nassau-Dillenberg (1578), Anhalt (1579), Bremen (1595), Baden-Durlach (1599), Lippe (1602), and Hessen-Kassel (1607).

49. Moltmann, *Christoph Pezel (1539–1604) und der Calvinismus in Bremen*.

50. Klein, *Der Kampf um die zweite Reformation in Kursachsen*.

51. Neuser, "Die Erforschung der 'Zweiten Reformation,'" 381.

52. Albrecht-Birkner, *Reformation des Lebens*, 82–84, 510–11.

53. Ibid., 34–37.

54. Nischan, *Lutherans and Calvinists in the Age of Confessionalism*, I, 211.

55. The *Pastorale Lutheri* by Conrad Porta (d. 1582); Dykema, "Handbooks for Pastors," 152–57; cf. Kolb, "Luther, the Master Pastor: Conrad Porta's *Pastorale Lutheri*, Handbook for Generations."

56. Koenigsberger, "The Unity of the Church and the Reformation," 415: "By the fourteenth and fifteenth centuries, the functional conditions for the survival of a unified Church had all but disappeared."

57. Decot, "Kirchenreform durch Konfessionalisierung."

58. Walls, "From Christendom to World Christianity," 306.

59. Donnelly, "Antonio Possevino's Plan for World Evangelization."

60. National Archives at Copenhagen, Treaty Collections, Supplement: The East Indies Inventory, Registratur 14, pp. 504–7, no. 5. For this reference I am indebted to Daniel Jeyaraj. On the Tranquebar mission, see Jeyaraj, *Inkulturation in Tranquebar*, and Hudson, *Protestant Origins in India*.

61. Young and Jebanesan, *The Bible Trembled*, 42–47; Young and Somartana, *Vain Debates*, 38–40.

62. Mundadan, *Sixteenth-Century Traditions of St. Thomas Christians*; Thekkudan, *Inculturation of Religious Formation among the St. Thomas Christians*; Kanichikattil, ed., *Church in Context*.

63. Firth, *An Introduction to Indian Church History*, 168–77; Chidester, *Christianity: A Global History*, 457–59.

64. Ziegenbalg, *Thirty Four Conferences between the Danish Missionaries and the Malabarian Brahmins . . .* , 94, cited in Young, "Some Hindu Perspectives on Christian Missionaries in the Indic World," 39–40.

65. Walls, *The Missionary Movement in Christian History*, 79–101.

66. Sanneh, "Translatability in Islam and in Christianity in Africa."

67. Barrett et al., *World Christian Encyclopedia*, 2nd ed., 12.

68. Walls, "From Christendom to World Christianity," 322.

69. Larson, "Capacities and Modes of Thinking."

70. Parry, "The Ottoman Empire 1520–1526"; Kafadar, "The Ottomans and Europe."

71. For the impact on Hungary, see Peter, "Hungary."

72. Kitching, "Broken Angels," 217.

73. Miller, "Luther on the Turks and Islam."
74. Bohnstedt, *The Infidel Scourge of God*; Miller, "Holy War and Holy Terror."
75. Keen, *Divine and Human Authority in Reformation Thought*, 130–32.
76. Pfister, "Reformation, Türken, und Islam," 346.
77. Zwingli to Philip of Hesse, 12 March 1530, in *Reformatorenbriefe*, 291.
78. Pfister, "Reformation, Türken, und Islam," 348–49.
79. Pfister, "Das Türkenbüchlein Theodor Biblianders."
80. Daniel, *Islam and the West*.
81. Luther to the city council of Basel, 27 October 1542, WABr 10:160–63.
82. For Luther's preface, see WA 53:569–72; for Melanchthon's, see *CR* 5:10–13 (no. 2616); see also Köhler, *Melanchthon und der Islam*, 23, 46–47.
83. Mau, "Luthers Stellung zu den Türken," 1:647–62, 2:962–63.
84. Luther, *Vom Kriege wider die Türken* (1529), WA 30,2:123.7–15; *LW* 46:177–78.
85. Ibid., WA 30,2:131.1–6; *LW* 46:186.
86. Luther, Preface to *Libellus de ritu et moribus Turcorum* (1530), WA 30,2:206.3–14. The *Libellus* had been written around 1480 by Georg von Muelbach, who had spent twenty years in Turkish captivity. See Henrich and Boyce, "Martin Luther—Translation of Two Prefaces on Islam"; see also Miller, "Luther on the Turks and Islam."
87. Luther, *Vom Kriege wider die Türken* (1529), WA 30,2:127.7–18; *LW* 46:182. Luther derived this "destruction" from the Qur'an. Although he saw the Qur'an in Latin by the early 1540s, his opinion was probably based on the *Libellus*, which he published in 1530.
88. Luther, Preface to *Libellus de ritu et moribus Turcorum* (1530), WA 30,2:206.31–34; cf. Henrich and Boyce, "Martin Luther—Translation of Two Prefaces on Islam," 259.
89. Fauth, "Die Bedeutung des Islam," 258–61.
90. Fauth, "Das Türkenbild bei Martin Luther."
91. Pfister, "Reformation, Türken, und Islam," 364–75; Mau, "Luthers Stellung zu den Türken," 1:647–62, 2:962–63 (n. 181); 2:965 (n. 222).
92. Luther, *Eine Heerpredigt wider den Türken* (1529), WA 30,2:194.28–195.4.
93. Luther, *Vermahnung zum Gebet wider den Türken* (1541), WA 51:585–625; *LW* 43:239.
94. Erasmus, *Utilissima consultatio de bello Turcis inferendo . . .*" (1530), in *Opera omnia Desiderii Erasmi Roterodami*, 5,3:62.614–18; Weiler, "The Turkish Argument and Christian Piety in Desiderius Erasmus."
95. Pfister, "Reformation, Türken, und Islam," 368–70.
96. For hopes of converting the Jews, see Friedman, "Sebastian Münster, the Jewish Mission, and Protestant Antisemitism"; Hendrix, *Tradition and Authority in the Reformation*, XI, 189–215.
97. Luther, *Dass Jesus Christus ein geborner Jude sei* (1523), WA 11:325.16–19; *LW* 45:213.
98. Carlebach, *Divided Souls*, 47, 59.
99. Alexander, *Religion in England 1558–1662*, 214.
100. Luther, *Von den Juden und ihren Lügen* (1543), WA 53:417–552; *LW* 47:122–306.
101. Friedman, *The Most Ancient Testimony*, 44–48; Friedman, "Sebastian Münster, the Jewish Mission, and Protestant Antisemitism."
102. Carlebach, *Divided Souls*, 54–56.
103. On this canon and the medieval debate, see Cohen, *Under Crescent and Cross*, 139–45.
104. Luther, *Von den Juden und ihren Lügen* (1543), WA 53:417–552; *LW* 47:121–306.

105. Rhegius, *Dialogus von der schönen Predigt*. The first edition of almost 500 pages was issued in 1537. Reprinted many times thereafter, the *Dialogus* also appeared in Latin, Low German, Dutch, Danish, English, and Czech translations.

106. Hendrix, *Tradition and Authority in the Reformation*, XI, 189–215. The *Dialogue* was probably conceived as a response to the late-medieval compilation of Jewish arguments called "The Old Book of Polemic" (*nitztzahon* or *Nizzahon*); see Cohen, *Under Crescent and Cross*, 143.

107. For prominent catechisms, see Greengrass, *The Longman Companion to the Reformation*, 251–52. See also Wengert, "Wittenberg's Earliest Catechism"; Kolb, "The Layman's Bible."

108. Bast, *Honor Your Fathers*.

109. The *Genevan Catechism* (1537, French), in *OS* 1:378–417; the 1545 Latin text, in *OS* 2:59–157. See McKee, *John Calvin: Writings on Pastoral Piety*, 101.

110. Calvin, "Address to the Ministers" (1564), in *John Calvin: Selections from His Writings*, 43.

111. Calvin, *Institution of the Christian Religion* (1536), 1: "My purpose was solely to transmit certain rudiments by which those who are touched with any zeal for religion might be shaped to true godliness. And I undertook this labor especially for our French countrymen, very many of whom I saw to be hungering and thirsting for Christ; very few who had been imbued with even a slight knowledge of him."

112. Luther to Philip Melanchthon, 13 July 1521, WABr 2:359.116–19; *LW* 48:262.

113. Rhegius, *Der xv. Psalm Davids*, B: "Und das ist nötig zu wissen / sonderlich itzt zur letzten zeit / da man mit dem heiligen namen Christ / Christenheit / Christliche Kirche / so geschwind gauckelt / und jederman die Christliche Kirche sein wil / wenn man schon erger lebt / denn Türcken und heiden."

114. Luther, *Vorrede auff die offenbarung Sanct Johannis* (1530), StA 1:412.15–28; *LW* 35:410. For the popularity of Revelation during the Reformation, see Backus, *Reformation Readings of the Apocalypse*.

115. Büsser, "H. Bullingers 100 Predigten über die Apokalypse." Mühling, *Heinrich Bullingers europäische Kirchenpolitik*, 36.

Bibliography

Sources

The Anglo-Saxon Missionaries in Germany. Ed. C. H. Talbot. London and New York: Sheed & Ward, 1954.

Die Bekenntnisschriften der evangelisch-lutherischen Kirche. 6th ed. Göttingen: Vandenhoeck & Ruprecht, 1967.

Bellarmine, Robert, S.J. *Disputationes . . . de controversiis christianae fidei*. Ingolstadt, 1586–1601.

The Book of Concord: The Confessions of the Evangelical Lutheran Church. Ed. Robert Kolb and Timothy J. Wengert. Minneapolis: Fortress, 2000.

Brenz, Johannes. *Godly Magistrates and Church Order: Johannes Brenz and the Establishment of the Lutheran Territorial Church in Germany 1524–1559*. Ed. and trans. James M. Estes. Toronto: Centre for Reformation and Renaissance Studies, 2001.

Bucer, Martin. *Correspondance de Martin Bucer*, vol. 1. Ed. Jean Rott. Leiden: Brill, 1979.

———. *De Regno Christi (1550)*. In *Martini Buceri opera latina*, vol. 15,1, ed. François Wendel. Paris: PUF; Gütersloh: C. Bertelsmann Verlag, 1955.

———. *The Kingdom of Christ*. In *Melanchthon and Bucer*, ed. Wilhelm Pauck, 153–394. LCC. Philadelphia: Westminster, 1969.

———. *Martin Bucers Deutsche Schriften*. Ed. Robert Stupperich. Gütersloh: GVH; Paris: PUF, 1960–.

Bugenhagen, Johannes. *Der Ehrbaren Stadt Hamburg Christliche Ordnung 1529: De Ordeninge Pomerani*. Ed. Annemarie Hübner and Hans Wenn. Hamburg: Friedrich Wittig, 1976.

Calvin, John. *Institutes of the Christian Religion*. Ed. John T. McNeill. Trans. Ford Lewis Battles. 2 vols. LCC. Philadelphia: Westminster, 1960.

———. *Institution of the Christian Religion, Embracing Almost the Whole Sum of Piety, and Whatever Is Necessary to Know [of] the Doctrine of Salvation* (Basel, 1536). Trans. Ford Lewis Battles. Atlanta: John Knox, 1975.

———. *John Calvin: Selections from His Writings*. Ed. John Dillenberger. Garden City: Doubleday Anchor, 1971.

———. *Sermon où il est montré quelle doit être la modestie des femmes en leurs habillements*. Geneva: Kundig, 1945.

———. *Tracts Relating to the Reformation*, vol. 1. Trans. Henry Beveridge. Edinburgh: Calvin Translation Society, 1844.

Calvin, John, and Jacopo Sadoleto. *A Reformation Debate: Sadoleto's Letter to the Genevans and Calvin's Reply*. Ed. John C. Olin. New York: Harper & Row, 1966.

Canons and Decrees of the Council of Trent. Ed. H. J. Schroeder. St. Louis: Herder, 1955.

Catharinus, Ambrosius. *Apologia pro veritate catholicae et apostolicae fidei ac doctrinae adversus impia ac valde pestifera Martini Lutheri dogmata* (1520). Ed. Josef Schweizer. Corpus Catholicorum 27. Münster: Aschendorff, 1956.

The Catholic Reformation: Savonarola to Ignatius Loyola. Ed. John Olin. 2nd ed. New York: Fordham University Press, 1992.

Christianity and Paganism, 350–750: The Conversion of Western Europe. Ed. J. N. Hillgarth. Philadelphia: University of Pennsylvania Press, 1986.

Christoph Scheurls Briefbuch. Ed. Franz Freiherr von Soden and J. K. F. Knaake. 2 vols. Aalen: Otto Zeller, 1962.

Convents Confront the Reformation: Catholic and Protestant Nuns in Germany. Ed. and trans. Joan Skocir and Merry Wiesner-Hanks. Milwaukee: Marquette University Press, 1996.

Denis the Carthusian. *D. Dionysii Cartusiani Opera Omnia*. Vol. 7, *Opera minora*. Tornaci: Typis Cartusiae S. M. de Pratis, 1910.

Documents on the Continental Reformation. Ed. William G. Naphy. New York: St. Martin's Press, 1996.

Donne, John. *John Donne: Selections from Divine Poems, Sermons, Devotions, and Prayer*. Ed. John Booty. New York: Paulist Press, 1990.

Eck, John. *Enchiridion of Commonplaces against Luther and Other Enemies of the Church*. Trans. Ford Lewis Battles. Grand Rapids: Baker, 1979.

Erasmus of Rotterdam. *Desiderius Erasmus Roterodamus Ausgewählte Werke*. Ed. Annemarie and Hajo Holborn. Munich: C. H. Beck, 1964.

———. *The Education of a Christian Prince*. Ed. and trans. Lisa Jardine. Cambridge: Cambridge University Press, 1997.

———. "A Journey for Religion's Sake." In *Scheming Papists and Lutheran Fools: Five Reformation Satires*, ed. Erika Rummel, 88–119. New York: Fordham University Press, 1993.

———. *Opera omnia Desiderii Erasmi Roterodami*. Amsterdam: North Holland, 1969–.

Die evangelischen Kirchenordnungen des XVI. Jahrhunderts. Ed. Emil Sehling. 15 vols. Tübingen: Mohr Siebeck, 1902–.

Exercitia spiritualia pro tyronibus FF. Capucinorum Ordinis Minorum S. P. Francisci simplici calamo excepta. Zug, 1683.

Flugschriften vom Bauernkrieg zum Täuferreich (1526–1535). Ed. Adolf Laube. 2 vols. Berlin: Akademie Verlag, 1992.

"Four Letters from the Socinus-Calvin Correspondence (1549)," ed. and trans. Ralph Lazzaro. In *Italian Reformation Studies in Honor of Laelius Socinus*, ed. John A. Tedeschi, 215–30. Florence: Felice Le Monnier, 1965.

Gerson, Jean. *Jean Gerson: Early Works*. Ed. and trans. Brian Patrick McGuire. New York and Mahwah: Paulist Press, 1998.

———. *Jean Gerson: Oeuvres complètes*. Ed. Palémon Glorieux. 10 vols. Paris: Desclée & Cie, 1960–1973.

Glaubenszeugnisse oberdeutscher Taufgesinnte, vol. 1. Ed. Lydia Müller. Leipzig: Heinsius, 1938.

Gregory of Tours. *History of the Franks*. Trans. Ernest Brehaut. New York: Columbia University Press, 1916.

Hus, John. *The Letters of John Hus.* Trans. Matthew Spinka. Manchester: Manchester University Press; Totowa, N.J.: Rowan & Littlefield, 1972.

Ignatius of Loyola. *The "Spiritual Exercises" and Selected Works.* Ed. George E. Ganss, S.J. New York: Paulist Press, 1991.

John of Damascus. *On the Divine Images: Three Apologies against Those Who Attack the Divine Images.* Trans. David Anderson. Crestwood, N.Y.: St. Vladimir's Seminary Press, 2000.

Knox, John. *The Works of John Knox,* vol. 4. Ed. David Laing. New York: AMS Press, 1966.

Luther's and Zwingli's Propositions for Debate. Ed. Carl S. Meyer. Leiden: Brill, 1963.

Das Marburger Religionsgespräch 1529. Ed. Gerhard May. Gütersloh: GVH, 1970.

More, Thomas. *Responsio ad Lutherum.* In *The Complete Works of St. Thomas More,* vol. 5, I-II. Ed. John M. Headley. New Haven and London: Yale University Press, 1969.

Müntzer, Thomas. *Schriften und Briefe: Kritische Gesamtausgabe.* Ed. Günther Franz. Gütersloh: GVH, 1968.

———. "Thomas Müntzer's *Protestation* and *Imaginary Faith,*" ed. James M. Stayer. *MQR* 55 (1981): 99–130.

Myconius, Oswald. *Vom Leben und Sterben Huldrych Zwinglis.* Ed. Ernst Gerhard Rusch. St. Gall: Fehr'sche Buchhandlung, 1979.

Oecolampadius, Johannes. *Briefe und Akten zum Leben Oekolampads.* Ed. Ernst Staehelin. 2 vols. Leipzig: M. Heinsius Nachfolger, 1927–1934.

Osiander, Andreas. *Gesamtausgabe,* vol. 3, *Schriften und Briefe 1528 bis April 1530.* Ed. Gerhard Müller and Gottfried Seebass. Gütersloh: GVH, 1979.

Peter Lombard. *Libri IV sententiarum.* 2nd ed. Ad Claras Aquas: Ex Typ. S. Bonventurae, 1916.

Pirckheimer, Willibald. *Willibald Pirckheimers Briefwechsel.* 4 vols. Munich: C. H. Beck, 1940–.

Quellen zur Geschichte der Täufer in der Schweiz, vol. 2, *Ostschweiz.* Ed. Heinold Fast. Zürich: Theologischer Verlag, 1973.

Quellen zur Geschichte des Papsttums und des Römischen Katholizismus, vol. 1. Ed. Carl Mirbt and Kurt Aland. 6th ed. Tübingen: Mohr Siebeck, 1967.

The Radical Reformation. Ed. Michael G. Baylor. Cambridge: Cambridge University Press, 1991.

Reformatorenbriefe: Luther, Zwingli, Calvin. Ed. Günter Gloede. Berlin: Evangelische Verlagsanstalt, 1973.

Registers of the Consistory of Geneva in the Time of Calvin, vol. 1, *1542–1544.* Ed. Robert M. Kingdon, Thomas A. Lambert, Isabella M. Watt, and Jeffrey R. Watt. Trans. M. Wallace McDonald. Grand Rapids and Cambridge: Eerdmans, 2000.

Registres de la Compagnie des Pasteurs de Genève au temps de Calvin, vol. 1. Ed. R. Kingdon and J.-F. Bergier. Geneva: Droz, 1964.

Rhegius, Urbanus. *Dialogus von der schönen Predigt die Christus Luc. 24. von Jerusalem bis gen Emaus den zweien jüngern am Ostertag aus Mose und allen Propheten gethan hat.* 2nd ed. Wittenberg: Josef Klug, 1539.

———. *Formulae quaedam caute et citra scandalum loquendi de praecipuis Christianae doctrinae locis, pro iunioribus Verbi Ministris in Ducatu Luneburgensi.* In *Preaching the Reformation: The Homiletical Handbook of Urbanus Rhegius,* ed. and trans. Scott Hendrix. Milwaukee: Marquette University Press, 2003.

———. *Der xv. Psalm Davids ausgelegt durch D. Urbanum Rhegium. Sampt einer Christlichen unterrichtung von einem unchristlichen unerhoerten wucher.* Magdeburg: Michael Lotther, 1537.

Sales, Francis de, and Jane de Chantal. *Letters of Spiritual Direction*. Mahwah: Paulist Press, 1988.

Servetus, Michael. *The Two Treatises of Servetus on the Trinity*, ed. and trans. Earl Morris Wilbur. Cambridge: Harvard University Press, 1932.

Simons, Menno. *The Complete Writings of Menno Simons c.1496–1561*. Ed. J. C. Wenger and trans. Leonard Verduin. Scottdale, Pa.: Herald Press, 1956.

———. *Dat Fundament des christelycken Leers*. Ed. H. W. Meihuizen. The Hague: Martinus Nijhoff, 1967.

Spiritual and Anabaptist Writers. Ed. George H. Williams. LCC. Philadelphia: Westminster Press, 1957.

Staupitz, Johann von. *Sämtliche Schriften, Abhandlungen, Predigten, Zeugnisse*. Ed. Lothar Graf zu Dohna and Richard Wetzel. Berlin and New York: W. de Gruyter, 1979–.

Teresa of Avila. *The Collected Works of St. Teresa of Avila*, vol. 1. Trans. Kieran Kavanaugh and Otilio Rodriguez. 2nd ed. Washington, D.C.: Institute of Carmelite Studies, 1987.

Thomas Aquinas. *Summa Theologiae*. 5 vols. 3rd ed. Madrid: Biblioteca de Autores Cristianos, 1961–1975.

La vraie piété: Divers traités de Jean Calvin et Confession de foi de Guillaume Farel. Ed. Irena Backus and Claire Chimelli. Geneva: Labor et Fides, 1986.

Zwingli, Ulrich. *Commentary on True and False Religion*. Ed. Samuel Macauley Jackson and Clarence Nevin Heller. Durham, N.C.: Labyrinth Press, 1981.

———. *Ulrich Zwingli: Early Writings*. Ed. Samuel Macauley Jackson. Durham, N.C.: Labyrinth Press, 1987.

———. *Ulrich Zwingli (1484–1531): Selected Works*. Ed. Samuel Macauley Jackson. Philadelphia: University of Pennsylvania Press, 1972.

Zwingli and Bullinger. Ed. G. W. Bromiley. LCC. Philadelphia: Westminster, 1953.

Literature

Abray, Lorna Jane. *The People's Reformation: Magistrates, Clergy, and Commons in Strasbourg, 1500–1598*. Ithaca, N.Y.: Cornell University Press, 1985.

Albrecht-Birkner, Veronika. *Reformation des Lebens: Die Reformen Herzogs Ernst des Frommen von Sachsen-Gotha und ihre Auswirkungen auf Frömmigkeit, Schule, und Alltag im ländlichen Raum (1640–1675)*. Leipzig: Evangelische Verlagsanstalt, 2002.

Alexander, H. G. *Religion in England 1558–1662*. London: University of London Press, 1968.

Almazán, Vincent. "The Pilgrim-Shell in Denmark." In *The Pilgrimage to Compostela in the Middle Ages*, ed. Maryjane Dunn and Linda Kay Davidson, 131–42. New York and London: Routledge, 1996.

Auer, Alfons. *Die vollkommene Frömmigkeit des Christen nach dem Enchiridion militis Christiani des Erasmus von Rotterdam*. Düsseldorf: Patmos-Verlag, 1954.

Backus, Irena. *Reformation Readings of the Apocalypse: Geneva, Zurich, and Wittenberg*. Oxford and New York: Oxford University Press, 2000.

Bagchi, David V. N. *Luther's Earliest Opponents: Catholic Controversialists, 1518–1525*. Minneapolis: Fortress, 1991.

Barrett, David B., George T. Kurian, and Todd M. Johnson. *World Christian Encyclopedia: A Comparative Survey of Churches and Religions in the Modern World*. 2nd ed. Oxford: Oxford University Press, 2001.

Bartlett, Robert. *The Making of Europe: Conquest, Colonization and Cultural Change 950–1350.* Princeton: Princeton University Press, 1993.

Bast, Robert J. *Honor Your Fathers: Catechisms and the Emergence of a Patriarchal Ideology in Germany 1400–1600.* Leiden: Brill, 1997.

Battles, Ford Lewis. "Against Luxury and License in Geneva: A Forgotten Fragment of Calvin." *Interpretation* 19 (1965): 182–202.

Becker, Petrus. "Benediktinische Reformbewegungen im Spätmittelalter: Ansätze, Entwicklungen, Auswirkungen." In *Untersuchungen zu Kloster und Stift,* ed. Max-Planck-Institut für Geschichte, 167–87. Göttingen: Vandenhoeck & Ruprecht, 1980.

———. "Benediktinische Reformbewegungen und klösterliches Bildungsstreben: Die rheinischen Abteien der Bursfelder Kongregation." *Rottenburger Jahrbuch für Kirchengeschichte* 11 (1992): 161–74.

Bell, Theo. *Divus Bernhardus: Bernhard von Clairvaux in Martin Luthers Schriften.* Mainz: Philipp von Zabern, 1993.

Berger, Heinrich. *Calvins Geschichtsauffassung.* Zurich: Zwingli-Verlag, 1955.

Biel, Pamela. *Doorkeepers at the House of Righteousness: Heinrich Bullinger and the Zurich Clergy 1535–1575.* Bern: Peter Lang, 1991.

Bilinkoff, Jodi. *The Avila of Saint Teresa: Religious Reform in a Sixteenth-Century City.* Ithaca, N.Y. and London: Cornell University Press, 1989.

Bireley, Robert. *The Refashioning of Catholicism, 1450–1700: A Reassessment of the Counter Reformation.* Washington, D.C.: Catholic University of America Press, 1999.

Black, Christopher F. "The Development of Confraternity Studies over the Past Thirty Years." In *The Politics of Ritual Kinship: Confraternities and Social Order in Early Modern Italy,* ed. Nicholas Terpstra, 9–29. Cambridge: Cambridge University Press, 2000.

Black, J. William. "From Martin Bucer to Richard Baxter: 'Discipline' and Reformation in Sixteenth- and Seventeeth-Century England." *CH* 70 (2001): 644–73.

Blickle, Peter. *Communal Reformation: The Quest for Salvation in Sixteenth-Century Germany.* Atlantic Highlands, N.J.: Humanities Press, 1992.

———. *Die Reformation im Reich.* Stuttgart: Eugen Ulmer, 1982.

———. "Politische Weiterungen der reformatorischen Theologie: Die Antwort des Gemeinen Mannes." In *Politische Institutionen im gesellschaftlichen Umbruch: Ideengeschichtliche Beiträge zur Theorie politischer Institutionen,* ed. Gerhard Göhler, Kurt Lenk, and Herfried Münkler, Manfred Walther, 160–69. Opladen: Westdeutscher Verlag, 1990.

———. *The Revolution of 1525: The German Peasants' War from a New Perspective.* Baltimore and London: Johns Hopkins University Press, 1981.

Blok, Marjan. "Discipleship in Menno Simons' *Dat Fundament*: An Exercise in Anabaptist Theology." In *Menno Simons: A Reappraisal,* ed. Gerald R. Brunk, 105–29. Harrisonburg, Va.: Eastern Mennonite College, 1992.

Bohnstedt, John W. *The Infidel Scourge of God: The Turkish Menace as Seen by German Pamphleteers of the Reformation Era.* Philadelphia: American Philosophical Society, 1968.

Boockmann, Hartmut. "Das 15. Jahrhundert und die Reformation." In *Kirche und Gesellschaft im Heiligen Römischen Reich des 15. und 16. Jahrhunderts,* ed. Hartmut Boockmann, 9–25. Göttingen: Vandenhoeck & Ruprecht, 1994.

———. *Einführung in die Geschichte des Mittelalters.* 6th ed. Munich: Beck, 1996.

Bossy, John. *Christianity in the West, 1400–1700.* Oxford and New York: Oxford University Press, 1987.

———. "The Counter-Reformation and the People of Catholic Europe." In *The Counter-Reformation: The Essential Readings*, ed. David M. Luebke, 85–104. Oxford: Blackwell, 1999.

Bouwsma, William J. *John Calvin: A Sixteenth-Century Portrait*. New York: Oxford University Press, 1988.

Bowd, Stephen D. *Reform before the Reformation: Vicenzo Querini and the Religious Renaissance in Italy*. Leiden: Brill, 2002.

Boyd, Stephen B. *Pilgram Marpeck: His Life and Social Theology*. Mainz: Verlag Philipp von Zabern, 1992.

Brady, Thomas A., Jr. *Protestant Politics: Jacob Sturm (1489–1553) and the German Reformation*. Atlantic Highlands, N.J.: Humanities Press, 1995.

Bräuer, Siegfried. "Thomas Müntzers Kirchenverständnis vor seiner Allstedter Zeit." In *Der Theologe Thomas Müntzer: Untersuchungen zu seiner Entwicklung und Lehre*, ed. Siegfried Bräuer and Helmar Junghans, 100–28. Göttingen: Vandenhoeck & Ruprecht, 1989.

Brecht, Martin. "Johannes Brenz und das Hexenwesen." *Zeitschrift der Savigny-Stiftung für Rechtsgeschichte* 117 [*Kanonistische Abteilung* 86] (2000): 386–97.

———. "Der mittelalterliche (Pseudo-)Augustinismus als gemeinsame Wurzel katholischer and evangelischer Frömmigkeit." In *Jansenismus, Quietismus, Pietismus*, ed. Hartmut Lehmann, Hans-Jürgen Schrader, and Heinz Schilling, 54–64. Göttingen: Vandenhoeck & Ruprecht, 2002.

———. "Was war Zwinglianismus?" In *Die Zürcher Reformation: Ausstrahlungen und Rückwirkungen*, ed. Alfred Schindler, Hans Stickelberger, and Martin Sallmann, 281–300. Bern: Peter Lang, 2001.

Brentano, Robert. *A New World in a Small Place: Church and Religion in the Diocese of Rieti, 1188–1378*. Berkeley and Los Angeles: University of California Press, 1994.

Brown, Christopher B. "Singing the Gospel: Lutheran Hymns and the Success of the Reformation in Joachimsthal." Ph.D. diss., Harvard University, 2001.

Brown, Peter. *The Cult of the Saints: Its Rise and Function in Latin Christianity*. Chicago: University of Chicago Press, 1981.

———. *The Rise of Western Christendom: Triumph and Diversity, A.D. 200–1000*. Oxford: Oxford University Press, 1995.

———. *The World of Late Antiquity, AD 150–750*. New York: Harcourt Brace Jovanovich, 1971.

Bubenheimer, Ulrich. "Andreas Bodenstein von Karlstadt und seine fränkische Heimat." In *Querdenker der Reformation—Andreas Bodenstein von Karlstadt und seine frühe Wirkung*, ed. Ulrich Bubenheimer and Stefan Oehmig, 15–41. Würzburg: Religion und Kultur Verlag, 2001.

Burger, Christoph. *Aedificatio, Fructus, Utilitas: Johannes Gerson als Professor der Theologie und Kanzler der Universität Paris*. Tübingen: Mohr Siebeck, 1991.

———. "Der Augustinereremit Martin Luther in Kloster und Universität bis zum Jahre 1512." In *Kloster Amelungsborn, 1135–1985*, ed. Gerhard Ruhbach and Kurt Schmidt-Clausen, 161–86. Hannover: Kloster Amelungsborn, 1985.

———. "Volksfrömmigkeit in Deutschland um 1500 im Spiegel der Schriften des Johannes von Paltz OESA." In *Volksreligion im hohen und späten Mittelalter*, ed. Peter Dinzelbacher and Dieter R. Bauer, 307–27. Paderborn: Ferdinand Schöningh, 1990.

Burke, Peter. "How to Become a Counter-Reformation Saint." In *The Counter-Reformation: The Essential Readings*, ed. David M. Luebke, 130–42. Oxford: Blackwell, 1999.

Burnett, Amy Nelson. *The Yoke of Christ: Martin Bucer and Christian Discipline.* Kirksville, Mo.: SCJ Publishers, 1994.

Büsser, Fritz. "H. Bullingers 100 Predigten über die Apokalypse." *Zwingliana* 27 (2000): 117–31.

———. *Die Prophezei: Humanismus und Reformation in Zürich. Ausgewählte Aufsätze und Vorträge,* ed. Alfred Schindler. Bern: Peter Lang, 1994.

Cameron, Euan. "The Late Renaissance and the Unfolding Reformation in Europe." In *Humanism and Reform: The Church in Europe, England and Scotland, 1400–1643: Essays in Honour of James K. Cameron,* ed. James Kirk, 15–36. Oxford: Blackwell, 1991.

———. *The Reformation of the Heretics: The Waldenses of the Alps, 1480–1580.* Oxford: Clarendon Press, 1984.

———. "The Search for Luther's Place in the Reformation." *JEH* 45 (1994): 475–85.

Carlebach, Elisheva. *Divided Souls: Converts from Judaism in Germany 1500–1750.* New Haven and London: Yale University Press, 2001.

Châtellier, Louis. *The Europe of the Devout: The Catholic Reformation and the Formation of a New Society.* Cambridge: Cambridge University Press, 1989.

———. *The Religion of the Poor: Rural Missions in Europe and the Formation of Modern Catholicism, c.1500–1800.* Cambridge: Cambridge University Press, 1997.

Chidester, David. *Christianity: A Global History.* New York: HarperCollins, 2000.

Chrisman, Miriam U. *Conflicting Visions of Reform: German Lay Propaganda Pamphlets, 1519–1530.* Atlantic Highlands, N.J.: Humanities Press, 1996.

Christensen, Carl C. *Art and the Reformation in Germany.* Athens: Ohio University Press, 1979.

———. *Princes and Propaganda: Electoral Saxon Art of the Reformation.* Kirksville, Mo.: SCJ Publishers, 1992.

Cohen, Mark R. *Under Crescent and Cross: The Jews in the Middle Ages.* Princeton: Princeton University Press, 1994.

Collinson, Patrick. *The Religion of Protestants: The Church in English Society 1559–1625.* Oxford: Clarendon, 1982.

Conrad, Anne. "Die Kölner Ursulagesellschaft und ihr 'weltgeistlicher Stand'—eine weibliche Lebensform im Katholizismus der frühen Neuzeit." In *Die katholische Konfessionalisierung,* ed. Wolfgang Reinhard and Heinz Schilling, 271–95. Gütersloh: GVH, 1995.

Constable, Giles C. *The Reformation of the Twelfth Century.* Cambridge: Cambridge University Press, 1996.

———. *Three Studies in Medieval Religious and Social Thought.* Cambridge: Cambridge University Press, 1995.

Cottret, Bernard. *Calvin: A Biography.* Grand Rapids and Cambridge: Eerdmans, 1999.

Cowdrey, H. E. J. *Popes and Church Reform in the 11th Century.* Aldershot, England, and Brookfield, Vt.: Ashgate, 2000.

Cummins, J. S., ed. *Christianity and Missions 1450–1800.* Aldershot, England, and Brookfield, Vt.: Ashgate, 1997.

Daly, William M. "Clovis: How Barbaric, How Pagan?" *Speculum* 69 (1994): 619–64.

Daniel, Norman. *Islam and the West: The Making of An Image.* Oxford: Oneworld Publications, 1997.

Dannenbauer, Heinz. *Luther als religiöser Volksschriftsteller 1517–1520: Ein Beitrag zu der Frage nach den Ursachen der Reformation.* Tübingen: Mohr Siebeck, 1930.

De Boer, Wietse. "Calvin and Borromeo: A Comparative Approach to Social Discipline." In *Early Modern Catholicism*, ed. Kathleen M. Comerford and Hilmar M. Pabel, 84–96. Toronto: University of Toronto Press, 2001.

———— *The Conquest of the Soul: Confession, Discipline, and Public Order in Counter-Reformation Milan*. Leiden: Brill, 2001.

Decot, Rolf. "Kirchenreform durch Konfessionalisierung: Überlegungen zu Luthers Reformation und ihren Wirkungen im Reich." In *700 Jahre Wittenberg: Stadt, Universität, Reformation*, ed. Stefan Oehmig, 155–70. Weimar: Böhlau, 1995.

Delaruelle, Étienne. *La piété populaire au moyen age*. Turin: Bottega d'Erasmo, 1975.

Delumeau, Jean. *Catholicism between Luther and Voltaire: A New View of the Counter-Reformation*. London: Burns & Oates; Philadelphia: Westminster, 1977.

————. *Sin and Fear: The Emergence of a Western Guilt Culture 13th–18th Centuries*, trans. Eric Nicholson. New York: St. Martin's Press, 1990.

Delumeau, Jean, and Monique Cottret. *Le Catholicisme entre Luther et Voltaire*. 6th ed. Paris: PUF, 1996.

DeMolen, Richard L. "Erasmus' Commitment to the Canons Regular of St. Augustine." *Renaissance Quarterly* 26 (1973): 437–43.

————. "The Interior Erasmus." In *Leaders of the Reformation*, ed. Richard L. DeMolen, 11–42. London and Toronto: Associated University Presses, 1984.

Deppermann, Klaus. "The Anabaptists and the State Churches." In *Religion and Society in Early Modern Europe 1500–1800*, ed. Kaspar von Greyerz, 95–106. London: George Allen & Unwin, 1984.

————. *Melchior Hoffman: Soziale Unruhen und apokalyptische Visionen im Zeitalter der Reformation*. Göttingen: Vandenhoeck & Ruprecht, 1979.

Despland, Michel. "How Close Are We to Having a Full History of Christianity? The Work of Jean Delumeau." *Religious Studies Review* 9 (1983): 24–33.

Diefendorf, Barbara B. *Beneath the Cross: Catholics and Huguenots in Sixteenth-Century Paris*. New York and Oxford: Oxford University Press, 1991.

Dinan, Susan Eileen. "Confraternities as a Venue for Female Activism during the Catholic Reformation." In *Confraternities and Catholic Reform in Italy, France, and Spain*, ed. John P. Donnelly, S.J., and Michael W. Maher, S.J., 191–214. Kirksville, Mo.: Thomas Jefferson University Press, 1999.

Dipple, Geoffrey. *Antifraternalism and Anticlericalism in the German Reformation: Johann Eberlin von Günzburg and the Campaign against the Friars*. Aldershot, England: Scolar Press, 1996.

Dohna, Lothar Graf zu. "Von der Ordensreform zur Reformation: Johann von Staupitz." In *Reformbemühungen und Observanzbestrebungen im spätmittelalterlichen Ordenswesen*, ed. Kaspar Elm, 571–84. Berlin: Duncker & Humblot, 1989.

Donnelly, John Patrick, S.J. "Antonio Possevino's Plan for World Evangelization." In *Christianity and Missions, 1450–1800*, ed. J. S. Cummins, 36–56. Aldershot, England, and Brookfield, Vt.: Ashgate, 1997.

————. "The New Religious Orders, 1517–1648." In *Handbook of European History, 1400–1600*, 2 vols., ed. Thomas A. Brady, Jr., Heiko A. Oberman, and James D. Tracy, 2:283–315. Grand Rapids: Eerdmans, 1996.

Donnelly, John P., S. J., and Michael W. Maher, S. J., eds. *Confraternities and Catholic Reform in Italy, France, and Spain*. Kirksville, Mo.: Thomas Jefferson University Press, 1999.

Dowden, Ken. *European Paganism: The Realities of Cult from Antiquity to the Middle Ages.* London and New York: Routledge, 2000.

Duffy, Eamon. *The Stripping of the Altars: Traditional Religion in England c. 1400–c. 1580.* New Haven and London: Yale University Press, 1992.

———. *The Voices of Morebath: Reformation and Rebellion in an English Village.* New Haven and London: Yale University Press, 2001.

Duke, Alastair, Gillian Lewis, and Andrew Pettegree, eds. *Calvinism in Europe, 1540–1610.* Manchester and New York: Manchester University Press, 1992.

Dülmen, Richard van. "Protestantismus und Kapitalismus: Max Webers These im Licht der neueren Sozialgeschichte." In *Max Weber: Ein Symposion,* ed. Christian Gneuss and Jürgen Kocka, 88–101. Munich: DTV, 1988.

Dykema, Peter. "Handbooks for Pastors: Late Medieval Manuals for Parish Priests and Conrad Porta's *Pastorale Lutheri* (1582)." In *Continuity and Change: The Harvest of Late-Medieval and Reformation History,* ed. Robert J. Bast and Andrew C. Gow, 143–62. Leiden: Brill, 2000.

Edwards, Mark U., Jr. *Luther and the False Brethren.* Stanford, Calif.: Stanford University Press, 1975.

———. *Luther's Last Battles: Politics and Polemics, 1531–46.* Ithaca, N.Y.: Cornell University Press, 1983.

———. *Printing, Propaganda, and Martin Luther.* Berkeley: University of California Press, 1994.

Eire, Carlos. *War against the Idols: The Reformation of Worship from Erasmus to Calvin.* Cambridge: Cambridge University Press, 1986.

Elm, Kaspar. "Antiklerikalismus im Deutschen Mittelalter." In *Anticlericalism in Late Medieval and Early Modern Europe,* ed. Peter A. Dykema and Heiko A. Oberman, 3–18. Leiden: Brill, 1993.

———. "Reform- und Observanzbestrebungen im spätmittelalterlichen Ordenswesen." In *Reformbemühungen und Observanzbestrebungen im spätmittelalterlichen Ordenswesen,* ed. Kaspar Elm, 3–19. Berlin: Duncker & Humblot, 1989.

———. "Verfall und Erneuerung des Ordenswesens im Spätmittelalter." In *Untersuchungen zu Kloster und Stift,* ed. Max-Planck-Institut für Geschichte, 188–238. Göttingen: Vandenhoeck & Ruprecht, 1980.

Erikson, Erik H. *Young Man Luther: A Study in Psychoanalysis and History.* New York: W. W. Norton, 1958.

Estes, James M. "Erasmus, Melanchthon, and the Office of Christian Magistrate." *Erasmus of Rotterdam Society Yearbook* 18 (1998): 21–39.

———. "Melanchthon's Confrontation with the 'Erasmian' *Via media* in Politics: The *De officio principum* of 1539." In *Dona Melanchthoniana: Festgabe für Heinz Scheible zum 70. Geburtstag,* ed. Johanna Loehr, 83–101. Stuttgart–Bad Cannstatt: frommann-holzboog, 2001.

———. "*Officium principis christiani*: Erasmus and the Origins of the Protestant State Church." *ARG* 83 (1992): 49–72.

Evennett, H. Outram. *The Spirit of the Counter-Reformation,* ed. John Bossy. Cambridge: Cambridge University Press, 1968.

Fasolt, Constantin. "Europäische Geschichte, zweiter Akt: Die Reformation." In *Die deutsche Reformation zwischen Spätmittelalter und Früher Neuzeit,* ed. Thomas A. Brady, 231–50. Munich: R. Oldenbourg, 2001.

Fast, Heinold. "The Dependence of the First Anabaptists on Luther, Erasmus, and Zwingli." *MQR* 30 (1956): 104–19.

———. "Reformation durch Provokation: Predigtstörungen in den ersten Jahren der Reformation in der Schweiz." In *Umstrittenes Täufertum 1525–1975: Neue Forschungen*, ed. Hans-Jürgen Goertz, 79–110. Göttingen: Vandenhoeck & Ruprecht, 1975.

Fata, Márta. *Ungarn, das Reich der Stephanskrone, im Zeitalter der Reformation und Konfessionalisierung: Multiethnizität, Land und Konfession 1500–1700*. Münster: Aschendorff, 2000.

Fauth, Dieter. "Die Bedeutung des Islam für die Erziehungs- und Bildungsvorstellungen vor allem in der radikalen Reformation und zu Nachwirkungen dieser Zeit." In *Der Umgang mit dem Fremden in der Vormoderne: Studien zur Akkulturation in bildungshistorischer Sicht*, ed. Christoph Lüth, Rudolf W. Keck, and Erhard Wiersing, 249–68. Cologne, Weimar, and Vienna: Böhlau, 1997.

———. "Das Türkenbild bei Martin Luther." *Berliner Theologische Zeitschrift* 11 (1994): 1–12.

———. "Verfassungs- und Rechtsvorstellungen im Bauernkrieg 1524/25." *Zeitschrift der Savigny-Stiftung für Rechtsgeschichte* 112 [kan. Abteilung 81] (1995): 225–48.

Feld, Helmut. "Konrad Summenhart: Theologe der kirchlichen Reform vor der Reformation." *Rottenburger Jahrbuch für Kirchengeschichte* 11 (1992): 85–116.

Firth, C. B. *An Introduction to Indian Church History*. Rev. ed. Madras: Christian Literature Society, 1976.

Fischer, Robert H. "Paltz und Luther." *LuJ* 37 (1970): 9–36.

Fletcher, Richard. *The Barbarian Conversion: From Paganism to Christianity*. New York: Henry Holt, 1997.

Flint, Valerie I. J. *The Rise of Magic in Early Medieval Europe*. Princeton: Princeton University Press, 1991.

Forster, Marc R. *The Counter-Reformation in the Villages: Religion and Reform in the Bishopric of Speyer, 1560–1720*. Ithaca, N.Y., and London: Cornell University Press, 1992.

French, Katherine L. *The People of the Parish: Community Life in a Late Medieval English Diocese*. Philadelphia: University of Pennsylvania Press, 2001.

Friedman, Jerome. *The Most Ancient Testimony: Sixteenth-Century Christian-Hebraica in the Age of Renaissance Nostalgia*. Athens: Ohio University Press, 1983.

———. "Sebastian Münster, the Jewish Mission, and Protestant Antisemitism." *ARG* 70 (1979): 238–59.

Friesen, Abraham. *Thomas Müntzer: A Destroyer of the Godless*. Berkeley: University of California Press, 1990.

Fudge, Thomas A. *The Magnificent Ride: The First Reformation in Hussite Bohemia*. Aldershot, England: Ashgate, 1998.

Gäbler, Ulrich. *Huldrych Zwingli: His Life and Work*. Trans. Ruth C. L. Gritsch. Philadelphia: Fortress Press, 1986.

Galpern, A. N. "The Legacy of Late Medieval Religion in Sixteenth-Century Champagne." In *The Pursuit of Holiness in Late Medieval and Renaissance Religion*, ed. Charles Trinkaus and Heiko A. Oberman, 141–76. Leiden: Brill, 1974.

Gäumann, Andreas. *Reich Christi und Obrigkeit: Eine Studie zum reformatorischen Denken und Handeln Martin Bucers*. Bern: Peter Lang, 2001.

Goertz, Hans-Jürgen. "Der fremde Menno Simons: Antiklerikale Argumentation im Werk eines melchioritischen Täufers." *Mennonitische Geschichtsblätter* 42, N.F., 37 (1985): 24–42.

————. *Konrad Grebel: Kritiker des frommen Scheins (1498–1526): Eine biographische Skizze.* Bolanden: Mennonitischer Geschichtsverein; Hamburg: Kümpers Verlag, 1998.

————. *Religiöse Bewegungen in der frühen Neuzeit.* Munich: R. Oldenbourg, 1993.

————, ed. *Umstrittenes Täufertum 1525–1975: Neue Forschungen.* Göttingen: Vandenhoeck & Ruprecht, 1975.

Goeters, J. F. Gerhard. *Ludwig Hätzer (ca. 1500 bis 1529): Spiritualist und Antitrinitarier.* Gütersloh: C. Bertelsmann, 1957.

Gordon, Bruce. "Religion and Change in Early Modern Germany." *German History* 16 (1998): 222–38.

Gordon, Bruce, and Peter Marshall, eds. *The Place of the Dead: Death and Remembrance in Late Medieval and Early Modern Europe.* Cambridge: Cambridge University Press, 2000.

Graham, W. Fred, ed. *Later Calvinism: International Perspectives.* Kirksville, Mo.: SCJ Publishers, 1994.

Grane, Leif. *Modus loquendi theologicus: Luthers Kampf um die Erneuerung der Theologie.* Leiden: Brill, 1975.

————. *Reformationsstudien: Beiträge zu Luther und zur dänischen Reformation,* ed. Rolf Decot. Mainz: Verlag Philipp von Zabern, 1999.

Greengrass, Mark. *The Longman Companion to the European Reformation, c. 1500–1618.* London and New York: Longman, 1998.

Gregory, Brad S. *Salvation at Stake: Christian Martyrdom in Early Modern Europe.* Cambridge and London: Harvard University Press, 1999.

Grieser, Jonathan. "Anabaptism, Anticlericalism, and the Creation of a Protestant Clergy." *MQR* 71 (1997): 515–43.

Guggisberg, Hans R. *Sebastian Castellio: Humanist und Verteidiger der religiösen Toleranz.* Göttingen: Vandenhoeck & Ruprecht, 1997.

Haliczer, Stephen. *Sexuality in the Confessional: A Sacrament Profaned.* New York and Oxford: Oxford University Press, 1996.

Hamm, Berndt. "Between Severity and Mercy: Three Models of Pre-Reformation Urban Preaching: Savonarola–Staupitz–Geiler." In *Continuity and Change: The Harvest of Late-Medieval and Reformation History,* ed. Robert J. Bast and Andrew C. Gow, 321–58. Boston: Brill, 2000.

————. "Frömmigkeit als Gegenstand theologiegeschichtlicher Forschung: Methodisch-historische Überlegungen am Beispiel von Spätmittelalter und Reformation." *Zeitschrift für Theologie und Kirche* 74 (1977): 464–97.

————. *Frömmigkeitstheologie am Anfang des 16. Jahrhunderts: Studien zu Johannes von Paltz und seinem Umkreis.* Tübingen: Mohr Siebeck, 1982.

————. "Normative Centering in the Fifteenth and Sixteenth Centuries: Observations on Religiosity, Theology, and Iconology." Trans. John M. Frymire. *Journal of Early Modern History* 3 (1999): 307–54.

————. "The Urban Reformation in the Holy Roman Empire." In *Handbook of European History, 1400–1600,* 2 vols., ed. Thomas A. Brady, Jr., Heiko A. Oberman, and James D. Tracy, 2:193–227. Grand Rapids: Eerdmans, 1996.

————. "Wie innovativ war die Reformation?" *Zeitschrift für historische Forschung* 27 (2000): 481–98.

————. *Zwinglis Reformation der Freiheit.* Neukirchen-Vluyn: Neukirchener Verlag, 1988.

Hamm, Berndt, Bernd Moeller, and Dorothea Wendebourg. *Reformationstheorien: Ein kirchenhistorischer Disput über Einheit und Vielfalt der Reformation.* Göttingen: Vandenhoeck & Ruprecht, 1995.

Hammann, Gottfried. "Ecclesiological Motifs behind the Creation of the 'Christlichen Gemeinschaften.'" In *Martin Bucer: Reforming Church and Community,* ed. D. F. Wright, 129–43. Cambridge: Cambridge University Press, 1994.

———. *Entre la secte et la cité: le projet d'église du réformateur Martin Bucer (1491–1551).* Geneva: Labor et Fides, 1984.

Harmening, Dieter. *Superstitio: Überlieferungs- und theoriegeschichtliche Untersuchungen zur kirchlich-theologischen Aberglaubensliteratur des Mittelalters.* Munich: Erich Schmidt Verlag, 1979.

Harrington, Joel F. *Reordering Marriage and Society in Reformation Germany.* Cambridge: Cambridge University Press, 1995.

Haskins, Charles Homer. *The Renaissance of the Twelfth Century.* Cambridge: Harvard University Press, 1927.

Haude, Sigrun. *In the Shadow of "Savage Wolves": Anabaptist Münster and the German Reformation during the 1530s.* Boston: Humanities Press, 2000.

———. "The Silent Monks Speak Up: The Changing Identity of the Carthusians in the Fifteenth and Sixteenth Centuries." *ARG* 86 (1995): 124–40.

Haustein, Jörg. *Martin Luthers Stellung zum Zauber- und Hexenwesen.* Stuttgart: W. Kohlhammer, 1990.

Headley, John. "Luther and the Problem of Secularization." *Journal of the American Academy of Religion* 55 (1987): 21–37.

Helmrath, Johannes. "Visitationsberichte als Geschichtsquellen." *Geschichte in Köln* 30 (December 1991): 137–41.

Hendrix, Scott. "American Luther Research in the Twentieth Century." *LQ* 15 (2001): 1–23.

———. "Beyond Erikson: The Relational Luther." *Lutheran Theological Seminary (Gettysburg) Bulletin* 75 (1995): 3–11.

———. "Luther and the Church." *LuJ* 52 (1985): 140–45.

———. "Luther on Marriage." *LQ* 14 (2000): 335–50.

———. "The Reform of Marriage in Calvin's Geneva." In *Caritas et Reformatio: Essays on Church and Society in Honor of Carter Lindberg,* ed. David M. Whitford, 113–31. St. Louis: Concordia, 2002.

———. "Rerooting the Faith: the Reformation as Re-Christianization." *CH* 69 (2000): 558–77.

———. *Tradition and Authority in the Reformation.* Aldershot, England, and Brookfield, Vt.: Ashgate, 1996.

———. "'We Are All Hussites': Hus and Luther Revisited." *ARG* 65 (1974): 134–61.

Henrich, Sarah, and James L. Boyce. "Martin Luther—Translation of Two Prefaces on Islam: Preface to the *Libellus de ritu et moribus Turcorum* (1530), and Preface to Bibliander's Edition of the Qu'ran (1543)." *Word and World* 16 (1996): 250–66.

Herrin, Judith. *The Formation of Christendom.* Princeton: Princeton University Press, 1987.

Hirsch, Elisabeth Feist. "Luther, Calvin, and the Doctrine of Tolerance of Sebastian Castellio." In *The Spanish Inquisition and the Inquisitorial Mind,* ed. Angel Alcalá, 625–42. Boulder, Colo.: Social Science Monographs; Highland Lakes, N.J.: Atlantic Research & Publications, 1987.

Hofacker, Hans-Georg. "'Vom alten und nüen Gott, Glauben und Ler': Untersuchungen zum Geschichtsverständnis und Epochenbewusstsein einer anonymen reformatorischen Flugschrift." In *Kontinuität und Umbruch: Theologie und Frömmigkeit in Flugschriften und Kleinliteratur an der Wende vom 15. zum 16. Jahrhundert*, ed. Josef Nolte, Hella Tompert, and Christof Windhorst, 145–77. Stuttgart: Klett-Cotta, 1978.

Hoffman, Philip T. *Church and Community in the Diocese of Lyon, 1500–1789*. New Haven and London: Yale University Press, 1984.

Holsten, Walter. "Reformation und Mission." *ARG* 44 (1953): 1–32.

Horowitz, Maryanne Cline. *Seeds of Virtue and Knowledge*. Princeton: Princeton University Press, 1998.

Howe, John. *Church Reform and Social Change in Eleventh-Century Italy: Dominic of Sora and His Patrons*. Philadelphia: University of Pennsylvania Press, 1997.

Hsia, R. Po-chia. *Society and Religion in Münster, 1535–1618*. New Haven and London: Yale University Press, 1984.

———. *The World of Catholic Renewal, 1540–1770*. Cambridge: Cambridge University Press, 1998.

Hudson, D. Dennis. *Protestant Origins in India: Tamil Evangelical Christians, 1706–1835*. Grand Rapids and Cambridge: Eerdmans, 2000.

Huizinga, Johan. *The Autumn of the Middle Ages*, ed. Rodney J. Payton and Ulrich Mammitzsch. Chicago: University of Chicago Press, 1996.

Iwand, Hans Joachim. *Luthers Theologie*. Ed. Johann Haar. Munich: Kaiser, 1983.

Jansen, Katherine L. *The Making of the Magdalen: Preaching and Popular Devotion in the Later Middle Ages*. Princeton, N.J.: Princeton University Press, 2000.

Jedin, Hubert. "Katholische Reformation oder Gegenreformation" (1946). In *The Counter-Reformation: The Essential Readings*, ed. David M. Luebke, 19–45. Oxford: Blackwell, 1999.

Jedin, Hubert, ed. *Handbuch der Kirchengeschichte*, 7 vols. Freiburg: Herder, 1962–1979.

Jeyaraj, Daniel. *Inkulturation in Tranquebar: Der Beitrag der frühen dänisch-halleschen Mission zum Werden einer indisch-einheimischen Kirche (1706–1730)*. Erlangen: Verlag der Ev.-Luth. Mission, 1996.

Jones, Martin D. W. *The Counter-Reformation: Religion and Society in Early Modern Europe*. Cambridge: Cambridge University Press, 1995.

Jones, Prudence, and Nigel Pennick. *A History of Pagan Europe*. London and New York: Routledge, 1995.

Jones, Serene. *Calvin and the Rhetoric of Piety*. Louisville: Westminster John Knox, 1995.

Junghans, Helmar. *Der junge Luther und die Humanisten*. Weimar: Hermann Böhlaus Nachfolger, 1984.

———. "Luthers Gottesdienstreform—Konzept oder Verlegenheit?" In *Herausforderung: Gottesdienst*, ed. Reinhold Morath and Wolfgang Ratzmann, 77–92. Leipzig: Evangelische Verlagsanstalt, 1997.

———. *Martin Luther und die Rhetorik*. Leipzig: Verlag der Sächsischen Akademie der Wissenschaften zu Leipzig, 1998.

———. *Martin Luther und Wittenberg*. Munich and Berlin: Koehler & Amelang, 1996.

———. "Martin Luthers Einfluss auf die Wittenberger Universitätsreform." In *Die Theologische Fakultät Wittenberg 1502 bis 1602: Beiträge zur 500. Wiederkehr des Gründungsjahres der Leucorea*, ed. Irene Dingel, Günther Wartenberg, and Michael Beyer, 55–70. Leipzig: Evangelische Verlagsanstalt, 2002.

————. Spätmittelalter, Luthers Reformation, Kirche in Sachsen: Ausgewählte Aufsätze, ed. Michael Beyer and Günther Wartenberg. Leipzig: Evangelische Verlagsanstalt, 2001.

Kafadar, Cemal. "The Ottomans and Europe." In Handbook of European History, 1400–1600, 2 vols., ed. Thomas A. Brady, Jr., Heiko A. Oberman, and James D. Tracy, 1:589–635. Grand Rapids: Eerdmans, 1996.

Kamen, Henry. Inquisition and Society in Spain in the Sixteenth and Seventeenth Centuries. Bloomington: Indiana University Press, 1985.

Kanichikattil, Francis, ed. Church in Context: Essays in Honour of Mathias Mundadan. Bangalore: Dharmaram Publications, 1996.

Karant-Nunn, Susan. The Reformation of Ritual: An Interpretation of Early Modern Germany. London and New York: Routledge, 1997.

————. "What Was Preached in German Cities in the Early Years of the Reformation? Wildwuchs Versus Lutheran Unity." In The Process of Change in Early Modern Europe: Essays in Honor of Miriam Usher Chrisman, ed. Phillip N. Bebb and Sherrin Marshall, 81–96. Athens: Ohio University Press, 1988.

Kavka, František. "Bohemia." In The Reformation in National Context, ed. Bob Scribner, Roy Porter, and Mikulâs Teich, 131–54. Cambridge: Cambridge University Press, 1994.

Keen, Ralph. Divine and Human Authority in Reformation Thought: German Theologians on Political Order, 1520–1555. Nieuwkoop: De Graaf, 1997.

Kingdon, Robert M. Adultery and Divorce in Calvin's Geneva. Cambridge and London: Harvard University Press, 1995.

————. "The Genevan Revolution in Public Worship." Princeton Seminary Bulletin 20 (1999): 264–80.

Kitching, Christopher. "Broken Angels: The Response of English Parishes to the Turkish Threat to Christendom, 1543–4." In The Church and Wealth, ed. W. J. Sheils and Diana Wood, 209–17. Oxford: Blackwell, 1987.

Kittelson, James M. Luther the Reformer: The Story of the Man and His Career. Minneapolis: Augsburg, 1986.

————. "Successes and Failures in the German Reformation: The Report from Strasbourg." ARG 73 (1982): 153–75.

Klein, Thomas. Der Kampf um die zweite Reformation in Kursachsen. Cologne and Graz: Böhlau, 1962.

Kloczowski, Jerzy. "Catholic Reform in the Polish-Lithuanian Commonwealth (Poland, Lithuania, the Ukraine, and Belorussia)." In Catholicism in Early Modern History: A Guide to Research, ed. John W. O'Malley, 83–111. St. Louis: Center for Reformation Research, 1988.

Koenigsberger, H. G. "The Unity of the Church and the Reformation." Journal of Interdisciplinary History 1 (1971): 407–17.

Kohler, Erika. Martin Luther und der Festbrauch. Cologne and Graz: Böhlau, 1959.

Köhler, Manfred. Melanchthon und der Islam: Ein Beitrag zur Klärung des Verhältnisses zwischen Christentum und Fremdreligionen in der Reformationszeit. Leipzig: Leopold Klotz Verlag, 1938.

Kohls, Ernst-Wilhelm. "Martin Bucer, 'Martinien.'" In Horizons européens de la réforme en Alsace: Mélanges offerts à Jean Rott pour son 65e anniversaire, ed. Marijn de Kroon and Marc Lienhard, 195–205. Strasbourg: Librairie Istra, 1980.

Kolb, Robert. For All the Saints: Changing Perceptions of Martyrdom and Sainthood in the Lutheran Reformation. Macon, Ga.: Mercer University Press, 1987.

———. "The Layman's Bible: The Use of Luther's Catechisms in the German Late Reformation." In *Luther's Catechisms—450 Years*, ed. David P. Scaer and Robert D. Preus, 16–26. Fort Wayne, Ind.: Concordia Theological Seminary Press, 1979.

———. "Luther, the Master Pastor: Conrad Porta's *Pastorale Lutheri*, Handbook for Generations." *Concordia Journal* 9 (1983): 179–87.

Kooi, Christine. "Converts and Apostates: The Competition for Souls in Early Modern Holland." *ARG* 92 (2001): 194–214.

Köpf, Ulrich. "Martin Luthers Lebensgang als Mönch." In *Kloster Amelungsborn 1135–1985*, ed. Gerhard Ruhbach and Kurt Schmidt-Clausen, 187–208. Hannover: Kloster Amelungsborn, 1985.

———. "Monastische Theologie im 15. Jahrhundert." *Rottenburger Jahrbuch für Kirchengeschichte* 11 (1992): 117–35.

Kowalski, Waldemar. "From the 'Land of Diverse Sects' to National Religion: Converts to Catholicism and Reformed Franciscans in Early Modern Poland." *CH* 70 (2001): 482–526.

Kuhr, Olaf. *"Die Macht des Bannes und der Busse": Kirchenzucht und Erneuerung der Kirche bei Johannes Oekolampad (1482–1531)*. Bern and New York: Peter Lang, 1999.

Kunzelmann, Adalbero. *Die sächsisch-thüringische Provinz und die sächsische Reformkongregation bis zum Untergang der beiden*. Geschichte der deutschen Augustiner-Eremiten 5. Würzburg: Augustinus-Verlag, 1974.

Laemmer, Hugo. *Die vortridentinisch-katholische Theologie des Reformations-Zeitalters aus den Quellen dargestellt*. Frankfurt: Minerva, 1966 (reprint of 1858 Berlin ed.).

Lambert, Thomas A. "Preaching, Praying, and Policing the Reform in Sixteenth-Century Geneva." Ph.D. diss., University of Wisconsin, 1998.

Lane, Anthony N. S. *Calvin and Bernard of Clairvaux*. Studies in Reformed Theology and History, n.s., 1. Princeton, N.J.: Princeton Theological Seminary, 1996.

Larson, Pier M. "'Capacities and Modes of Thinking': Intellectual Engagements and Subaltern Hegemony in the Early History of Malagasy Christianity." *AHR* 102 (1997): 969–1002.

Lau, Franz. *Luther*. Berlin: De Gruyter, 1959.

Lauster, Jörg. "Religion als Lebensform: Zur Erinnerung an Marsilio Ficinos Programm eines platonischen Christentums." *Theologie und Philosophie* 76 (2001): 206–28.

Lazar, Lance. "The First Jesuit Confraternities and Marginalized Groups in Sixteenth-Century Rome." In *The Politics of Ritual Kinship: Confraternities and Social Order in Early Modern Italy*, ed. Nicholas Terpstra, 132–49. Cambridge: Cambridge University Press, 2000.

Lehmann, Hartmut. *Max Webers "Protestantische Ethik": Beiträge aus der Sicht eines Historikers*. Göttingen: Vandenhoeck & Ruprecht, 1996.

Lehmann, Hartmut, ed. *Säkularisierung, Dechristianisierung, Rechristianisierung im neuzeitlichen Europa: Bilanz und Perspektiven der Forschung*. Göttingen: Vandenhoeck & Ruprecht, 1997.

Le Roy Ladurie, E. *Montaillou: The Promised Land of Error*. Trans. Barbara Bray. New York: George Braziller, 1978.

Lienhard, Marc. "Glaube und Skepsis im 16. Jahrhundert." In *Bauer, Reich und Reformation*, ed. Peter Blickle, 160–81. Stuttgart: Eugen Ulmer, 1982.

Lilienfein, Heinrich. *Lukas Cranach und seine Zeit*. Bielefeld and Leipzig: Velhagen & Klasing, 1942.

Lindberg, Carter. *The European Reformations*. Oxford: Blackwell, 1996.

Locher, Gottfried W. *Huldrych Zwingli in neuer Sicht.* Zurich and Stuttgart: Zwingli Verlag, 1969.

Lohse, Bernhard. "Luther und Bernhard von Clairvaux." In *Bernhard von Clairvaux: Rezeption und Wirkung im Mittelalter und in der Neuzeit,* ed. Kaspar Elm, 271–301. Wiesbaden: Harrassowitz, 1994.

Lottes, Günther. "Luther und die Frömmigkeitskrise des Spätmittelalters." In *Luther in seiner Zeit: Persönlichkeit und Wirken des Reformators,* ed. Martin Greschat and Günther Lottes, 13–28. Stuttgart: W. Kohlhammer, 1997.

MacCormack, Sabine. "Ubi Ecclesia? Perceptions of Medieval Europe in Spanish America." *Speculum* 69 (1994): 74–100.

MacCulloch, Diarmaid. *Thomas Cranmer: A Life.* New Haven, Conn., and London: Yale University Press, 1996.

MacMullen, Ramsay. *Christianity and Paganism in the Fourth to Eighth Centuries.* New Haven, Conn., and London: Yale University Press, 1997.

———. *Christianizing the Roman Empire (A.D. 100–400).* New Haven, Conn., and London: Yale University Press, 1984.

Maron, Gottfried. "Die nachtridentinische Kodifikationsarbeit in ihrer Bedeutung für die katholische Konfessionalisierung." In *Die katholische Konfessionalisierung,* ed. Wolfgang Reinhard and Heinz Schilling, 104–24. Gütersloh: GVH, 1995.

Martin, Dennis D. "The Via Moderna, Humanism, and the Hermeneutics of Late Medieval Monastic Life." *Journal of the History of Ideas* 51 (1990): 179–97.

Martin, Francis Xavier. "The Augustinian Observant Movement." In *Reformbemühungen und Observanzbestrebungen im spätmittelalterlichen Ordenswesen,* ed. Kaspar Elm, 325–45. Berlin: Duncker & Humblot, 1989.

Martin, Hervé. *Mentalités médiévales, XIe–XVe siècle.* Paris: PUF, 1996.

Matheson, Peter. *The Imaginative World of the Reformation.* Edinburgh: T. & T. Clark, 2000.

Mau, Rudolf. "Luthers Stellung zu den Türken." In *Leben und Werk Martin Luthers von 1526 bis 1546,* 2 vols., ed. Helmar Junghans, 1:647–62, 2:956–66. Berlin: Evangelische Verlagsanstalt, 1983.

Mauer, Wilhelm. *Der junge Melanchthon zwischen Humanismus und Reformation.* Vol. 1, *Der Humanist.* Göttingen: Vandenhoeck & Ruprecht, 1967.

McKee, Elsie Anne. *John Calvin: Writings on Pastoral Piety.* New York: Paulist Press, 2001.

———. *Katharina Schütz Zell.* 2 vols. Leiden: Brill, 1999.

McKitterick, Rosamond. *Books, Scribes, and Learning in the Frankish Kingdoms, 6th–9th Centuries.* Aldershot, England, and Brookfield, Vt.: Ashgate, 1994.

McKitterick, Rosamond, ed. *Carolingian Culture: Emulation and Innovation.* Cambridge and New York: Cambridge University Press, 1994.

Mehlhausen, Joachim. "*Forma Christianismi*: Die theologische Bewertung eines kleinen katechetischen Lehrstücks durch Luther und Erasmus von Rotterdam." In *Humanism and Reform: The Church in Europe, England, and Scotland, 1400–1643; Essays in Honour of James K. Cameron,* ed. James Kirk, 57–75. Oxford: Blackwell, 1991.

Milis, Ludovicus J., ed. *The Pagan Middle Ages.* Trans. Tanis Guest. Woodbridge: Boydell, 1998.

Miller, Gregory J. "Holy War and Holy Terror: Views of Islam in German Pamphlet Literature, 1520–1545." Ph.D. diss., Boston University, 1994.

———. "Luther on the Turks and Islam." *LQ* 14 (2000): 79–97.

Moeller, Bernd. "Die frühe Reformation in Deutschland als neues Mönchtum." In *Die frühe Reformation in Deutschland als Umbruch*, ed. Bernd Moeller and Stephen E. Buckwalter, 76–91. Gütersloh: Gütersloher Verlagshaus, 1998.

———. *Imperial Cities and the Reformation: Three Essays*. Ed. and trans. H. C. Erik Midelfort and Mark U. Edwards, Jr. Philadelphia: Fortress Press, 1972.

———. *Luther-Rezeption: Kirchenhistorische Aufsätze zur Reformationsgeschichte*. Ed. Johannes Schilling. Göttingen: Vandenhoeck & Ruprecht, 2001.

———. "Piety in Germany around 1500." In *The Reformation in Medieval Perspective*, ed. Steven Ozment, 50–75. Chicago: Quadrangle, 1971.

———. *Reichsstadt und Reformation*. Rev. ed. Berlin: Evangelische Verlagsanstalt, 1987.

———. "Die Ursprünge der reformierten Kirche." *Theologische Literaturzeitung* 100 (1975): 641–53.

———. "Was wurde in der Frühzeit der Reformation in den deutschen Städten gepredigt?" *ARG* 75 (1984): 176–93.

Molitor, Hansgeorg. "Frömmigkeit in Spätmittelalter und früher Neuzeit als historisch-methodisches Problem." In *Festgabe für Ernst-Walter Zeeden*, ed. Horst Rabe, Hansgeorg Molitor, and Hans-Christoph Rublack, 1–20. Münster: Aschendorff, 1976.

Moltmann, Jürgen. *Christoph Pezel (1539–1604) und der Calvinismus in Bremen*. Bremen: Einkehr, 1958.

Monter, E. William. "Popular Piety in Late Medieval Europe." In E. William Monter, *Ritual, Myth, and Magic in Early Modern Europe*, 6–22. Athens: Ohio University Press, 1983.

Moorhead, John. "Clovis' Motives for Becoming a Catholic Christian." *Journal of Religious History* 13 (1985): 329–59.

Mühling, Andreas. *Heinrich Bullingers europäische Kirchenpolitik*. Bern: Lang, 2001.

Muir, Edward. *Ritual in Early Modern Europe*. Cambridge: Cambridge University Press, 1997.

Münch, Paul. *Zucht und Ordnung: Reformierte Kirchenverfassungen im 16. und 17. Jahrhundert (Nassau-Dillenburg, Kurpfalz, Hessen-Kassel)*. Stuttgart: Klett-Cotta, 1978.

Mundadan, A. Mathias. *Sixteenth-Century Traditions of St. Thomas Christians*. Bangalore: Dharmaram College, 1970.

Nalle, Sara T. *God in La Mancha: Religious Reform and the People of Cuenca, 1500–1650*. Baltimore and London: Johns Hopkins University Press, 1992.

Neidiger, Bernhard. "Die Observanzbewegungen der Bettelorden in Südwestdeutschland." *Rottenburger Jahrbuch für Kirchengeschichte* 11 (1992): 175–96.

Neuser, Wilhelm. "Bucers Programm einer 'guten leidlichen Reformation' (1539–1541)." In *Horizons européens de la réforme en Alsace: Mélanges offerts à Jean Rott pour son 65e anniversaire*, ed. Marijn de Kroon and Marc Lienhard, 227–39. Strasbourg: Librairie Istra, 1980.

———. "Die Erforschung der 'Zweiten Reformation'—eine wissenschaftliche Fehlentwicklung." In *Die reformierte Konfessionalisierung in Deutschland—Das Problem der "Zweiten Reformation,"* ed. Heinz Schilling, 379–86. Gütersloh: GVH, 1986.

Nichols, James Hastings. *History of Christianity 1650–1950: Secularization of the West*. New York: Ronald Press, 1956.

Niebuhr, H. Richard. *Christ and Culture*. New York: Harper, 1956.

Nischan, Bodo. *Lutherans and Calvinists in the Age of Confessionalism*. Aldershot, England, and Brookfield, Vt.: Ashgate, 1999.

———. *Prince, People, and Confession: The Second Reformation in Brandenburg*. Philadelphia: University of Pennsylvania Press, 1994.

Norman, Corrie E. *Humanist Taste and Franciscan Values: Cornelio Musso and Catholic Preaching in Sixteenth-Century Italy.* New York: Peter Lang, 1998.

Oberman, Heiko A. "*Europa afflicta*: The Reformation of the Refugees." *ARG* 83 (1992): 91–111.

———. *The Harvest of Medieval Theology: Gabriel Biel and Late Medieval Nominalism.* Rev. ed. Grand Rapids: Eerdmans, 1967.

———. "*Initia Calvini*: The Matrix of Calvin's Reformation." In *Calvinus Sacrae Scripturae Professor / Calvin as Confessor of Holy Scripture,* ed. Wilhelm H. Neuser, 113–54. Grand Rapids: Eerdmans, 1994.

———. *Luther: Man between God and the Devil.* New Haven, Conn., and London: Yale University Press, 1989.

———. "Martin Luther: Vorläufer der Reformation." In *Verifikationen: Festschrift für Gerhard Ebeling zum 70. Geburtstag,* ed. Eberhard Jüngel, Johannes Wallmann, and Wilfrid Werbeck, 91–119. Tübingen: Mohr Siebeck, 1982.

———. *Die Reformation: Von Wittenberg nach Genf.* Göttingen: Vandenhoeck & Ruprecht, 1986.

———. "'Tuus sum, salvum me fac.' Augustinréveil zwischen Renaissance und Reformation." In *Scientia Augustiniana: Studien über Augustinus, den Augustinismus und den Augustinerorden,* ed. Cornelius Petrus Mayer and Willigis Eckermann, 349–94. Würzburg: Augustinus-Verlag, 1975.

Oehmig, Stefan. "'Christliche Bürger'—'christliche Stadt'? Zu Andreas Bodensteins von Karlstadt Vorstellungen von einem christlichen Gemeinwesen und den Tugenden seiner Bürger." In *Querdenker der Reformation—Andreas Bodenstein von Karlstadt und seine frühe Wirkung,* ed. Ulrich Bubenheimer and Stefan Oehmig, 151–85. Würzburg: Religion und Kultur Verlag, 2001.

Oestreich, Gerhard. *Geist und Gestalt des frühmodernen Staates: Ausgewählte Aufsätze.* Berlin: Duncker & Humblot, 1969.

———. *Strukturprobleme der frühen Neuzeit,* ed. Brigitta Oestreich. Berlin: Duncker & Humblot, 1980.

Old, Hughes Oliphant. *The Reading and Preaching of the Scriptures in the Worship of the Christian Church.* Vol. 3, *The Medieval Church.* Grand Rapids and Cambridge: Eerdmans, 1999.

O'Malley, John W. *The First Jesuits.* Cambridge and London: Harvard University Press, 1993.

———. *Religious Culture in the Sixteenth Century: Preaching, Rhetoric, Spirituality, and Reform.* Aldershot, England, and Brookfield, Vt.: Ashgate, 1993.

———. *Trent and All That: Renaming Catholicism in the Early Modern Era.* Cambridge and London: Harvard University Press, 2000.

Ozment, Steven. *The Reformation in the Cities: The Appeal of Protestantism to Sixteenth-Century Germany and Switzerland.* New Haven, Conn., and London: Yale University Press, 1975.

Packull, Werner O. *Hutterite Beginnings: Communitarian Experiments during the Reformation.* Baltimore and London: Johns Hopkins University Press, 1995.

———. "The Origins of Peter Riedemann's *Account of Our Faith.*" *SCJ* 30 (1999): 61–69.

Pannen, Friedemann. "Luther über Johannes Gerson." *Luther* 71 (2000): 117–25.

Parry, V. J. "The Ottoman Empire 1520–1526." In *The New Cambridge Modern History,* vol. 2, *The Reformation, 1520–1559,* 2nd ed., ed. G. R. Elton, 570–94. Cambridge: Cambridge University Press, 1990.

Pegg, Mark G. *The Corruption of Angels: The Great Inquisition of 1245–1246.* Princeton: Princeton University Press, 2001.

Peter, Katalin. "Hungary." In *The Reformation in National Context*, ed. Bob Scribner, Roy Porter, and Mikulás Teich, 155–67. Cambridge: Cambridge University Press, 1994.

Peters, Frank C. "The Ban in the Writings of Menno Simons." *MQR* 29 (1955): 16–33.

Petri, Heinrich. "Zur Frage nach dem eigentlich Christlichen." *Catholica* 30 (1976): 1–19.

Pettegree, Andrew W., ed. *The Reformation World.* London and New York: Routledge, 2000.

Pfister, Rudolf. "Reformation, Türken, und Islam." *Zwingliana* 10 (1956): 345–75.

———. "Das Türkenbüchlein Theodor Biblianders." *Theologische Zeitschrift* 9 (1953): 438–54.

Pósfay, George. "'The Whole Christian Church on Earth'—Luther's Conception of the Universality of the Church." *Lutheran Theological Seminary (Gettysburg) Bulletin* 72 (1992): 20–43.

Poska, Allison M. *Regulating the People: The Catholic Reformation in Seventeenth-Century Spain.* Leiden: Brill, 1998.

Ranke, Leopold von. *Deutsche Geschichte im Zeitalter der Reformation.* 6 vols. 2nd ed. Berlin: Duncker & Humblot, 1842–1847.

Rapley, Elizabeth. *The Dévotes: Women and Church in Seventeenth-Century France.* Kingston, Ont.: McGill–Queens University Press, 1990.

Reid, W. Stanford, ed. *John Calvin: His Influence in the Western World.* Grand Rapids: Zondervan, 1982.

Reinhard, Wolfgang. "Gegenreformation als Modernisierung? Prolegomena zu einer Theorie des konfessionellen Zeitalters." *ARG* 68 (1977): 226–52.

———. "Reformation, Counter-Reformation, and the Early Modern State: A Reassessment." In *The Counter-Reformation: The Essential Readings*, ed. David M. Luebke, 105–28. Oxford: Blackwell, 1999.

———. "Was ist katholische Konfessionalisierung?" In *Die katholische Konfessionalisierung*, ed. Wolfgang Reinhard and Heinz Schilling, 419–52. Gütersloh: GVH, 1995.

Reinhard, Wolfgang, and Heinz Schilling, eds. *Die katholische Konfessionalisierung.* Gütersloh: GVH, 1995.

Rieske-Braun, Uwe. "Glaube und Aberglaube: Luther's Auslegung des Ersten Gebotes 1516/1518." *LuJ* 69 (2002): 21–46.

Rieth, Ricardo Willy. *"Habsucht" bei Martin Luther: Ökonomisches und theologisches Denken, Tradition und soziale Wirklichkeit im Zeitalter der Reformation.* Weimar: Hermann Böhlaus Nachfolger, 1996.

———. "Luther on Greed." *LQ* 15 (2001): 336–51.

Riley-Smith, Jonathan. *The First Crusaders, 1095–1131.* Cambridge: Cambridge University Press, 1997.

Ritter, Moriz. *Deutsche Geschichte im Zeitalter der Gegenreformation und des Dreissigjährigen Krieges, 1555–1648.* 3 vols. Stuttgart: J. G. Cotta, 1889–1908.

Rogge, Joachim. *Anfänge der Reformation: Der junge Luther 1483–1521 / Der junge Zwingli 1484–1523.* Berlin: Evangelische Verlagsanstalt, 1983.

Roper, Lyndal. *The Holy Household: Women and Morals in Reformation Augsburg.* Oxford: Clarendon Press, 1989.

Rosman, Doreen. *From Catholic to Protestant: Religion and the People in Tudor England.* London: UCL Press, 1996.

Rott, Jean. "Die 'Gartner,' der Rat, und das Thomaskapitel." In *Investigationes historicae: Églises et société au XVIe siècle*, 2 vols., ed. Marijn de Kroon and Marc Lienhard, 2:177–80. Strasbourg: Librairie Oberlin, 1986.

Rott, Jean, and Marc Lienhard. "Die Anfänge der evangelischen Predigt in Strassburg und ihr erstes Manifest: Der Aufruf des Karmeliterlesemeisters Tilman von Lyn (Anfang 1522)." In *Investigationes historicae: Églises et société au XVIe siècle*, ed. Marijn de Kroon and Marc Lienhard, 1:444–63. 2 vols. Strasbourg: Librairie Oberlin, 1986.

Rubin, Miri. *Corpus Christi: The Eucharist in Late Medieval Culture.* Cambridge: Cambridge University Press, 1991.

Rublack, Hans-Christoph. "Anticlericalism in German Reformation Pamphlets." In *Anticlericalism in Late Medieval and Early Modern Europe*, ed. Peter A. Dykema and Heiko A. Oberman, 461–89. Leiden: Brill, 1993.

———. "Reformation und Moderne: Soziologische, theologische und historische Ansichten." In *The Reformation in Germany and Europe: Interpretations and Issues*, ed. Hans R. Guggisberg and Gottfried G. Krodel, 17–38. Gütersloh: GVH, 1993.

Rublack, Hans-Christoph, ed. *Die lutherische Konfessionalisierung in Deutschland.* Gütersloh: GVH, 1992.

Rummel, Erika. *The Confessionalization of Humanism in Reformation Germany.* Oxford and New York: Oxford University Press, 2000.

———. "*Monachatus non est pietas:* Interpretations and Misinterpretations of a Dictum." In *Erasmus' Vision of the Church*, ed. Hilmar M. Pabel, 41–55. Kirksville, Mo.: SCJ Publishers, 1995.

———. "Voices of Reform from Hus to Erasmus." In *Handbook of European History, 1400–1600*, 2 vols., ed. Thomas A. Brady, Jr., Heiko A. Oberman, and James D. Tracy, 2:61–91. Grand Rapids: Eerdmans, 1996.

Saak, Eric L. *High Way to Heaven: The Augustinian Platform between Reform and Reformation, 1292–1524.* Leiden: Brill, 2002.

Sallmann, Martin. *Zwischen Gott und Mensch: Huldrych Zwinglis theologischer Denkweg im De vera et falsa religione commentarius (1525).* Tübingen: Mohr Siebeck, 1999.

Salmon, J. H. M. "Clovis and Constantine: The Uses of History in Sixteenth-Century Gallicanism." *JEH* 41 (1990): 584–605.

Sánchez, Magdalena. "Confession and Complicity: Margarita de Austria, Richard Haller, S.J., and the Court of Philip III." *Cuadernos de Historia Moderna* 14 (1993): 133–49.

Sanneh, Lamin. "The Gospel, Language and Culture: The Theological Method in Cultural Analysis." *International Review of Missions* 84 (1995): 47–64.

———. "Translatability in Islam and in Christianity in Africa: A Thematic Approach." In *Religion in Africa: Experience and Expression*, ed. Thomas D. Blakely, Walter E. A. van Beek, and Dennis L. Thomson, 22–45. London: James Curry, 1994.

Sautman, Francesca Canadé. *La religion du quotidien: rites et croyances populaires de la fin du moyen âge.* Florence: Leo S. Olschki Editore, 1995.

Scarisbrick, J. J. *The Reformation and the English People.* Oxford: Blackwell, 1984.

Schilling, Heinz. "Confessional Europe." In *Handbook of European History, 1400–1600*, 2 vols., ed. Thomas A. Brady, Jr., Heiko A. Oberman, and James D. Tracy, 2:641–81. Grand Rapids: Eerdmans, 1996.

———. "Die Konfessionalisierung im Reich: Religiöser und Gesellschaftlicher Wandel in Deutschland zwischen 1555 und 1620." *Historische Zeitschrift* 246 (1988): 1–45.

———. "Die Konfessionalisierung von Kirche, Staat und Gesellschaft—Profil, Leistung, Defizite und Perspektiven eines geschichtswissenschaftlichen Paradigmas." In *Die katholische Konfessionalisierung*, ed. Wolfgang Reinhard and Heinz Schilling, 1–49. Gütersloh: GVH, 1995.

———. *Konfessionskonflikt und Staatsbildung*. Gütersloh: GVH, 1981.

———. "Zwang zur Konfessionalisierung? Prolegomena zu einer Theorie des konfessionellen Zeitalters." *Zeitschrift für historische Forschung* 10 (1983): 257–77.

Schilling, Heinz, ed. *Die reformierte Konfessionalisierung in Deutschland—Das Problem der "Zweiten Reformation."* Gütersloh: GVH, 1986.

Schilling, Johannes. *Gewesene Mönche: Lebensgeschichten in der Reformation*. Munich: Stiftung Historisches Kolleg, 1990.

Schindling, Anton, and Walter Ziegler, eds. *Die Territorien des Reichs im Zeitalter der Reformation und Konfessionalisierung: Land und Konfession 1500–1650*. 7 vols. Münster: Aschendorff, 1989–1997.

Schmidt, Heinrich Richard. "Die Ethik der Laien in der Reformation." In *Die frühe Reformation in Deutschland als Umbruch*, ed. Bernd Moeller and Stephen E. Buckwalter, 333–70. Gütersloh: GVH, 1998.

———. "Gemeinde und Sittenzucht im protestantischen Europa der Frühen Neuzeit." In *Theorien kommunaler Ordnung in Europa*, ed. Peter Blickle, 181–214. Munich: R. Oldenbourg, 1996.

———. *Konfessionalisierung im 16. Jahrhundert*. Munich: R. Oldenbourg, 1992.

———. "Sozialdisziplinierung? Ein Plädoyer für das Ende des Etatismus in der Konfessionalisierungsforschung." *Historische Zeitschrift* 265 (1997): 639–82.

Schneider, Hans. "Zwinglis Marienpredigt und Luthers Magnifikat-Auslegung: Ein Beitrag zum Verhältnis Zwinglis zu Luther." *Zwingliana* 23 (1996): 105–41.

Schwarz, Reinhard. *Die apokalyptische Theologie Thomas Müntzers und der Taboriten*. Tübingen: Mohr Siebeck, 1977.

———. "Luthers unveräusserte Erbschaft an der monastischen Theologie." In *Kloster Amelungsborn 1135–1985*, ed. Gerhard Ruhbach and Kurt Schmidt-Clausen, 209–31. Hannover: Kloster Amelungsborn, 1985.

Scribner, Robert W. *For the Sake of Simple Folk: Popular Propaganda for the German Reformation*. Oxford and New York: Oxford University Press, 1994.

———. "The Reformation, Popular Magic, and the 'Disenchantment of the World.'" *Journal of Interdisciplinary History* 23 (1993): 475–94.

Scribner, Robert, Roy Porter, and Mikulâs Teich, eds. *The Reformation in National Context*. Cambridge: Cambridge University Press, 1994.

Seebass, Gottfried. *Artikelbrief, Bundesordnung und Verfassungsentwurf: Studien zu drei zentralen Dokumenten des südwestdeutschen Bauernkrieges*. Heidelberg: Carl Winter, 1988.

———. "Das Zeichen der Erwählten: Zum Verständnis der Taufe bei Hans Hut." In Gottfried Seebass, *Die Reformation und die Aussenseiter: Gesammelte Aufsätze und Vorträge*, ed. Irene Dingel, 203–26. Göttingen: Vandenhoeck & Ruprecht, 1997.

———. "Der 'linke Flügel der Reformation.'" In Gottfried Seebass, *Die Reformation und die Aussenseiter: Gesammelte Aufsätze und Vorträge*, ed. Irene Dingel, 151–64. Göttingen: Vandenhoeck & Ruprecht, 1997.

Seegets, Petra. *Passionstheologie und Passionsfrömmigkeit im ausgehenden Mittelalter: Der Nürnberger Franziskaner Stephan Fridolin (gest. 1498) zwischen Kloster und Stadt*. Tübingen: Mohr Siebeck, 1998.

Seidel Menchi, Silvana. *Erasmus als Ketzer: Reformation und Inquisition im Italien des 16. Jahrhunderts.* Leiden: Brill, 1993.

Selderhuis, H. J. *Marriage and Divorce in the Thought of Martin Bucer.* Trans. John Vriend and Lyle D. Bierma. Kirksville, Mo.: Thomas Jefferson University Press, 1999.

Selwyn, Jennifer D. "Reverberations from the New World: The Jesuits' Civilizing Mission in the Early Modern Period." Unpublished Essay, 2000.

Soergel, Philip M. *Wondrous in His Saints: Counter-Reformation Propaganda in Bavaria.* Berkeley: University of California Press, 1993.

Sparn, Walter. "'Wahrlich, dieser ist ein frommer Mensch gewesen!' Überlegungen zu einem evangelischen Begriff von Frömmigkeit." In *Post-Theism: Reframing the Judeo-Christian Tradition,* ed. Henri A. Krop, Arie L. Molendijk, and Hent de Vries, 447–65. Leuven: Peeters, 2000.

Spencer, Mark. "Dating the Baptism of Clovis 1886–1993." *Early Medieval Europe* 3 (1994): 97–116.

Spitz, Lewis W. "Luther and Humanism." In *Luther and Learning: The Wittenberg University Luther Symposium,* ed. Marilyn J. Harran, 69–94. London and Toronto: Associated University Presses, 1985.

Stafford, William S. *Domesticating the Clergy: The Inception of the Reformation in Strasbourg, 1522–1524.* Missoula, Mont.: Scholars Press, 1976.

Stahl, Friedrich Julius. *Die lutherische Kirche und die Union: Eine wissenschaftliche Erörterung der Zeitfrage.* Berlin: Verlag von Wilhelm Hertz, 1859.

Stayer, James M. *Anabaptists and the Sword.* Lawrence, Kans.: Coronado Press, 1972.

———. *The German Peasants' War and Anabaptist Community of Goods.* Montreal: McGill–Queen's University Press, 1991.

———. "The Passing of the Radical Moment in the Radical Reformation." *MQR* 71 (1997): 147–52.

Steinmetz, David C. "Calvin and the Monastic Ideal." In *Anticlericalism in Late Medieval and Early Modern Europe,* ed. Peter A. Dykema and Heiko A. Oberman, 605–16. Leiden: Brill, 1993.

———. *Luther and Staupitz: An Essay in the Intellectual Origins of the German Reformation.* Durham: Duke University Press, 1980.

Stephens, W. P. "Zwingli and the Salvation of the Gentiles." In *The Bible, the Reformation and the Church: Essays in Honour of James Atkinson,* ed. W. P. Stephens, 224–44. Sheffield: Sheffield Academic Press, 1995.

Stierle, Beate. *Capito als Humanist.* Gütersloh: GVH, 1974.

Stokes, Gale. "The Fate of Human Societies: A Review of Recent Macrohistories." *AHR* 106 (2001): 508–25.

Stolt, Birgit. *Martin Luthers Rhetorik des Herzens.* Tübingen: Mohr Siebeck, 2000.

Strauss, Gerald. *Luther's House of Learning: Indoctrination of the Young in the German Reformation.* Baltimore and London: Johns Hopkins University Press, 1978.

———. "Success and Failure in the German Reformation." *Past & Present* 67 (1975): 30–63.

Strom, Jonathan. *Orthodoxy and Reform: The Clergy in Seventeenth Century Rostock.* Tübingen: Mohr Siebeck, 1999.

Swanson, R. N. *Religion and Devotion in Europe, c. 1215–c. 1515.* Cambridge: Cambridge University Press, 1995.

———. *The Twelfth-Century Renaissance.* Manchester: Manchester University Press, 1999.

Tazbir, Janusz. "Poland." In *The Reformation in National Context,* ed. Bob Scribner, Roy Porter, and Mikuláš Teich, 168–80. Cambridge: Cambridge University Press, 1994.

Terpstra, Nicholas, ed. *The Politics of Ritual Kinship: Confraternities and Social Order in Early Modern Italy.* Cambridge: Cambridge University Press, 2000.

Thekkudan, Anto P. *Inculturation of Religious Formation among the St. Thomas Christians.* Rome: Pontificia Universitas Gregoriana, 1987.

Thurnhofer, Franz Xaver. *Bernhard Adelmann von Adelmannsfelden, Humanist und Luthers Freund (1457–1523).* Freiburg: Herder, 1900.

Tolley, Bruce. *Pastors and Parishioners in Württemberg during the Late Reformation, 1581–1621.* Stanford: Stanford University Press, 1995.

Tracy, James D. "Public Space: Restriction of Non-Calvinist Religious Behavior in the Province of Holland, 1572–1591." In *Continuity and Change: The Harvest of Late-Medieval and Reformation History,* ed. Robert J. Bast and Andrew C. Gow, 98–110. Leiden: Brill, 2000.

Trinkaus, Charles. *"In Our Image and Likeness": Humanity and Divinity in Italian Humanist Thought.* 2 vols. Chicago: University of Chicago Press, 1979.

Trompf, G. W. "The Concept of the Carolingian Renaissance." *Journal of the History of Ideas* 34 (1973): 3–26.

Tyler, J. Jeffrey. "Refugees and Reform: Banishment and Exile in Early Modern Augsburg." In *Continuity and Change: The Harvest of Late-Medieval and Reformation History,* ed. Robert J. Bast and Andrew C. Gow, 77–97. Leiden: Brill, 2000.

Valone, Carolyn. "The Pentecost: Image and Experience in Late Sixteenth-Century Rome." *SCJ* 24 (1993): 801–28.

Van Engen, John. "The Christian Middle Ages as an Historiographical Problem." *AHR* 91 (1986): 519–52.

———. "The Church in the Fifteenth Century." In *Handbook of European History, 1400–1600,* 2 vols., ed. Thomas A. Brady, Jr., Heiko A. Oberman, and James D. Tracy, 1:305–30. Grand Rapids: Eerdmans, 1996.

———. "The 'Crisis of Cenobitism' Reconsidered: Benedictine Monasticism in the Years 1050–1150." *Speculum* 61 (1986): 269–304.

———. "Faith as a Concept of Order in Medieval Christendom." In *Belief in History: Innovative Approaches to European and American Religion,* ed. Thomas Kselman, 19–67. Notre Dame and London: University of Notre Dame Press, 1991.

———. "The Sayings of the Fathers: An Inside Look at the New Devout in Deventer." In *Continuity and Change: The Harvest of Late-Medieval and Reformation History,* ed. Robert J. Bast and Andrew C. Gow, 279–320. Leiden: Brill, 2000.

Verkamp, Bernard. "The Zwinglians and Adiaphorism." *CH* 42 (1973): 486–504.

Vogler, Bernard. "Die Entstehung der protestantischen Volksfrömmigkeit in der rheinischen Pfalz zwischen 1555 and 1619." *ARG* 73 (1982): 158–95.

Vogler, Günter. "Gab es eine radikale Reformation? Bemerkungen zur Konzeption von G. H. Williams." *Wissenschaftliche Zeitschrift der Karl-Marx-Universität Leipzig* 14 (1965): 495–500.

Voolstra, Sjouke. *Menno Simons: His Image and Message.* North Newton, Kan.: Bethel College, 1997.

———. "Themes in the Early Theology of Menno Simons." In *Menno Simons: A Reappraisal,* ed. Gerald R. Brunk, 37–55. Harrisonburg, Va.: Eastern Mennonite College, 1992.

Waldburg Wolfegg, Christoph Graf zu. *Venus and Mars: The World of the Medieval Housebook.* Munich and New York: Prestel-Verlag, 1998.

Walls, Andrew F. "From Christendom to World Christianity: Missions and the Demographic Transformation of the Church." *Princeton Seminary Bulletin* 22 (2001): 306–30.

————. *The Missionary Movement in Christian History: Studies in the Transmission of Faith.* Maryknoll, N.Y.: Orbis, 1996.

Walsham, Alexandra. *Church Papists: Catholicism, Conformity, and Confessional Polemic in Early Modern England.* Woodbridge, England: Boydell Press, 1993.

Walter, Peter. "Kirche und Kirchenreform nach Erasmus von Rotterdam." *Rottenburger Jahrbuch für Kirchengeschichte* 11 (1992): 137–48.

Wandel, Lee Palmer. *Always among Us: Images of the Poor in Zwingli's Zurich.* Cambridge and New York: Cambridge University Press, 1990.

————. "The Reform of the Images: New Visualizations of the Christian Community at Zurich." *ARG* 80 (1989): 105–24.

Wassermann, Dirk. *Dionysius der Kartäuser: Einführung in Werk und Gedankenwelt.* Salzburg: Institut für Anglistik und Amerikanistik, 1996.

Weber, Max. *The Protestant Ethic and the Spirit of Capitalism.* Trans. Talcott Parsons. Los Angeles: Roxbury, 1996.

Weigelt, Horst. *Sebastian Franck und die lutherische Reformation.* Gütersloh: GVH, 1972.

Weiler, A. G. "The Turkish Argument and Christian Piety in Desiderius Erasmus' 'Consultatio de Bello Turcis Inferendo' (1530)." In *Erasmus of Rotterdam: The Man and the Scholar,* ed. Jan Sperna Weiland and Willem Th. M. Frijhoff, 30–39. Leiden: Brill, 1988.

Wendel, François. *Calvin: The Origins and Development of His Religious Thought.* London: Collins, 1965.

Wengert, Timothy J. "Luther and Melanchthon on Consecrated Communion Wine (Eisleben 1542–43)." *LQ* 15 (2001): 24–42.

————. "Philip Melanchthon and a Christian *Politics.*" *LQ* 17 (2003): 29–62.

————. "Wittenberg's Earliest Catechism." *LQ* 7 (1993): 247–60.

Wiesner-Hanks, Merry. *Gender in History.* Oxford: Blackwell, 2001.

————. "Ideology Meets the Empire: Reformed Convents and the Reformation." In Merry Wiesner-Hanks, *Gender, Church and State in Early Modern Germany,* 47–62. London and New York: Longman, 1998.

Wiest, Jean-Paul. "Bringing Christ to the Nations: Shifting Models of Mission among Jesuits in China." *CHR* 83 (1997): 654–90.

Wilcox, Peter. "The Lectures of John Calvin and the Nature of His Audience, 1555–1564." *ARG* 87 (1996): 136–48.

Williams, George H. *The Radical Reformation.* 3rd ed. Kirksville, Mo.: SCJ Publishers, 1992.

————. "The Radical Reformation Revisited." *Union Seminary Quarterly Review* 39 (1984): 1–24.

Winston-Allen, Anne. *Stories of the Rose: The Making of the Rosary in the Middle Ages.* University Park, Pa.: Pennsylvania State University Press, 1997.

Witt, Ronald G. "The Humanist Movement." In *Handbook of European History, 1400–1600,* 2 vols., ed. Thomas A. Brady, Jr., Heiko A. Oberman, and James D. Tracy, 2:93–125. Grand Rapids: Eerdmans, 1996.

Witte, John, Jr. *Law and Protestantism: The Legal Teachings of the Lutheran Reformation.* Cambridge: Cambridge University Press, 2002.

Wriedt, Markus. "Kirche und Kolonien in der frühen Neuzeit: Der Aufbau des lateinamerikanischen Kirchenwesens im 16. Jahrhundert." *Saeculum: Jahrbuch für Universalgeschichte* 44 (1993): 220–42.

————. "Seelsorgerliche Theologie am Vorabend der Reformation: Johann von Staupitz als Fastenprediger in Nürnberg." *ZKG* 63 (1994): 1–12.

Wunder, Heide. "'iusticia, Teutonice fromkeyt.' Theologische Rechtfertigung und bürger-liche Rechtschaffenheit: Ein Beitrag zur Sozialgeschichte eines theologischen Konzepts." In *Die frühe Reformation in Deutschland als Umbruch*, ed. Bernd Moeller and Stephen E. Buckwalter, 307–32. Gütersloh: GVH, 1998.

Young, Richard F. "Some Hindu Perspectives on Christian Missionaries in the Indic World of the Mid Nineteenth Century." In *Christians, Cultural Interactions, and India's Religious Traditions*, ed. Judith M. Brown and Robert Eric Frykenberg, 37–60. Grand Rapids and Cambridge: Eerdmans, 2002.

Young, Richard F., and S. Jebanesan. *The Bible Trembled: The Hindu-Christian Controversies of Nineteenth-Century Ceylon.* Vienna: De Nobili Research Library, 1995.

Young, Richard F., and G. P. V. Somartana. *Vain Debates: The Buddhist-Christian Controversies of Nineteenth-Century Ceylon.* Vienna: De Nobili Research Library, 1996.

Zardin, Danilo. "Relaunching Confraternities in the Tridentine Era: Shaping Consciences and Christianizing Society in Milan and Lombardy." In *The Politics of Ritual Kinship: Confraternities and Social Order in Early Modern Italy*, ed. Nicholas Terpstra, 190–209. Cambridge: Cambridge University Press, 2000.

Zeeden, Ernst Walter. *Katholische Überlieferungen in den lutherischen Kirchenordnungen des 16. Jahrhunderts.* Münster: Aschendorff, 1959.

———. *Das Zeitalter der Glaubenskämpfe, 1555–1648.* Handbuch der Deutschen Geschichte 9. 3rd ed. Munich: DTV, 1978.

Zeller, Reimar. *Prediger des Evangeliums: Erben der Reformation im Spiegel der Kunst.* Regensburg: Schnell & Steiner, 1998.

Ziegler, Walter. "Reformation und Klosterauflösung: Ein ordensgeschichtlicher Vergleich." In *Reformbemühungen und Observanzbestrebungen im spätmittelalterlichen Ordenswesen*, ed. Kaspar Elm, 585–614. Berlin: Duncker & Humblot, 1989.

Zschoch, Hellmut. "Gehorsamschristentum: Die 'göttliche und gründliche Offenbarung' des Augsburger Täuferführers Jakob Dachser." *Zeitschrift für bayerische Kirchengeschichte* 63 (1994): 30–45.

———. "Graf Friedrich Spee von Langenfeld (1591–1635)." *TRE* 31:635–41.

———. *Klosterreform und monastische Spiritualität im 15. Jahrhundert: Conrad von Zenn OESA (+1460) und sein Liber de vita monastica.* Tübingen: Mohr Siebeck, 1988.

———. "Das Recht der Mächtigen und die Macht der Gerechten: Bemerkungen zur gesellschaftlichen Selbstwahrnehmung des frühen Täufertums." In *Recht, Macht, Gerechtigkeit*, ed. Joachim Mehlhausen, 470–84. Munich: Chr. Kaiser; Gütersloh: GVH, 1998.

Zumkeller, Adolar. *Erbsünde, Gnade, Rechtfertigung und Verdienst nach der Lehre der Erfurter Augustinertheologen des Spätmittelalters.* Würzburg: Augustinus-Verlag, 1984.

Scripture Index

Person/Place Index

Subject Index

Brothers and Sisters of the Common Life,
    23–24, 27
Buddhism, 161
business, Luther on, 62–63

Calvinism, 145, 146, 150, 155–56, 158, 159.
    See also Calvin, John in Person/Place
    Index
Camaldolese Order, 25, 27, 121
Cambridge University, 84
Capuchins, 25, 121, 128, 129, 141–42, 144
Carmelites, 138, 139, 144
Carolingian Renaissance, 5
Carolingian theologians, 10
Carthusians, 28, 141, 147
catechisms, 155–56, 172
Catechisms (England), 155
Cathars, 7, 11
Catholic church. *See also* papacy
    on Bible, 53
    Christianization and, xxi–xxii, 21–22,
        124–52
    clerical reform and, 21, 23
    confessionalization and, 156
    Counter-Reformation and, xxii, 121–23
    in medieval Europe, 2
    missionary activities of, 127, 129, 130,
        131, 142–47, 161, 162, 163
    new devotion in, 134–42, 148–49,
        152, 155
    and pre-creedal sources of Christian-
        ity, 115
    religious orders in sixteenth century,
        121, 128–34
    sacraments and, 127
    sixteenth-century reform in, 121–24
    and teaching Christianity, 128–34
celibacy
    Bucer on, 81
    of clergy, 23, 79, 81, 110–11
    Luther on marriage versus, 62
    of women in religious orders, 139
Celifodina (Paltz), 188 n.102
charity
    almsgiving and, 2, 47
    Augustinian theology on good works, 14
    Catholic church and, 150

Jesuits and, 140
    by lay fraternities, 16
    Luther on, 19, 47, 64–65
    monasticism and, 27
    nuns and, 129–30
    Protestants and, 151
    Zwingli on, 74, 76
Choice and Freedom of Fools (Zwingli), 71
Christ
    Bride of Christ, 107
    Erasmus on, 32, 65, 66, 73, 117, 171
    Hus on, 20
    Ignatius of Loyola's devotion to, 130,
        171
    imitation of, by Christians, 14–15,
        32–33
    last judgment by, 16
    Luther on, 19, 54–56, 77–78
    as mediator, 5, 76, 135, 171, 172
    as Messiah, 168, 169
    passion of, 13
    Reformation and Christology, 171–72
    Sermon on the Mount and, 26, 60,
        90, 153
    Servetus on, 115, 117
    as sole agent of redemption, 19
    Zwingli on, 74, 76, 77–78, 192 n.55
Christian Freedom (Luther), 18–19
Christianization
    Catholic church and, xxi–xxii, 21–22,
        124–51
    Catholic missionary movement and,
        127, 129, 130, 131, 142–47
    confessionalization and, 155–60
    definition of, 3
    in Geneva, 69–71, 87–96
    as goal of Reformation, xvii–xxii, 17–24,
        34–35
    Islam and Judaism and, 164–70
    Jesuits and, 130–34
    Luther and, 17–20, 37–45, 54–56,
        63–67, 70, 71, 102, 147
    Magisterial Reformation and, 119
    of medieval Europe, 1–9, 161
    radical Christianization, 100–108
    in Strasbourg, 69–71, 79–88
    translations of Bible and, 172–73

CPSIA information can be obtained at www.ICGtesting.com
Printed in the USA
BVOW02s1243230914

367863BV00009B/154/P